UNDERSTANDING
TRUMAN CAPOTE

UNDERSTANDING CONTEMPORARY AMERICAN LITERATURE
Matthew J. Bruccoli, Founding Editor
Linda Wagner-Martin, Series Editor

Volumes on
Edward Albee I Sherman Alexie I Nelson Algren I Paul Auster
Nicholson Baker I John Barth I Donald Barthelme I The Beats
Thomas Berger I The Black Mountain Poets I Robert Bly I T. C. Boyle
Truman Capote I Raymond Carver I Michael Chabon I Fred Chappell
Chicano Literature I Contemporary American Drama
Contemporary American Horror Fiction
Contemporary American Literary Theory
Contemporary American Science Fiction, 1926–1970
Contemporary American Science Fiction, 1970–2000
Contemporary Chicana Literature I Robert Coover I Philip K. Dick
James Dickey I E. L. Doctorow I Rita Dove I John Gardner I George Garrett
Tim Gautreaux I John Hawkes I Joseph Heller I Lillian Hellman I Beth Henley
James Leo Herlihy I David Henry Hwang I John Irving I Randall Jarrell
Charles Johnson I Diane Johnson I Adrienne Kennedy I William Kennedy
Jack Kerouac I Jamaica Kincaid I Etheridge Knight I Tony Kushner
Ursula K. Le Guin I Denise Levertov I Bernard Malamud I David Mamet
Bobbie Ann Mason I Colum McCann I Cormac McCarthy I Jill McCorkle
Carson McCullers I W. S. Merwin I Arthur Miller I Stephen Millhauser
Lorrie Moore I Toni Morrison's Fiction I Vladimir Nabokov I Gloria Naylor
Joyce Carol Oates I Tim O'Brien I Flannery O'Connor I Cynthia Ozick
Suzan-Lori Parks I Walker Percy I Katherine Anne Porter I Richard Powers
Reynolds Price I Annie Proulx I Thomas Pynchon I Theodore Roethke
Philip Roth I May Sarton I Hubert Selby, Jr. I Mary Lee Settle I Sam Shepard
Neil Simon I Isaac Bashevis Singer I Jane Smiley I Gary Snyder I William Stafford
Robert Stone I Anne Tyler I Gerald Vizenor I Kurt Vonnegut
David Foster Wallace I Robert Penn Warren I James Welch I Eudora Welty
Edmund White I Tennessee Williams I August Wilson I Charles Wright

UNDERSTANDING

TRUMAN CAPOTE

Thomas Fahy

The University of South Carolina Press

Published by the University of South Carolina Press
Columbia, South Carolina 29208

www.sc.edu/uscpress

Manufactured in the United States of America

23 22 21 20 19 18 17 16 15 14   10 9 8 7 6 5 4 3 2 1

Library of Congress Cataloging-in-Publication Data

Fahy, Thomas Richard.
  Understanding Truman Capote / Thomas Fahy.
    pages cm
  Includes bibliographical references and index.
    ISBN 978-1-61117-341-3 (hardbound : alk. paper) — ISBN 978-1-61117-342-0
  (ebook) 1. Capote, Truman, 1924–1984—Criticism and interpretation. I. Title.
  PS3505.A59Z645 2014
  813'.54—dc23

                                                    2013041090

This book was printed on recycled paper with 30 percent postconsumer waste content.

For my son Nicolai, with love

CONTENTS

Series Editor's Preface *ix*
Acknowledgments *xi*

Chapter 1
Understanding Truman Capote *1*

Chapter 2
A Tree of Night and Other Stories *16*

Chapter 3
Other Voices, Other Rooms *43*

Chapter 4
The Grass Harp *61*

Chapter 5
The Muses Are Heard *79*

Chapter 6
Breakfast at Tiffany's *95*

Chapter 7
In Cold Blood *112*

Chapter 8
Three Stories, *Answered Prayers,* and Capote in the
Twenty-First Century *149*

Notes *157*
Bibliography *167*
Index *175*

SERIES EDITOR'S PREFACE

The Understanding Contemporary American Literature series was founded by the estimable Matthew J. Bruccoli (1931–2008), who envisioned these volumes as guides or companions for students as well as good nonacademic readers, a legacy that will continue as new volumes are developed to fill in gaps among the nearly one hundred series volumes published to date and to embrace a host of new writers only now making their marks on our literature.

As Professor Bruccoli explained in his preface to the volumes he edited, because much influential contemporary literature makes special demands, "the word 'understanding' in the titles was chosen deliberately. Many willing readers lack an adequate understanding of how contemporary literature works; that is, of what the author is attempting to express and the means by which it is conveyed." Aimed at fostering this understanding of good literature and good writers, the criticism and analyses in the series provide instruction in how to read certain contemporary writers—explicating their material, language, structures, themes, and perspectives—and facilitate a more profitable experience of the works under discussion.

In the twenty-first century Professor Bruccoli's prescience gives us an avenue to publish expert critiques of significant contemporary American writing. The series continues to map the literary landscape and to provide both instruction and enjoyment. Future volumes will seek to introduce new voices alongside canonized favorites, to chronicle the changing literature of our times, and to remain, as Professor Bruccoli conceived, contemporary in the best sense of the word.

Linda Wagner-Martin, Series Editor

ACKNOWLEDGMENTS

I want to begin by thanking Linda Wagner-Martin and the University of South Carolina Press for their help with this project. It is a pleasure to be part of this series.

I am grateful for the invaluable feedback and support of John Lutz, Jessica O'Hara, and Kirsten Ringelberg. Their generosity and patience have improved this book every step of the way. I also benefited greatly from my conversations about Capote with James MacDonald, Jeanie Attie, and numerous other colleagues and friends. Thank you all for your enthusiasm and encouragement.

I also wish to thank the Archives and Manuscripts division of the New York Public Library, my wonderful colleagues in the English department at Long Island University-Post, and two journals, *Mississippi Quarterly* and the *Journal of the Midwest Modern Language Association*, for permission to reprint some of the material here.

Last, I am always humbled by the loving support of my family and friends. I especially want to mention Tatyana Tsinberg, who has lived with this project for quite some time. I cannot thank her enough for helping me cross the finish line. Again.

CHAPTER 1

Understanding Truman Capote

Lillie Mae Faulk desperately wanted an abortion. Within a few weeks of her marriage to Archulus ("Arch") Persons in 1923, she realized she had made a terrible mistake. At first Arch seemed like her ticket out of small-town America. A natural salesman with a charming personality, Arch came from a well-respected Alabama family, and his talk of money-making schemes dazzled the sixteen-year-old girl, who dreamed of going to the big city. She would finally escape Monroeville, a town with no paved streets and a population of just over one thousand people . . . or so she thought. She soon discovered that her new husband was not what he appeared to be. Arch ran out of money on their honeymoon along the Gulf Coast, and after deciding to stay in New Orleans to find work, he scraped together enough cash to buy his wife a return ticket to Alabama. Lillie Mae felt duped. She was right back where she started, living with her three spinster cousins and their bachelor brother in the family house. She was not going to let these circumstances dim her aspirations, though. She enrolled in business school with plans of making it on her own, but a few weeks later she realized she was pregnant. The thought of having a permanent connection with Arch chilled her, but it was difficult to get an abortion in the 1920s—particularly in the South. As a result Truman Streckfus Persons (whose name would later be changed to Truman Capote after his mother's second marriage) was born on September 30, 1924.

Neither Arch nor Lillie Mae had much interest in parenthood. Arch, who possessed P. T. Barnum's hunger for get-rich-quick schemes but lacked the showman's acumen, spent much of his life moving from one fruitless enterprise to another. One of his more curious ventures involved managing the Great Pasha, a sideshow performer who could survive being buried alive for nearly five hours. (Capote would later resurrect this figure in his haunting short story "A Tree of Night.") As Arch's entrepreneurial efforts became less scrupulous (particularly through his habit of writing bad checks), he would find himself in legal trouble and behind bars numerous times throughout his life. Truman's mother was preoccupied with her own affairs—literally. She began seeing other men a few months after Truman's birth, and her young son witnessed a number of these dalliances firsthand. In short, Truman was a neglected child who, not surprisingly, developed a profound fear of abandonment—a fear his parents did little to assuage. When the family traveled together, for instance, Arch and Lillie Mae had no scruples about locking Truman in their hotel room (sometimes in a dark closet) and leaving him for the evening. They simply told the hotel staff to ignore the boy if he started screaming, which was often the case. His parents came back on those nights, but in the summer of 1930, with Arch away to pursue yet another scheme, Lillie Mae left Truman with her relatives in Monroeville indefinitely. She decided to follow her own dreams in New York City.

The three Faulk sisters, Jennie, Callie, and Nanny Rumbly ("Sook"), became Truman's family for the next two years, and they would inspire the central characters in a number of his works, including *The Grass Harp* and "A Christmas Memory." Jennie, the most authoritarian member of the family, owned a successful hat shop that sold a variety of women's goods. Her volatile temper helped fuel a contentious relationship with her youngest sister, the proper and sanctimonious Callie. Though she had been a schoolteacher, Callie eventually managed the finances of Jennie's store. Sook possessed a childlike spirit and rarely left the property. Only twice a year did she walk to the nearby forest to scavenge ingredients for her dropsy cure and Christmas fruitcakes. Two African American women, "Aunt" Liza and Anna Stabler, also spent a great deal of time at the Faulk house, and as hired help they did much of the cooking and cleaning. The cantankerous Anna, who would become Catherine in *The Grass Harp*, lived in a shed behind the house, had no teeth, played a mean accordion, and argued fearlessly with whites. She also denied having any black blood.

Truman spent most of his time with Sook, who played games with him in the attic, and Nelle Harper Lee—a neighbor and the future author of *To Kill a Mockingbird* (1960). The three of them shared a sense of separateness. Sook was largely isolated at the house before Truman arrived, and Nelle, who could whup most boys her age, did not behave like a conventional girl. She also felt estranged from her sickly mother. Truman's effeminate behavior, soft features, affectionate nature, and small frame (he never grew taller than 5'3") ostracized him, making him an easy target for verbal and physical abuse. Nelle protected him from bullies on a number of occasions, and both children frequently took refuge in the chinaberry tree in her backyard—a space where they hid from peers, shared dreams, and read their favorite books. This tree would become the setting for Capote's *The Grass Harp,* and Nelle would provide the model for Idabel, the tomboy in *Other Voices, Other Rooms.* Truman's experiences in Monroeville also inspired his engagement with social issues. On one occasion he hosted a Halloween party that included the participation of an African American servant who had once killed several people with a revolver. This enraged the local chapter of the Ku Klux Klan, but their planned march was thwarted, which Capote viewed as a personal victory: "Nobody will back them. We saw the Ku Klux Klan commit suicide" (quoted in Schultz 27). Perhaps it is not entirely surprising that Capote felt his calling to be a writer while living in this town: "When I was nine or ten, I was walking along the road, kicking stones, and I realized that I wanted to be a writer, an artist. How did it happen? . . . I don't believe in possession, but something took over inside me, some little demon that made me a writer" (quoted in Clarke 48–49).

Lillie Mae eventually sent for her son in September 1932, but his arrival in New York was not the homecoming Truman had hoped for. His mother, who had remarried and changed her name to Nina Capote (just as Lulamae would rename herself Holly Golightly in *Breakfast at Tiffany's*), was preoccupied with the active society life that her husband's (Joseph Garcia Capote's) income as a Wall Street broker enabled.[1] She also lavished most of her affection on Joe Capote. Not only was she in love with her husband, but she was also ashamed of and repelled by Truman's effeminacy. In fact she would terminate two pregnancies with Joe in large part because she refused to have another child like Truman. Mostly Nina feared that her son was becoming a homosexual, and she tried desperately to prevent this. She took him to numerous psychiatrists and then sent him to a military academy in the fall of 1936 (just before his twelfth birthday). After a disastrous year of being verbally and sexually abused by other cadets,[2] he returned to the city and resumed his studies at Trinity—an elite private school on the Upper West Side. Nina, however, remained vigilant in her disapproval of Truman. She ridiculed him publically and privately, calling him a "fairy," a "pansy," and a "monster." She even set up an appointment with a doctor to give her son male-hormone shots.[3] These humiliations and torments intensified when she drank, which was increasingly the case after the Capotes moved to an exclusive suburb in Greenwich, Connecticut, in 1939. It is no wonder that Capote later described her as "the single worst person in my life" (quoted in Clarke 41).

When he entered Greenwich High School as a tenth-grader, Capote continued his horrendous career as a student—failing various subjects, ditching classes, and refusing to participate in any athletic activities. Despite all of this, his English teacher Catherine Wood began to mentor him, inviting him for dinner, speaking to Nina about his talent, and encouraging his writing. He also developed an important friendship with Phoebe Pierce during this period. On Sunday evenings they would train into Manhattan to explore numerous jazz clubs and spend time at either the Stork Club or El Morocco. Truman's grades, however, prevented him from graduating with his classmates in 1942. That summer the Capotes moved to an apartment on Park Avenue, and Truman entered Franklin School to retake his senior year. During this year (from 1942 through 1943) he became close friends with Carol Marcus, Oona O'Neill (daughter of the playwright Eugene O'Neill and future wife of Charlie Chaplin), and the heiress Gloria Vanderbilt—all of whom achieved celebrity status at an early age. This foursome frequented the club scene as well, and these experiences solidified Capote's lifelong passion for the glamorous nightlife of New York City. Each of these women would subsequently claim to be the model for Capote's Holly Golightly in *Breakfast at Tiffany's*.

After a brief and thankless job as a copyboy at the *New Yorker*, Capote returned to Monroeville to work on *Summer Crossing*—a novel about a wealthy seventeen-year-old debutant who rebels against her parents by marrying a Jewish parking lot attendant. Being back in Alabama changed Capote's focus, however. He set aside *Summer Crossing* to begin *Other Voices, Other Rooms,* mining his childhood for material and returning to his interest in the problem of southern racism. More specifically, recent news about the gang rape of an African American woman in Alabama inspired Capote to include a similar incident in this new novel. In 1945 Capote returned to New York with his manuscript well under way and several completed short stories in hand. His career as a fiction writer was about to take off. *Mademoiselle* accepted "Miriam" for its June issue, and *Harper's Bazaar* published "A Tree of Night" a few months later.

During these months he befriended several important figures in New York's literary and social scene, including Carson McCullers. McCullers felt an immediate connection with Capote (both were southern writers interested in issues of alienation and loneliness), and she took the young writer under her wing. She found him an agent and sent a letter on his behalf to the senior editor at Random House. On October 22, 1945, Capote signed a contract with the press for *Other Voices, Other Rooms.* McCullers then used her influence to secure him a spot at Yaddo, the artists' colony in Saratoga Springs.

This retreat would give him enough time—and quiet—to finish his book. This fast and intense friendship would characterize Capote's relationships throughout his life. He learned at an early age that he charmed people. His wit, emotional generosity, flamboyant behavior, and startling willingness to share deeply personal information drew people to him. After working with Capote on the film set of John Huston's *Beat the Devil,* for example, Hollywood tough guy Humphrey Bogart said, "At first you can't believe him, he's so odd, and then you want to carry him around with you always in your pocket" (quoted in Clarke 222).

Other Voices, Other Rooms, published in 1948, leaped onto the *New York Times* best-seller list and sold over twenty-six thousand copies in just nine weeks.[4] Not surprisingly, a novel about a young boy's struggles to come to terms with and accept his homosexuality caused a stir. Many critics railed against the protagonist's acquiescence to an older man's sexual advances at the end of the book. The publication of Alfred Kinsey's *Sexual Behavior in the Human Male* (1948) was startling many with its statistics about male sexuality as well. Based on over five thousand interviews, Kinsey and his team reported that 37 percent of men had reached orgasm through homosexual contact.[5] Such a report played into pervasive fears about masculinity and homosexuality at the time, and Capote, who consciously tapped into these social issues, added fuel to the fire with this novel, as did the jacket photograph of the precocious novelist lounging suggestively on a Victorian couch.

Shortly after the novel's publication, Capote traveled to England and Europe with his lover Jack Dunphy. As did many Jazz Age expatriates, Capote often wrote his best works about American life while living overseas, and he spent considerable time abroad throughout the next fifteen years. He may have been thousands of miles away from his beloved New York, which he once referred to as a "diamond iceberg," but he never lost touch with the happenings at home. He corresponded daily with friends and read several U.S. newspapers every afternoon. His travels also inspired him to work as a journalist. In addition to his exploration of the anxieties characterizing 1940s American life in *A Tree of Night and Other Stories* (1949), his first collection of short fiction, he compiled some recent travel writing for a book titled *Local Color* (1950). Whether through the profile of a New Orleans jazz musician named Shotgun, a piece about the stigma of being a Brooklynite, or his recollections about overreacting to the sound of gunfire while traveling on a Spanish train, the essays in *Local Color* demonstrated an early interest in bringing together the directness of journalism with the techniques of fiction.

Capote was eager to get back to his new novel, but his struggles with *Summer Crossing* continued. He put aside the manuscript again and turned to his experiences in Alabama for inspiration. The result was his 1951 novella, *The Grass Harp*. This fable recalls the teenage years of Collin Fenwick, a boy sent to live with his father's spinster sisters and a toothless African American housekeeper. As with *Other Voices, Other Rooms,* Capote modeled the protagonist on himself; he also based several characters on the Faulk family and their servants. This elegant, comic novel not only is a coming-of-age story but also celebrates the collective efforts of several misfits who reject social conformity and American materialism by living in a tree house. In many ways Capote's nostalgic impulse to return to his childhood—instead of writing about contemporary American life—can be seen as a reaction against the cultural climate of the Cold War. Furthermore the maniacal efforts of McCarthyism included a highly publicized attack on homosexuality, and these attitudes were undoubtedly an affront to Capote's identity. In all likelihood, they reminded him of his own mother's aggressive disapproval and persecution

Over the next few years Capote took a hiatus from serious fiction writing to pursue other projects. The success of *The Grass Harp* inspired a Broadway producer to approach Capote about writing a theatrical adaptation. The play, which premiered on March 27, 1952, was a critical and popular failure, as was Capote's second attempt at writing for the stage—a musical adaptation of his short story "House of Flowers." Capote also dabbled with screenwriting, penning *Beat the Devil* (1953) and cowriting *The Innocents* (1961). His work as a journalist continued as well. *The Muses Are Heard,* his firsthand account of Everyman Opera Company's performances of *Porgy and Bess* in the Soviet Union, was released in 1956. Its portrait of Russian culture and racial integration challenged Cold War prejudices, reflecting Capote's ongoing interest in the political issues of the period. The following year he published a controversial profile of Marlon Brando ("The Duke and His Domain") in the *New Yorker.* Capote's technique as an interviewer here would be crucial to his later success with *In Cold Blood.* He tended to disclose personal information to disarm his subjects, to encourage them to speak frankly. Furthermore he committed his interviews to memory (he never took notes or used a tape recorder), making people feel less inhibited. Brando was no exception. In their interview, which lasted over five hours, Brando spoke frankly about his contempt for acting, his mother's alcoholism, and his own need to dominate those around him. After reading the publication, the actor told a friend, "I'll kill him!" (quoted in Clarke 303).

With *Breakfast at Tiffany's* (1958) Capote returned to fiction writing, and his subject matter was once again controversial. The novella revolves around the adventures of a young woman who thoroughly enjoys her sexual and social freedom. Holly Golightly does exactly as her name implies: she goes lightly from one man to another and from one self-constructed identity to another. Having abandoned her life as a country girl and her fleeting career in movies, she has become an unabashed gold digger who charges men for her company and seeks a wealthy husband. She sums up her philosophy to the narrator: "I'd steal two bits off a dead man's eyes if I thought it would contribute to the day's enjoyment. . . . Be anything but a coward, pretender and emotional crook, a whore. I'd rather have cancer than a dishonest heart" (83). *Harper's Bazaar* had originally agreed to publish the book but opted out after reading it. The editors found Holly's lifestyle (as a woman who earns a living through her romantic/sexual relationships) and the use of profanity offensive. The response by *Harper's* can largely be understood as a reflection of contemporary anxieties about female sexuality in the late 1950s (though the text is set in the immediate aftermath of World War II). The success of *Playboy* magazine, the popularity of Marilyn Monroe, and the shocking findings of Kinsey's report on female sexuality undermined the popular images of white womanhood on television shows such as *Father Knows Best* and *Leave It to Beaver*. Instead Kinsey's study revealed that 50 percent of women had engaged in premarital sex, 26 percent had been unfaithful to their husbands, and over 20 percent had gotten abortions.[6] Holly's sexual proclivities reflected the kinds of behaviors that Kinsey reported and that mainstream America wanted to suppress. Perhaps it is not surprising that the film adaptation of the novel, which was released in 1961 and starred Audrey Hepburn, presented a much more palatable version for public consumption. The screenplay transforms the book into a romantic comedy in which the narrator and Holly fall in love at the end—"saving" her from her dissolute lifestyle.

Though Capote was disappointed with the film, he was already embroiled in his next project, which would make him one of the most celebrated writers of the twentieth century. Capote was reading the *New York Times* on November 16, 1959, when he came across a story about four brutal murders in Holcomb, Kansas. Four weeks later Capote arrived in the town of Holcomb with Nelle Harper Lee, who helped him with his initial research and interviews.Six years after the execution of the killers, he completed *In Cold Blood: A True Account of a Multiple Murder and Its Consequences*. The book offers a powerful commentary on American culture in its portrait of poverty, violence, and Cold War fears. Capote could not have hoped for a greater success. His "nonfiction novel," as he called it, first appeared in four installments in the *New Yorker* and garnered record sales for the magazine. Columbia Pictures optioned the book for five hundred thousand dollars, and foreign and domestic sales soon topped one million dollars.[7] Yet the emotional and psychological toll of this project was debilitating. Capote once remarked, "No one will ever know what *In Cold Blood* took out of me. It scraped me right down to the marrow of my bones. It nearly killed me. I think, in a way, it *did* kill me" (quoted in Clarke 398). Capote did find the energy to appear on a variety of television programs to talk about the project, and he was frequently consulted as an expert on capital punishment—even testifying before a Senate subcommittee about the issue in July 1966. That same year he hosted a social event that was nicknamed the "party of the century" at the Plaza Hotel in Manhattan. Guests for Capote's masked ball were asked to wear only black and white, and some of the most famous people in the country attended, including Frank Sinatra, Irving Berlin, Jacqueline Kennedy, and Thornton Wilder.

In the aftermath of *In Cold Blood,* Capote's addiction to alcohol and drugs worsened, and he would be in and out of rehabilitation clinics for the rest of his life. Meanwhile he spoke in wildly exaggerated terms about the progress on his next novel, a massive work of Proustian proportions entitled *Answered Prayers*. Several chapters finally appeared in *Esquire* in 1976, but Capote's searing indictment of the ultrarich as disillusioned, bitter, and cruel alienated him from most of his wealthy friends—friends who immediately recognized themselves in the text. Capote was surprised and hurt by this response. Only in 1979 did he regain enough control over his alcoholism to have a productive year of writing, and he completed a beautiful collection of short works entitled *Music for Chameleons* (1980). Despite its success (the book stayed on the best-seller list for sixteen weeks, selling 84,471 copies), Capote was unable to do any meaningful work on *Answered Prayers*. The manuscript remained disjointed and incomplete at the time of his death from a fatal overdose on August 24, 1984.

Capote Studies and the Literary Canon

Truman Capote's writing has rarely been discussed in relation to Cold War culture, and this oversight can be attributed in large part to the tendency among scholars to view his work ahistorically. Such an approach may also explain why his fiction is rarely anthologized and taught in college courses. Even his most famous book, *In Cold Blood,* holds a rather ambiguous place in the academy. In 2009 Harold Bloom assembled a new anthology of criticism on Capote, and the introductory note reiterates his concern over the "survival possibilities of Capote's work" (vii). He goes on to question whether or not *In Cold Blood* "deserves canonical status" (2) and suggests

that comparing Capote to contemporary writers only exacerbates the problem. Flannery O'Connor "dwarfs poor Capote" (vii), Bloom laments, and
he cites my essay on Capote and Carson McCullers as an example of that
risk.[8] Though I would argue that exploring the intersection between different
literary works enhances our understanding of them (Capote can enrich readings of O'Connor just as she can illuminate elements of his work), this kind
of scholarship has not solved the problem of Capote's place in the academy.
Given his status (then and now) as a well-known literary and cultural figure,
how can we explain his precarious position in the canon?

Two types of criticism—biographical and New Critical—continue to
shape Capote scholarship, contributing to the perception of his writing as
removed from sociopolitical concerns. In the biographical school Capote,
the man, remains a larger-than-life figure. Recent films such as *Capote*
(2005) and *Infamous* (2006) point to an ongoing fascination with his life,
particularly in regard to *In Cold Blood*. William Todd Schultz's recent psy-
chobiography of Capote, *Tiny Terror: Why Truman Capote (Almost) Wrote
Answered Prayers*, offers another example of this tendency to privilege biographical over sociopolitical interpretations of the author's work. In short,
people still seem far more interested in Capote's relationships with Jacqueline Kennedy, Humphrey Bogart, Marilyn Monroe, and Andy Warhol, for
example, than with contextualizing his fiction. Likewise New Criticism has
encouraged a similar view of Capote as disconnected from cultural politics.
New Criticism was the dominant mode of literary scholarship in the 1940s
when Capote first started publishing. Most practitioners, including Robert
Penn Warren, John Crowe Ransom, and Allen Tate, were poets and literary
critics who first identified themselves as the Fugitives and Southern Agrar-
ians in the 1920s and 1930s. By the 1940s several influential books had
emerged from this group—most notably Ransom's volume of essays *The
New Criticism* (1941) and Cleanth Brooks's *Understanding Fiction* (1943).
These works emphasized the importance of close reading and viewing the
text as a self-sufficient object that could be understood apart from a broader
cultural context, authorial intention, and reader response. As Terry Eagleton
has argued, the New Critics wrestled with the task of "rescuing the text from
author and reader . . . [and] disentangling it from any social or historical
context" (42).

This school of thought strongly influenced early Capote scholarship,
which struggled to reconcile the gothic elements of his work with its moments
of hope and black humor. Specifically, the notion of Capote as vacillating
between two styles—"daylight" and "nocturnal"—emerged. As Paul Levine

explained in 1958, the "daylight stories" are preoccupied with "surfaces, the interest and humor deriving from the situation and the action. . . . In the nocturnal stories the hero is forced to come to grips with the destructive element—the power of blackness which resides in each of us. The confrontation of the psyche leads to the exposure of the constructive and destructive elements: the wish for death and the wish for life" (83–84). The critic Ihab H. Hassan used the same terminology two years later,[9] and Clarke reinforced this framework in his 1988 biography, arguing that "Truman's short fiction alternated between the dark and the sunny, the terrifying and the amusing" (86). Helen S. Garson's comprehensive study of Capote's short fiction explicitly relies on Levine's thesis as well[10], and even Robert Emmet Long's recent book *Truman Capote—Enfant Terrible* continues this tradition by focusing almost exclusively on the nocturnal stories in his discussion of the author's early career. While New Critical approaches to Capote, as typified by Levine, have provided a helpful framework for interpretation, the characterization of "daylight" works as superficial (about "surfaces") and "nocturnal" works as psychological (about internal struggles) has contributed to the perception of his writing as lacking political and social intent.

Even though queer theory and the field of Southern Literary Studies provide logical approaches for examining Capote, they continue to have a conflicted relationship with his work. Queer theory has been critical of the author's sexual politics. As Peter G. Christensen explains, "Capote's apparent indifference to gay liberation has . . . lost him potentially sympathetic critics in the highly visible field of gay and queer studies" ("Major" 222). This resistance also stems from Capote's depiction of homosexuality. The author, according to Christensen, seemed "unable even at a later date to imagine a story in which the love of two adult men would lead to mutual salvation or even help" ("Capote" 63). Gary Richards's recent examination of homosexual desire in *Other Voices, Other Rooms* makes a similar observation about the depictions of physical sex between men, and he notes Capote's problematic tendency to equate "gender transitivity and homosexuality" (33). It is understandable, then, that queer theorists would be concerned with these elements of Capote's fiction. One could also argue that Capote lost potential allies within Southern Literary Studies for distancing himself from the label "southern writer." As he explained in a 1964 interview, "I, personally, have never thought of myself as a writer regionally oriented. . . . Now, of course, the South is so far behind me that it has ceased to furnish me with subject matter" (Inge 42–43). This has not prevented insightful work about Capote's relationship with other southern contemporaries, but it has contributed to his marginalization within this critical community.

Nevertheless Capote's early writing has been fruitfully linked with the gothic tradition in southern literature, and this association can provide an effective starting point for reconceptualizing his work as socially, culturally, and politically engaged. In the United States, Washington Irving, Nathaniel Hawthorne, and Edgar Allan Poe first used the gothic genre to explore troubling aspects of American culture such as the legacy of Puritanism and the horrors of slavery. As Teresa A. Goddu argues in *Gothic America: Narrative, History, and Nation,* the gothic should be understood as historically and socially situated: "Instead of being gateways to other, distant worlds of fantasy, . . . gothic stories are intimately connected to the culture that produces them. . . . If the gothic is informed by its historical context, the horrors of history are also articulated through gothic discourse" (2). The horrors of history preoccupied not only these early American authors; they were also of central concern to southern writers such as William Faulkner, Truman Capote, and Flannery O'Connor, who revived the gothic tradition in the twentieth century. Even though the terror within the new gothic usually stems from "internal weakness and character flaws rather than some external force" (Garson, *Truman Capote,* 4), it should not be separated from its cultural context. Instead Capote's depiction of the terrors of the hidden self can be more fully appreciated when understood relative to the social anxieties of 1940s and 1950s America.

In many respects *Understanding Truman Capote* places the author's works in dialogue with the field of American Studies as an act of recuperation. There is an attempt in this work to provide a new direction for Capote studies that can bring him back into the classroom and the literary canon.[11] Reading his works in their historical context reveals the politics shaping Capote's writing. Such an approach aligns with Linda Wagner-Martin's assertions about the "new fiction" of this period: "Such writers as Truman Capote, Gore Vidal, Carson McCullers, and other southerners . . . during the 1940s and 1950s created a new category of American letters—that of the minority viewpoint (though white), the literature of the anti-dream. Expressing themselves in nonrealistic, or at least unconventionally structured, works, these newer writers insisted on the dreamlike (or, sometimes, hallucinatory) quality of much human experience. At their most ephemeral, novels by these visionary if fragile writers were written *to disguise the narratives being conveyed*" (83–84, my emphasis). Though Wagner-Martin discusses only Capote's *Other Voices, Other Rooms* here, the bogeyman figure in his short fiction, the tree house setting in *The Grass Harp,* mythmaking/propaganda in *The Muses Are Heard,* Holly Golightly's reveries, and the haunting aftermath of the Clutter murders endow the respective works with dreamlike qualities that mask sociopolitical narratives. My emphasis on the field of American Studies offers a way to reclaim these disguised narratives. It refutes the notion of Capote as disconnected from the political. Instead *Understanding Truman Capote* positions him as a writer deeply engaged with the social anxieties surrounding race relations, gender, sexuality, communism, capitalist culture, the atomic age, poverty, and delinquency in the 1940s and 1950s. His writing captures the isolation, marginalization, and persecution of those who deviated from or failed to achieve white middle-class ideals. His works highlight the artificiality of mainstream idealizations about American culture. They reveal the deleterious consequences of nostalgia, the insidious impact of suppression, the dangers of Cold War propaganda, and the importance of equal rights. Ultimately they reflect a critical engagement with American culture that challenges us to rethink our own biases and fears.

Overview

Each chapter examines elements of 1940s and 1950s American culture that help illuminate the sociopolitical subtext of Capote's work. The book begins with *A Tree of Night and Other Stories,* and although this collection appeared in 1949 (one year after his debut novel, *Other Voices, Other Rooms*), he wrote and published most of these stories between 1944 and 1947. Capote's short fiction portrays individuals, like the decade of the 1940s itself, as fragmented—torn between security and fear, communal engagement and isolationism, public and private identity. These fragmented characters have withdrawn from others in an attempt to escape both the dangers of modern life and a history (personal and social) that they do not wish to confront. They hope that isolation will protect them from present-day threats and past failures, but the act of turning inward only exacerbates their fears. Capote uses these anxieties as metaphors for the tensions characterizing contemporary American culture, which longed to retreat from its global responsibilities as a result of World War II, from the terrifying implications of the atomic age, and from dramatic social changes at home. Ultimately *A Tree of Night and Other Stories* depicts the disconcerting unease of American life at the time and portrays isolation (through turning inward and nostalgia) as dangerous for the individual and society as a whole.

Chapter three examines Capote's use of freak shows and rape in *Other Voices, Other Rooms* (1948) as vehicles for condemning homophobia and racism. Acts of gender/sexual ambiguity and racist depictions of nonwhites were staples on the sideshow stage, and both appear in the novel to indict the ways society relegated same-sex desire and nonwhites to the realm of the freakish. Not only does the protagonist, Joel Harrison Knox, begin to accept his sexuality at a circus, but in addition the freakishness of all the characters points to Capote's larger concerns about intolerance. Likewise the allusion to Recy Taylor's rape in *Other Voices, Other Rooms* contributes to the novel's scathing portrait of race relations in the South. The brutal sexual assault of Missouri "Zoo" Fever initially seems out of place in Joel's dreamlike narrative, but within the context of 1940s Alabama, her experiences highlight the ongoing use of rape as a tool for oppressing black women in America. In Capote's hands this incident also connects the social injustices facing African Americans with those of homosexuals in the early days of the civil rights movement. Ultimately Capote's juxtaposition of Joel's fantasy world with the social realities of southern life offers a powerful critique of the silence surrounding violence against black women and homosexuals.

Like most postwar Americans, Capote followed the news of Communist expansion and the atomic age with increasing angst. As an openly gay man he must have been particularly concerned by the overt link between homosexuality and communism in the early years of the Cold War. In the wake of the Alger Hiss affair (in which the man accusing him of espionage was widely characterized as his jilted gay lover) and the shocking findings of the Kinsey report on male sexuality, the vilification of homosexuals became commonplace in the fight against Communist subversion. When placed against this backdrop, the nostalgic sentiment and pastoral setting of *The Grass Harp* carry a complex sociocultural critique, and this critique is the focal point of chapter four. Nostalgia comes from discontent, from a desire to escape the crises of the present by imagining another time as better. The seeming idealization of the past and rural life in *The Grass Harp* can therefore be read as capturing Cold War–era disillusionment; it tapped into a yearning among Americans to establish a stable identity in a past undisturbed by the threat of nuclear weapons and homosexuality. Despite the novel's failure to provide an alternate way of achieving lasting happiness in the present, it depicts the dangers of conformity, points to the corrosive nature of gossip, portrays human sexuality as complex, and argues for the importance of social tolerance. In these ways Capote uses the characters' ultimate capitulation to the establishment to condemn the conformist, homophobic values of 1950s America and the methods used to enforce them.

In 1955 Capote turned his attention to journalism and accompanied the Everyman Opera Company to the Soviet Union for its performances of George Gershwin's *Porgy and Bess*. For Capote, this trip provided an opportunity to write about the intersection of fears over Communists and racial discrimination in America. As he remarked afterward, "Everybody in the West seemed to be so fantastically naïve about Russia . . . as though it were different from any other country. Well, it basically isn't, because human nature is what it is" (quoted in Clarke 305).[12] Capote's notion of human nature here provides a central key for understanding *The Muses Are Heard.* Specifically, chapter five looks at Capote's indictment of anti-Communist propaganda during the McCarthy era and the racial ideologies that justified discrimination. His narrative links mythmaking (as manifested through gossip and propaganda) with racism to suggest that U.S. fears of the "other" were constructed from falsehoods that served a political agenda. For Capote, art offers one solution to this problem. Just as his book (and art more broadly) humanizes people from different cultures, political perspectives, and ethnicities, it also has the power to bridge cultural differences and to lessen the possibilities of war.

In his next major work, *Breakfast at Tiffany's* (1958), Capote sparked controversy with his critique of sexual repression and the social practices that limited female autonomy. Holly Golightly takes pleasure in sex, enjoys material comforts, and is in no rush to the altar. One of the characters in *Breakfast at Tiffany's* labels this quality in Holly as a kind of "phoniness," but Capote uses the term to raise questions about the investment American culture places on outward appearances. These questions reflect on the novel's concerns about materialism as well. None of the wealthy characters finds personal or romantic fulfillment, which undercuts Holly's vision of Tiffany's as a place of stability and contentment. Financial security may be an essential ingredient for living an autonomous single life, but it does not seem to help women break free from the ideology of domesticity in America. They still seek meaning in men and marriage. When Holly fails to do both, she must flee the country. This moment suggests that America denies a lasting place for people who reject or resist this ideology—particularly single women (who are single for too long) and homosexuals.

In 1959 the brutal murder of four members of the Clutter family would become the focal point of Capote's life for nearly six years. Chapter seven specifically examines Capote's portrait of the intersection among poverty, juvenile delinquency, Beat culture, and violence during the Cold War. Many sociologists in the 1950s viewed poverty as a breeding ground for male violence, and a debate about the causes and implications of juvenile delinquency raged throughout the decade. Dick Hickock and Perry Smith, who had been delinquents themselves, became the logical extension of such behavior—adult criminals. The violent disillusionment driving delinquency also linked it with the Beat movement. On-the-road culture created a new kind of space—one defined by movement, not stasis; by personal freedom, not repression; and by homosocial bonds, not heterosexual marriage. Like Jack Kerouac's

On the Road, Capote's *In Cold Blood* makes artistry, movement, and theft central themes, and these thematic elements reveal the darker, more dangerous consequences of the Beat life. Perry and Dick, in essence, embodied the worst possible outcome of the Beat life. They never transcended the rootlessness, poverty, and artistic struggles that the Beats tended to glamorize; instead they remained in a state of never-ending transience and criminality, ultimately leaving them with feelings of resentment and rage. When understood in the context of the 1950s, the importance of *In Cold Blood* consists in its exposure of the myths of American prosperity and suburban harmony and the realization that such myths—because they were unrealizable for so many—actually contributed to eruptions of violent, murderous rage.

Understanding Truman Capote concludes with a discussion of the three stories published with *Breakfast at Tiffany's* and the recently discovered excerpt from *Answered Prayers.* Since I primarily focus on Capote as a writer shaped by 1940s and 1950s American culture, his final two books (*Music for Chameleons* and *Answered Prayers*) fall outside the scope of this study, and I do not give them detailed consideration. I believe, however, that the methodology presented here can be applied effectively to these later works. It is my hope that this book will provide a way to reconsider Capote's place in literary criticism, the canon, and the classroom.

CHAPTER 2

A Tree of Night and Other Stories

Truman Capote hoped his part-time job at the *New Yorker* would put him on the path to becoming a published author, and in rather unexpected ways it did. The magazine hired him in 1942—along with a variety of sketchy assistants who were "either old and decrepit, thieves, or whistlers"—only as an act of desperation (Clarke 70). Most of the staff had left because of the war, and the *New Yorker* needed the help. At any other time someone with Capote's flamboyance, childlike appearance, high-pitched voice, and writerly aspirations would never have been considered. Not only did his demeanor run counter to the image of a typical copyboy, who was expected to be invisible and silent, but his submissions to the fiction department also irritated editors, who did not view employees as potential writers. It is not surprising that they rejected all of Capote's work. The young upstart did not become discouraged, however. He continued to write as often as he could and increasingly desired more time to dedicate to his craft—a wish that the *New Yorker* inadvertently granted in the summer of 1944. While attending the Bread Loaf Writers' Conference in Vermont, Capote overstated his position with the magazine and was given a front-row seat at Robert Frost's poetry reading. Capote decided to attend despite having just contracted the flu, and shortly into the event he felt too lightheaded and nauseated to stay.[1] He tried to leave quietly, but Frost took immediate offence: "Well, if that's what the representative of *The New Yorker* thinks of my reading, I shall stop" (quoted in Clarke 76). He then threw his book at Capote. After the *New Yorker* received several angry letters, including one from Frost, Capote was fired.

His termination provided just the opportunity he was looking for. Capote returned to Monroeville, Alabama, and the town brought back such vivid childhood memories that he set aside *Summer Crossing,* his manuscript about a seventeen-year-old girl in New York, and began *Other Voices, Other Rooms*. He also drafted several short stories—a genre he later described as his "great love."[2] In January 1945 Capote left Alabama for New Orleans, where he rented a room in the heart of the French Quarter and continued to polish his short fiction. Capote drank in the city's vibrant nightlife. The jazz-filled streets pulsed with tourists and soldiers on leave. He rode the streetcars and tried to make extra money as a painter—though, as Capote himself admitted, his paintings were awful. After a few months he returned to New York with a suitcase full of manuscripts. He wasted no time before marching into the office of *Mademoiselle* with a short story. When the receptionist asked for his contact information, Capote explained that he would simply wait while someone read it. The magazine's fiction editor sent his assistant Rita Smith to meet the boy. She liked "The Walls Are Cold" enough to recommend it for publication, but the senior editor disagreed. Nevertheless her enthusiastic response inspired Capote to return with "My Side of the Matter," which he had recently sold to *Story* magazine. Smith greatly admired this work as well, and she asked to see more. Soon after Capote gave her a copy of "Miriam," *Mademoiselle* accepted it for the June 1945 issue. This publication began a domino effect of opportunity for Capote. When the fiction editor at *Harper's Bazaar* read "Miriam," she sought out the young writer for a story, and the magazine published "A Tree of Night" in October 1945. Two months later "Jug of Silver" appeared in *Mademoiselle,* and *Harper's Bazaar* included "Headless Hawk" in the November 1946 issue—the same year Capote received an O. Henry Award for "Miriam." Most of these stories, along with a few others composed in 1947 and 1948, would comprise his first collection, *A Tree of Night and Other Stories* (1949).

Capote's collection portrays individuals, like the decade of the 1940s itself, as fragmented—torn between security and fear, communal engagement and isolationism, public and private identity. The end of World War II certainly produced a sense of relief, but almost immediately the country seemed to face even greater threats with the global spread of communism and the realities of the atomic age. As the historian William S. Graebner has argued, "To be sure, the forties were witness to considerable prosperity and to the nation's rise to the pinnacle of world power. But neither achievement generated the culture of optimism, confidence, and security that has generally been seen as characteristic of the decade. Instead, uncertainty reigned" (xi). Capote captures this climate of uncertainty through these fragmented characters, who have withdrawn from others in an attempt to escape both the dangers of modern life and a history (personal and social) that they do not wish to confront. They hope that isolation will protect them from present-day threats and past failures, but the act of turning inward only exacerbates their fears. Capote uses these anxieties as metaphors for the tensions characterizing contemporary American culture, which longed to retreat from its global responsibilities as a result of World War II, from the terrifying implications of the atomic age, and from dramatic social changes at home. Ultimately *A Tree of Night and Other Stories* depicts this disconcerting unease and portrays isolation (through turning inward and nostalgia) as dangerous for the individual and the country.

Historical Horrors and Consumer Comforts in the 1940s

From the onset of World War II to the emergence of the Cold War, the events of the 1940s profoundly unsettled American life. One's community, employment, morality, and safety could be threatened at any moment. Like the shadowy rooms and dark alleyways of film noir, the prospect of violent danger seemed to lurk around every corner. Retreating from the world offered one possibility for achieving and maintaining safety. At the end of the 1930s, isolationism appealed to a country that was still reeling from the hardships of an economic depression at home. Domestic concerns were daunting enough without the burdens of geopolitical engagement. Even though 84 percent of Americans supported the Allies in 1939,[3] the country as a whole, according to David M. Kennedy, "hung quivering between hope and fear—hope that with American help the Allies could defeat Hitler, and fear that events might yet suck the United States into the conflict" (434). This hope of remaining largely uninvolved eroded daily, however. At the end of 1939 President Franklin Roosevelt passed a revised Neutrality Act, which allowed belligerent nations to order war materials, and the implementation of the Lend-Lease program in March 1941 enabled the United States to supply Britain and the other Allies directly with aircraft, weaponry, tanks, food, and other essential goods. When the Japanese bombed Pearl Harbor on December 7, 1941, killing 2,403 people, the illusion of political isolationism in America ended. Congress declared war the following day, and the United States would eventually deploy 16 million troops to the conflict. America emerged from the war as the most powerful nation in the world, but the celebrations did not last long. Tensions with the Soviet Union had eased during the conflict only out of necessity. Postwar debates about the political influence over occupied territories reignited long-held suspicions and distrust. Soon angry exchanges between both countries set the stage for the Cold War, and once again many Americans wanted to retreat from the concerns of global politics.

The postwar economy made fantasies about isolation—or turning inward —unrealistic as well. Fueled in part by bitter memories of the Depression and an anemic job market, business owners, government leaders, and the public feared that the country could not support millions of returning veterans. Between May and August 1945, for example, "employment in shipyards and aircraft and arms plants was cut in half. The government cancelled $35 billion of war contracts within one month of V-J Day, and between June 1945 and June 1946 it discharged 9 million service men and women. Unemployment climbed from 1 million in 1945 to 2.3 million in 1946" (Hartmann 7). These economic realities carried a psychological toll as well. According to one national poll, 70 percent of Americans expected their lives to worsen after the war, and few citizens believed that their children would achieve a better standard of living (Chafe 29–30). Government officials quickly realized that the only solution to mass unemployment involved rebuilding European markets and expanding international trade, which would irrevocably link the United States with the global economy.

Although isolationism gradually became a political and economic impossibility, it did manifest itself culturally in a new emphasis on the individual. The war demanded collective engagement, sacrificing oneself for the broader goals of the country. President Roosevelt often called on businesses and factories to work tirelessly to prepare the United States for war and to assist Allied nations. Throughout the first half of the decade, America thus became a nation of producers, making useful goods instead of generating money for consumption. Individual income rose dramatically as a result. Annual wages climbed from $754 at the start of the decade to $1,289 in 1944 (Hartmann 4), and personal savings swelled 300 percent between 1941 and 1945, leaving Americans with $140 billion of liquid capital (Chafe 10). This new income created a desire for material goods, and after 1945 individual Americans were ready to celebrate the nation's new prosperity—largely through consumerism. They began to treat themselves to cars, houses, and a wide array of consumer goods.[4] For example, approximately 7 million cars were purchased annually throughout the 1950s, and a record 7.9 million sold in 1955 (Tom McCarthy 100). Single-family home construction, which totaled only 114,000 in 1944, jumped to 1,692,000 in 1950 (Jackson 233), and the television set became a staple of domestic life: "In 1948, there were 148,000. By 1950, 4.4 million families had a TV, and people bought them at a feverish rate—20,000 *a day* by 1956" (Miller and Nowak 344). While consumer culture became increasingly equated with prosperity and personal contentment, the range of choices also generated anxiety. As Graebner explains, "In the absence of accepted moral and ethical principles of conduct and belief, an infinity of actions and beliefs became possible and the anxiety of choice unavoidable. For instance, consumer anxiety was experienced in a marketplace stocked with virtually indistinguishable goods, each bearing a brand name and claiming superiority over all others" (104). It seemed that Americans were exchanging one set of anxieties for another.

Although consumer goods promised the public happiness, they also offered a means for escaping fears about the atomic age. The world's capacity for destruction—as evidenced by more than 60 million casualties during World War II—was too overwhelming for the individual to comprehend. Atomic bombs, which killed an estimated 340,000 Japanese citizens within five years of the blasts,[5] made small-town America just as vulnerable to attack as any other city or military target. Like the citizens of Nagasaki and Hiroshima, Americans could suffer a similar fate one day. In fact a 1950 poll showed that 53 percent of Americans believed that "there was a good or fair chance that their community would be bombed in the next war, and nearly three-fourths assumed that American cities would be bombed. Most agreed that since Russia now had the bomb, the likelihood of another war increased" (May 25). These responses point to the psychological impact of the atomic age.According to one *Saturday Review* editorial, the aftermath of the bomb magnified the climate of fear in America. It unleashed "a primitive fear, the fear of the unknown, the fear of forces man can neither channel nor comprehend. . . . It is the fear of irrational death. But overnight it has become intensified, magnified. It has burst out of the subconscious and into the conscious, filling the mind with primordial apprehension" (quoted in Graebner 20). These fears of irrational death coincided with profound moral questions about such warfare. How could America justify using atomic bombs against a civilian population? How could one account for human behavior in the 1940s that included events such as the siege of Leningrad, the Holocaust, and nuclear warfare? These questions inspired feelings of guilt and encouraged many Americans to seek an escape from this oppressive past.

While a variety of forces—patriarchal hierarchies, economic discrimination, and psychological discouragement—marginalized women throughout the Great Depression, the labor needs of World War II offered them significant opportunities for achieving greater recognition as workers and citizens. According to Susan M. Hartmann, "Between 1940 and 1945, the female labor force grew by more than 50 percent, as the number of women at work outside the home jumped from 11,970,000 (with an additional 2.19 million unemployed) in 1940 to 18,610,000 (420,000 unemployed) in 1945" (21). Women were motivated by a sense of patriotism, an opportunity to earn money, and a desire to access professional roles previously denied to them. Some inspiration also came from propaganda. The War Manpower Commission created Rosie the Riveter, a tool-wielding worker who wore denim and proudly displayed her flexed arm, to represent the millions of women called to support the war effort in factories. Despite the number of women who joined the ranks of heavy industry, however, the majority found work in clerical and service jobs such as waitressing.[6]

Regardless all of these employment opportunities came with significant caveats. It was made abundantly clear to women that part of their patriotic duty included relinquishing their jobs at the war's end and returning to the domestic sphere. "They were reminded," Hartmann explains, "that their new positions were temporary, that retaining the traditional feminine characteristics was essential, and that their familiar roles continued to take precedence over all others" (23). Not surprisingly, millions of women left work (both by force and voluntarily) after 1945 as the country tried to reestablish old hierarchies and relegate women to the home. By 1946 the female labor force dropped from 19,170,000 to 16,896,000 (Hartmann 24), but it climbed again quickly. Many women, including a high percentage of wives who assumed that they would be happy to return home at the end of the war, changed their minds. They wanted to continue working. In fact the number of women in the workplace rose to nearly war-time peaks by 1947. America's patriarchal culture may not have been able to prevent women from working, but it did devalue this work through limited opportunities, wage discrimination, and an ongoing psychological campaign that insisted on women having an innate duty to raise children.

Fear and Isolation in *A Tree of Night and Other Stories*

To capture the war's place at the center of American life and consciousness in the 1940s, Capote placed "Miriam" at the center of *A Tree of Night and Other Stories*. First published in June 1945, "Miriam" depicts the psychological deterioration of Mrs. H. T. Miller after she witnesses newsreel footage of World War II. The sixty-one-year-old widow has tried to insulate herself from outside events by living alone in a small apartment, maintaining no friendships, and traveling no farther than the corner grocery store. No one in her building notices her, and she has even cultivated her external appearance in the most "plain and inconspicuous" way possible, wearing nondescript clothing, cutting her hair short, and never using makeup. Mrs. Miller's self-imposed isolation does enable her to control the world around her for a while. She keeps her rooms immaculate and follows the same pattern of cooking meals and feeding her canary every day. Such insularity not only prevents her from dealing with the complexities of human interaction but also shields her from the realities of World War II. She has escaped into a mundane routine, which Capote reinforces through the dry, repetitive sentence structure in the first paragraph: "Her interests were narrow. . . . Her clothes were matter-of-fact . . . ; her features were plain. . . . Her activities were seldom spontaneous" (163). The predictable sentence structure parallels the predictability of her life.

On the night Mrs. Miller hears/sees the newsreel, she begins encountering an imaginary girl named Miriam, and the two events force her to confront her own fears about mortality and the dangers of the war. In an uncharacteristic break from her routine, Mrs. Miller decides to see a movie. She is waiting in line to buy a ticket when she first notices a thin, fragile girl with silver-white hair and hazel eyes that "seemed to consume her small face" (164). The child is wearing an elegant dark blue dress, a plum-velvet coat, and a gold necklace. Her extravagant clothing (she will later appear at Mrs. Miller's doorstep wearing a silk dress) and jewelry contrast with the plainness of Mrs. Miller, whose finery remains hidden in closets and a jewelry box at home. After Mrs. Miller buys the girl a ticket, the two enter the theater together. Capote then introduces a war newsreel as the backdrop for their conversation: "The rumble of the newsreel bombs exploded in the distance. Mrs. Miller rose, tucking her purse under her arm. 'I guess I'd better be running now if I want to get a seat'" (165). Although Mrs. Miller wants to view this news/propaganda as nothing more than an announcement for the start of the film, the footage serves as a reminder of the destructive, global conflict that she has tuned out by isolating herself. The sound of exploding bombs, like the *New York Times* articles that she will either read or skim in her apartment the following week, brings the war to the forefront of her consciousness. Her newfound awareness coincides with Miriam's arrival, and Capote reinforces this connection by linking the sounds of this violent military battle with the harsh doorbell that Miriam rings to gain access to Mrs. Miller's apartment: "The doorbell . . . rang and rang and settled to a persistent buzz" (165). The bell's noise intrudes upon the peacefulness of the apartment, suggesting that Miriam represents unwanted knowledge about the self and the horrors of war.

Two other significant details emerge in this initial encounter with Miriam, and Capote ties both to his critique of isolationism. First, Mrs. Miller agrees to buy the girl a movie ticket but expresses regrets a moment later: "I feel just like a genuine criminal. . . . I mean that sort of thing's against the law, isn't it? I do hope I haven't done the wrong thing. Your mother knows where you are, dear? I mean she does, doesn't she?" (164). The ticket becomes an image for guilt and for questions of individual morality. In Mrs. Miller's case, she has chosen to remain disengaged throughout the war while others have sacrificed themselves at home and abroad. She has justified this in part by implying that the responsibility lies with someone else (such as Miriam's absent mother). Nevertheless she recognizes at some level that her actions are "wrong," even "criminal." Second, Mrs. Miller learns that she and the girl share the same first name—Miriam. This doubling can suggest a number of things. Some critics interpret the girl as a manifestation of schizophrenia, while others view the younger, elegantly dressed Miriam as a reflection of longing on Mrs. Miller's part. She is a woman who desires to shed her aged body and plainness for the girl's youthful glamour. Helen Garson offers a synthesis of these analyses: "One may subscribe to the particulars of any of these readings, but they all share the view that Mrs. Miller is a woman who finds her life intolerable, and who therefore creates another self, a person she simultaneously longs to be and rejects. She is destroyed by the revelation and can escape it only through madness" (*Truman Capote*, 14). If we place this story in the context of the 1940s, this doubling also captures the split between wanting to remain isolated from the realities of the war and confronting its horrors. Mrs. Miller repeatedly feels debilitated and exhausted from her encounters with the imaginary Miriam, and Capote presents this deterioration as an image for the emotional and psychological toll of social engagement. Like Miriam, who pushes her way into Mrs. Miller's apartment and refuses to leave, one cannot remain isolated from the world. By the time Capote wrote this story, for instance, the American public had known about Nazi concentration camps for years, and Pearl Harbor had long since shattered any hope that geographical distance would insulate the United States from the battlefield. These truths, like the name of the little girl, are buried inside Mrs. Miller. Her psychological state speaks both to her loneliness and to her pattern of disengagement. She has not wanted to confront what the war reveals about humanity's horrifying capacity for violence, the fragility of human life, and the moral culpability that every citizen shoulders for the actions of their country.

Finally, "Miriam" takes place during the winter, and snow imagery connects Capote's message about isolationism with the fear of mortality. Snow covers the city landscape. Plants and trees are dead, and the cold, wet weather makes even the voices of "a few children who romped high on mountains of gutter snow [seem] lonely and cheerless" (170). In fact the snow has a deadening effect on everything: "Wheels and footsteps moved soundlessly on the street, as if the business of living continued secretly behind a pale but impenetrable curtain. In the falling quiet there was no sky or earth, only snow lifting in the wind, frosting the window glass, chilling the rooms, deadening and hushing the city. At all hours it was necessary to keep a lamp lighted, and Mrs. Miller lost track of the days" (165). Capote's language reinforces the common association between winter and death; yet he depicts death in particularly sweeping terms. The snow blankets everything here, falling without any borders and implying a vastness on the scale of war. The incomprehensible loss of life during the 1940s is something Mrs. Miller has tried assiduously to ignore, in part, as a response to her own fears about mortality. Like knowledge about the war, death is something from which she ultimately cannot hide. She may try to keep it at bay by leaving the lights on, but death/darkness/cold air threatens to seep through the windowpanes at any moment. When she learns of Miriam's intention to move into the apartment, for example, Mrs. Miller cries but can produce only an "unnatural, tearless sort of weeping, as though, not having wept for a long time, she had forgotten how" (172). She has experienced her husband's death, but this tearless weeping suggests an emotional distance from that isolating loss. The cold snow thus serves as an image for the lack of warmth (that is, human contact) in her life. Her molelike blindness to the events of the war and the needs of others has taken away some fundamental aspect of her humanity. This absence of touch is also juxtaposed with Miriam's utter physicality. The girl pushes her way into the apartment, eats ravenously, touches everything, and smashes a vase of paper roses, which represent the artificiality of Mrs. Miller's existence and of isolationism in general. She even demands to be kissed at one point. Her physical connection to things offers another stark contrast with Mrs. Miller's aloofness. For Capote, emotional and physical disengagement—particularly in regard to the suffering and needs of others—is one danger of isolation.

In the first and final stories of the collection, Capote focused on women haunted by predatory figures. As with the relationship between Mrs. Miller and Miriam, this dynamic again captures the tension between isolation and social engagement in the 1940s. On one level "Master Misery" appears to be a coming-of-age story about a young woman, Sylvia, who has recently moved to New York City to shed her midwestern roots and to experience life on her own. Her independence and maturity are limited, however, by her fear of sexuality. For example, she is frustrated with her job at the SnugFare underwear company, whose products focus on body parts that she does not want to think about. Likewise she finds her friend's married life upsetting. When her friend tries to talk about sex, Sylvia refuses to listen: "'Estelle! For Christ's sake!' Sylvia sat bolt upright in bed, anger on her cheeks like rouge. . . . 'I didn't mean to shout. Only I wish you wouldn't talk like that'" (103). Her anger stems from embarrassment about her own sexual inexperience and a fear of sexual intimacy. She is too frightened to view sex as a positive stage of development. Not surprisingly, Sylvia's only friendship is with a former clown who reminds her of her childhood: "When I was a little girl I only liked clown dolls. . . . My room at home was like a circus" (107). She considers the weekend spent in her apartment with this friend to be one of the best experiences of her life and compares it to "the most beautiful party" (116). Circuses and parties typify the carefree pleasures of childhood, and here they represent her desire to remain in that state perpetually.

Capote also presents Sylvia's reluctance to embrace sexuality and adulthood as a metaphor for the nostalgic impulse in 1940s America. The world seemed to become a much more dangerous place after the Holocaust and the atomic bomb, and many Americans felt that the country had lost its innocence after 1945. Sylvia shares this desire to return to a simpler time in order to escape the dangers of modern life. Juvenile delinquency in the story provides one vivid example of these contemporary dangers: "two boys: pimple-faced, grinning, they loomed in the dusk like menacing flames, and Sylvia, passing them, felt a burning all through her, quite as though she'd brushed fire. They turned and followed her past a deserted playground, one of them bump-bumping a stick along an iron fence, the other whistling" (102). The images of heat suggest the sexual nature of the threat posed by the boys as well as Sylvia's own desires. Later that night she even feels a sense of loss "as though she'd been the victim of some real or even moral theft, as though, in fact, the boys encountered in the park had snatched (abruptly she switched on the light) her purse" (105). The "real or moral theft" implies rape, and the purse symbolizes something Sylvia still wants to protect—her virginity and sexual innocence.

Delinquent subculture first became a heated topic of discussion in the late 1940s, and public concerns over adolescent violence intensified into the next decade. By the mid-1950s a Senate subcommittee on juvenile delinquency conducted televised hearings on the matter, and Hollywood explored the issue in films such as *The Wild One, Blackboard Jungle,* and *Rebel without a Cause.* For many Americans, delinquency offered one manifestation of a world irrevocably changed by the horrors of war. Young people suddenly seemed to use violence to reject social norms and to express personal dissatisfaction. As the sociologist Harrison E. Salisbury argues in *The Shook-Up Generation,* "When we look at life today, the tensions between peoples, the constant threat of war, the preoccupation with weapons of unequaled power, the universal training of young men in the arts of death and destruction, we cannot fail to see in adolescent gang hostility a distorted reflection of the atmosphere of the world itself" (192). Cold War culture, in other words, was manifesting itself in juvenile violence and crime. For Capote, male delinquency (with the implied threat of rape here) anchored this story in one of the pervasive anxieties of the time.

Much like Mrs. Miller in "Miriam," Sylvia responds to the problems of the outside world through isolation, which emerges as an unrealistic choice for the individual and the country as a whole. Sylvia abandons living with her friend to rent a shabby, furnished apartment with a daybed, a bureau "with a mirror like a cataracted eye," and "one window" (109). The mirror captures Sylvia's willful blindness to the truth about herself and the world at large. Instead she surrounds herself with unread books, "antique newspapers," and the detritus of day-to-day life. Her insularity suggests a desire to cling to the past, to remain in a state of suspended animation by staying inside, eating cupcakes, and being cared for by the former clown Oreilly. Just as she fears the loss of sexual innocence, she wants to remain insulated from the hardships of modern life. At one point, however, she hears snippets of news on the radio: "*Lana Denies, Russia Rejects, Miners Conciliate:* of all things this was saddest, that life goes on: if one leaves one's lover, life should stop for him, and if one disappears from the world, then the world should stop, too; and it never did. And that was the real reason for most people getting up in the morning: not because it would matter but because it wouldn't" (114–15).

The realities of the Cold War and union strikes press upon Sylvia here. In fact the United States was reeling from labor unrest in 1945 over working conditions, pay, and pension plans. Toward the end of November 1945, for example, "225,000 auto workers at General Motors went on strike. Two months later they were joined by 174,000 electrical workers, and then 800,000 steel workers. Within a year of V-J Day more than 5 million men and women walked off the job" (Chafe 93–94). Sylvia's sadness comes from recognizing her desire to "disappear from the world" as untenable. Remaining isolated is merely another act of blindness. It is an attempt to disengage from one's moral and social responsibilities—choices that ultimately make Sylvia feel as if she has nothing meaningful to contribute. For Capote, Sylvia's idealization of childhood parallels the nostalgic desire in America for isolation. Throughout much of the 1940s the country was either yearning for a time before World War II (and the Great Depression) or escaping into a haze of consumerist excess, but neither option offered lasting comfort. These fantasies failed to shield the individual from the social and global implications of the Cold War and class strife at home.

Capote positions Mr. Revercomb as a metaphor for postwar fears as well. Sylvia first learns of Mr. Revercomb, who combs through people's dreams (*reve* being the French word for "dream"), while overhearing a conversation at the Automat. Something inexplicable draws her to his house, and she begins reciting her dreams to him, which he records and places in an elaborate filing system. After quitting her job, she becomes dependent on these sessions for money even though the encounters have a debilitating effect. Capote immediately crafts Revercomb as a mythical figure. He possesses a "graying invisibility" and has "flat gray eyes planted like seed in the anonymity of his face" (108). Oreilly even refers to Revercomb as Master Misery, a variant of the bogeyman: "All mothers tell their kids about him: he lives in hollows of trees, he comes down chimneys late at night, he lurks in graveyards and you can hear his step in the attic. The sonofabitch, he is a thief and a threat: he will take everything you have and end by leaving you nothing" (108–9). What exactly is the adult version of the bogeyman? Capote suggests that the terrors inhabiting the fantasy world of children have gotten replaced by the real terrors of mass executions and catastrophic weapons. Revercomb's/ Master Misery's graying invisibility and amorphous threat thus represent the visible dangers facing the country in the first half of the decade and the invisible ones of the Cold War, such as the prospect of another global war, the use of atomic bombs, and the fear of Communist infiltration. It is not surprising that Revercomb's home gets associated with death. The floors evoke the sound of ice cubes, and Sylvia imagines that the chrysanthemums in the entryway would "if touched . . . shatter, splinter . . . into frozen dust" (101).

A kind of misery did, in fact, shatter beauty by forcing the world to witness a virtually incomprehensible display of suffering during World War II. These events robbed many people of their dreams for a better future, and in the context of the war, many individual aspirations had been replaced by waking nightmares. When Sylvia explains that she wants to get her dreams back, Oreilly asks what she would do with them: "I would go home. . . . And that is a terrible decision, for it would mean giving up most of my other dreams" (117). Sylvia now realizes that her desire for isolation and nostalgic yearning for a simple past are incompatible with postwar life. As Capote suggests, the war created a new culture of uncertainty, leaving many people, such as Sylvia, fearful and disillusioned about the future. As she walks down the street at the end of the story, she claims to be unafraid of the boys following her because "there was nothing left to steal" (118). The human capacity to harm others and to inflict misery has left Sylvia uncertain about what she can hope for in her own life.

The eerie conclusion to the collection, "A Tree of Night" (published in October 1945), was written before the end of the war, and it returns to the image of the bogeyman in Capote's portrait of an isolated woman, Kay, who must confront death as she races toward an uncertain future. Once again the author uses youthful innocence and a journey into darkness as a metaphor for America's ongoing role in the war. At the outset of the story, Kay waits uncomfortably on an empty train platform after attending her uncle's funeral. Everything about the setting connotes death: the wintry landscape, the icicles hanging from the "station-house eaves like some crystal monster's vicious teeth," and the coffinlike train with its "decaying interior" and the stifling "dead smoke" of the compartments (206). These "vicious teeth" suggest something violent about death. It is an image of life being devoured by monsters—by abrupt losses such as those resulting from war, not nature. The nineteen-year-old protagonist, however, is insulated from these cold surroundings, protected by consumer goods such as her gray flannel suit, raincoat, and plaid scarf. Her wrapped body parallels the emotional insulation she feels about her uncle's death. The funeral was "an event, to tell the truth, that had not much affected her since she had scarcely known him" (213). Kay represents a country involved yet far removed from a distant war. Like many other of Capote's isolated characters, Kay has not really confronted or examined the implication of war-time losses. She has remained aloof from war's tragedies through her wealth and college education. When she feels most afraid, she clings to her sense of self—the engraved name on her purse and her nice clothing, glossy magazines, age, and status as a college sophomore. These details, like Mrs. Miller's daily routine and Sylvia's friendship with Oreilly, reveal Kay's attempt to avoid engaging with some of the more terrifying aspects of adult life—the war, mortality, and even sexuality.

Capote returns to the bogeyman figure to challenge such a sheltered existence amid the real-world adult horrors of violence. After entering the garbage-filled train car, Kay takes the only available seat across from two traveling sideshow performers—an intoxicated woman and a disabled man who can neither speak nor hear. Their act features the man, Lazarus, being buried alive. The woman wears a "black veil and a black dress," and the man dresses in a "gorgeous made-to-order bridegroom suit and a turban and lotsa talcum on his face" (212). In some ways by alluding to the biblical story of Lazarus, this performance offers an escapist fantasy about mortality. It taps into the audience's fear of death. Not surprisingly, some people cry during the performance, "especially the old ones" (212). The elderly patrons are certainly more aware of their own mortality than is a nineteen-year-old college student, for instance, but in the context of the early to mid-1940s this reaction can also be understood as a response to war-time casualties. America desired to stay out of the war, hoping it would be resolved without U.S. involvement and sacrifice. As the country took a more active role in military conflict, however, families soon had to cope with dead loved ones.

The disabled man also reminds Kay of something she cannot quite iden-
tify, and only after learning about his act does she recall a childhood memory
about the bogeyman: "Kay knew of what she was afraid: it was a . . . childish
memory of terrors that once, long ago, had hovered above her like haunted
limbs on a tree of night. Aunts, cooks, strangers—each eager to spin a tale
or teach a rhyme of spooks and death, omens, spirits, demons. And always
there had been the unfailing threat of the wizard man: stay close to the house,
child, else a wizard man'll snatch you and eat you alive! He lived everywhere,
the wizard man, and everywhere was danger. At night, in bed, hear him tapping at the window? Listen!" (216). The wizard man, like other mythical
figures of terror from her childhood, represents the mortal dangers that lurk
everywhere, that tap against the window demanding to be let inside. For Kay,
adults used these tales to frighten children into obedience (through warnings
to stay close to home) and, perhaps less consciously, to prepare them for the
terrors of adult life—namely death. Death, like haunting tree branches, casts
an unnerving shadow over everyday life. It will eventually devour everyone,
swallowing people whole as does the wizard man. As Capote makes clear
throughout the collection, war was the bogeyman. It tapped at the window
of most American homes and forced people to deal with the reality of sudden
death and brutality.

Alternating between Anxiety and Humor: The Internal
Structure of *A Tree of Night and Other Stories*

In addition to this framework, the collection alternates between tales of
gothic horror and black comedy as it builds toward and then moves away
from "Miriam." All of the stories share similar themes with "Master Misery," "Miriam," and "A Tree of Night." Dread, anxiety, and uncertainty
hang over the main characters. Most of them retreat into isolated spaces and
share a nostalgic idealization of childhood in attempts to escape uncomfort-
able personal truths and social horrors. In many respects this alternating
structure mirrored the zeitgeist of the decade. It reflected the tensions that
characterized American life—shifting between hope and fear, personal need
and national responsibility, and nostalgia and anxiety.

Composed in 1948, "Children on Their Birthdays" extends the themes
established in the opening story of the collection; even though its black humor offers some respite from the brooding quality of "Master Misery," it
portrays isolation and the idealization of childhood as dangerous. The story
recounts the year a ten-year-old girl named Miss Lily Jane Bobbit lived in a
small Alabama town with her mostly mute mother, and it details the lasting

impression she made with her unorthodox behavior and Hollywood aspirations. Like Sylvia, the narrator of "Children" is an isolated figure. Identified as Mr. C, he not only lacks an individual identity but also remains aloof from the family he lives with. As he observes, "She came on Sunday and I was there alone, the family having gone to church" (127). The narrator's exclusion from this weekly outing highlights his role as an observer in the town as opposed to a participant. He also shares Sylvia's fascination with childhood innocence: "It was almost nightfall, a firefly hour, blue as milkglass; and birds like arrows swooped together and swept into the folds of tress. Before storms, leaves and flowers appear to burn with a private light, color, and Miss Bobbit, got up in a little white skirt like a powder-puff and with strips of gold-glittering tinsel ribboning her hair, seemed set against the darkening all around, to contain this illuminated quality" (122). The lush description and magical imagery transform Miss Bobbit into a mythical figure, and yet her presence gets illuminated only because of the blackness around her.

This image can be understood in terms of adult nostalgia as well. Amid so much anxiety in the 1940s, the idea of children in small towns was an alluring one. It called to mind carefree innocence, happiness, and fun. However, this story reveals that clichéd images about childhood often masked darker truths. Mr. C's absent family, for example, is never discussed, and Miss Bobbit's father resides in a penitentiary. In the world of Capote's short stories, characters such as Mr. C must eventually come to terms with their nostalgic idealizations through social engagement. Just as Sylvia from "Master Misery" abandons her childish regression to enter the dangers of city life, the narrator of "Children" assumes a similar role after Miss Bobbit's death. He decides to tell her story even though he is not sure "what there is to be said about it; . . . still I know no one of us in this town will forget her" (119). His experiences with Miss Bobbit connect him with others. As the narrator/writer, he records events (including his own private conversations with her) that have value for the town, and this recording brings him into the community.

In addition Capote seems critical of the way American popular culture can transform history into a vehicle for consumerism. Miss Bobbit's talent-show performance, for example, invokes patriotic imagery to manipulate the crowd and to win a competition for a Hollywood screen test. Along with singing a racy song ("I was born in China, and raised in Jaypan . . . if you don't like my peaches, stay away from my can") and exposing her blue-lace underwear to the audience, she concludes her number by doing the splits, holding a Roman candle that "burst into fiery balls of red, white and blue," and "singing 'The Star Spangled Banner'" (133). Patriotism, which functions as a prop for the performance here, has been completely divorced from a meaningful context. Similarly Billy Bob, one of the boys who falls in love with Miss Bobbit, wears his "daddy's World War khakis" (125) while stirring up trouble and tormenting an African American girl. His behaviors and outfit are merely part of his performance to impress Miss Bobbit. In both cases the gap between these performances (for fame and romance respectively) and the nationalistic fervor that shaped American culture during the war suggest that popular culture has the power to devalue the real sacrifices of the past. It can transform history into something tawdry and artificial. Even the origins of the show reinforce this message. The event, which was hosted by a con artist who breezes through town and steals everyone's money, promises the winner a Hollywood screen test. In many respects he functions like Mr. Revercomb, who steals people's dreams—dreams based on the idealizations and false promises of popular culture.

Capote also uses the idea of sudden annihilation and the devil to tap into fears about the atomic age. The juxtaposition of the title ("Children on Their Birthdays") and the first line ("Yesterday afternoon the six-o'clock bus ran over Miss Bobbit") announces the chance event, the possibility of sudden annihilation, as a contributing factor to the shattering of American innocence. The realities of the atomic age threatened anyone at any moment, and this fear weighed heavily on the country at the time. Similarly the devil can be seen as an image for the dangerous "deal" that the United States made by developing the atomic bomb. Miss Bobbit, who wishes for fame and fortune as depicted in glossy magazines and Hollywood films, explains her pragmatic relationship with the devil: "Love the Devil like you do Jesus: because he is a powerful man, and will do you a good turn if he knows you trust him. . . . I always called on the Devil to help me get the biggest part in our annual show. That is common sense; you see, I knew Jesus wouldn't have any truck with dancing" (127). On the surface she offers a comforting philosophy in which morality (good/evil, right/wrong, Jesus/devil) exists in polarized terms. Yet she has embraced an odd fusion of these categories by loving both Jesus and the devil equally. Her moral framework has been complicated and blurred much like that of postwar America. The bombing of Hiroshima and Nagasaki raised profound ethical questions about U.S. military action and the specter of such destruction at home.

"Shut a Final Door," which first appeared in the August 1947 issue of *Atlantic* and earned Capote an O. Henry Award the following year, returns to the foreboding atmosphere of "Master Mystery" and the theme of isolationism. Specifically this frame story focuses on Walter Ranney, a man who has locked himself in a New Orleans hotel room to escape the truth about his callous treatment of others and his own sexuality. As he stares at the circular motion of the ceiling fan ("there was no beginning to its action, and no end" [137]), Walter confronts two aspects of his personality. First, he recognizes his own circular pattern of using people to get ahead: befriending Irving to meet people in New York (then having an affair with his girlfriend); using Margaret to get a job (before abandoning her); charming his boss to gain access to an upper-class social circle; lying about an engagement to a wealthy heiress to promote his public image; and spreading lies about others to harm their reputations. Second, the central point of the fan inspires Walter to contemplate his own center—namely the truth about his sexuality. Although by the end of the story he has not learned to accept his homosexuality, he does run out of places to hide and doors to shut himself behind. It becomes clear that he will soon receive another call from the mysterious stranger who seems to be pursuing him. Just as a little girl stalks Mrs. Miller in "Miriam," Walter receives a series of calls from an imaginary source (his own subconscious): "'Oh, you know me, Walter,'" the anonymous caller says. "'You've known me a long time'"; this "dry and sexless" voice speaks with such clarity that it sounds as if the speaker were "standing beside him with lips pressed against his ear" (146). The proximity of this voice implies that it comes from Walter himself, and the increasing frequency of these calls suggests that he can no longer suppress his homosexuality. All of Walter's rooms—the New Orleans hotel, his New York apartment, Margaret's place, and the rented room of the disabled woman—are, in fact, temporary spaces. Capote makes clear that Walter will never belong anywhere until he accepts the truth about himself. He must, in a sense, become like the club-footed woman who travels to Florida to display her disability at a medical conference. He must recognize his isolation and repression as disabling.

Like most of the characters throughout *A Tree of Night and Other Stories,* Walter tries to escape painful truths through a nostalgic idealization of childhood. After his social circle crumbles in New York, he decides to leave the city. Uncertain where to go next, he recalls childhood memories about the circus and his father: "silk caps, cherry-colored and lemon, and little, wise-faced men wearing exquisite polka-dot shirts. Closing his eyes, he was suddenly five years old, and it was delicious remembering the cheers, the hot dogs, his father's big pair of binoculars. Saratoga!" (145). Much like Sylvia, Walter wants to return to a time before the complexities of adult sexuality, and this dream inspires him to take a train to Saratoga. These fantasies also require Walter to reconstruct other aspects of his past, namely his relationship with his family. At the outset of the story, Walter admits that he left home because he needed "to get out of the house" (137). He later has a dream in which his father severs his son's fingers: "a man, his father, invitingly held open the door. Daddy, he yelled, running forward, and the door slammed shut, mashing off his fingers, and his father, with a great belly-laugh, leaned out of the window to toss an enormous wreath of roses" (146). This dream reflects Walter's desire for the fatherly affection he remembers from his childhood trips to the circus—a time characterized by affection ("Daddy") and unconditional acceptance. Instead his father cuts off the possibility of a physical connection between them (literally destroying Walter's hand), and in effect he severs their emotional bond.

His derisive laughter also suggests condemnation, which Capote explains through a parallel scene earlier in the story. After flirting with a homosexual man in a bookstore, Walter encourages the man to follow him down the street for several blocks: "Then I turned around and gave this guy a long, long look, and he came rushing up, all smiles. And I jumped in the cab, and slammed the door and leaned out the window and laughed out loud" (142). Walter's response to the man's sexuality parallels his father's actions in the dream. Together these moments expose Walter's fear of rejection for being homosexual: "It was like paying back all the people who've ever hurt me, but it was something else, too" (143). The "something else" involves Walter's feelings about his own sexuality, and he lashes out at the man in an expression of self-hatred. Thus childhood nostalgia functions like his mistreatment of homosexuals. It provides a temporary escape from truths about himself. Ultimately Capote presents nostalgia as dangerous for the individual and for a country that still wanted to retreat to an idealized past instead of confronting present-day problems. This central theme is expressed near the end of the story: "more and more he came to understand experience is a circle of which no moment can be isolated, forgotten" (148). Like Walter's memories of the circus, America's longing for a mythic point in the past to remain isolated from geopolitical issues cannot be understood ahistorically. The past and the present need to be reconciled.

Capote also links this desire for isolation with anxieties about changing gender roles in America. Walter often uses gossip as a weapon for expressing his anger about the role of women in the workplace. Walter's girlfriend, Margaret, offers to get him a job at an advertising agency, but his subsequent position as her assistant enrages him: "One of these days, though, he was going to have to get rid of her, and soon. It was degrading, his working for Margaret. And besides, the tendency from now on would be to keep him down" (140). Even though Walter's laziness has prevented his finding a job on his own and in all likelihood would keep him from earning a promotion, he blames his limitations on Margaret. The workplace changed dramatically during the war, and the highly visible role of women in the public sphere continued to be a source of anxiety for men. Walter's jealousy, resentment, and fear about working for women offer one example of this: "I told Kuhnhardt [her boss] a lot of lies about Margaret; I suppose that's pretty rotten, but she would do the same for me; and anyway my idea is not for him to fire her, but maybe transfer her to the Chicago office" (142). Walter's actions stem from both personal and social matters—his discomfort with her knowledge of his disreputable treatment of others and his resentment at having to work for a woman. He perceives the latter as emasculating, equating his job with feelings about homosexuality as antithetical to manhood. (He repeatedly perceives effeminate men, such as Irving for instance, in disparaging terms.)

Capote pairs "Shut a Final Door" with "Jug of Silver," and the latter offers a meditation on the tension between hope and disappointment in American consumer culture. As is the case with "Children," the narrator of "Jug of Silver" recalls a childhood memory with lasting importance for a small town. Capote reinforces its nostalgic dimensions, in part, through various details that evoke fairy tales and myths. The "Valhalla" drugstore, for instance, alludes to the paradise for slain warriors in Norse mythology, and it is rumored that Mr. Hamurabi comes from royal lineage in Egypt. Likewise the central figure of the story goes by the name Appleseed, which links him with the frontier myth of Johnny Appleseed. Every day for months this boy journeys to Valhalla to study the jug of silver coins. He claims to be able to count the coins by merely looking at them because a Louisiana witch once told him that he "could see things other folks couldn't" (154). In addition the antique soda fountain resembles a magic mirror that reflects customers "as though by candlelight, in a row of ancient, mahogany-framed mirrors" (150). Even the landscape has an otherworldly quality. Frost freezes the town in time, transforming it into "a picture postcard of a Northern scene, what with icicles sparkling whitely on the trees and frost flowers coating all windowpanes" (159). All of these details make "Jug of Silver" a modern fairy tale that reflects the nostalgic fantasies Capote's characters typically have about childhood innocence. The world of the story appears shiny, enchanting, and preserved from the outside world much like a scene in a snow globe.

Through his portrait of consumer culture, Capote quickly reveals the ways nostalgia glosses over painful truths. "Jug of Silver" recalls the narrator's part-time job at Mr. Ed Marshall's drugstore. When a new drugstore opens across the courthouse square and threatens business, Mr. Marshall comes up with an idea to crush the competition. He fills an empty wine jug with nickels and dimes, and any customer who buys "a quarter's worth of stuff" can guess the total amount to win the entire thing. His business thrives as a result, and yet this ploy inspires resentment on the part of the other store owner, Rufus McPherson. Rufus will try anything to bring back customers. He publishes a hysterical letter in the town paper about Mr. Marshall's unethical behavior ("turning innocent little children into confirmed gamblers and sending them down the path to Hell!" [153]) and later hires a man to disrupt the announcement of the prize winner. Such tactics change Rufus's reputation in town, in many respects deservedly so: "Nobody had anything for McPherson but scorn" (153). Yet his desperation also reveals a ruthless aspect of capitalism. Economic competition has social consequences in this town, and Rufus pays this price as well. While the narrator admits his own bias as Mr. Marshall's nephew ("This old Rufus McPherson was a villain; that is, he took away my uncle's trade" [151]), he presents Rufus's social marginalization as justified.

A certain degree of spitefulness characterizes Mr. Marshall's actions as well. When first learning of Mr. Marshall's plan, Mr. Hamurabi announces that he could write a book called "*The Skillful Murder of Rufus McPherson*" (152). Mr. Hamurabi recognizes that his friend Mr. Marshall wants to "kill" Rufus as an economic and social threat. Since the drugstore is a gathering place for this sleepy community, it has social as well as financial value, and Mr. Marshall does not want to lose either. In part he does so by tapping into the community's hopes and desires for material goods. As Mr. Hamurabi observers, the mystery of the silver jug intrigues people. It makes one wonder, "*how* much? And that's a profound question, indeed. It can mean different things to different people" (152). For most of Mr. Marshall's customers, though, it provokes consumer fantasies. Everyone participates in the contest: "Even the poolhall bums who never spent a cent on anything not connected with whiskey or women took to investing their spare cash in milkshakes" (152). Soon the town's favorite pastime is discussing how one might spend the prize money. Some of the answers include "a trip to and a permanent wave in Birmingham, a second-hand piano, a Shetland pony, a gold bracelet, a set of *Rover Boy* books and a life insurance policy" (157). Just as the frost converts the town into a postcard image (into something that can be consumed by the marketplace), people want this money to transform some aspect of their lives—whether through physical appearance (through a hairstyle or a new set of teeth), an image of class (jewelry, ponies), or through the pleasures of escapist fantasies (*Rover Boy* books, music). Capote suggests that everyone in town views money as essential for achieving one's dreams—similar to poor girls becoming princesses in fairy tales.

These questions about consumer culture are linked with broader concerns about American class hierarchies as well. The socioeconomic realities of the town and its surroundings further challenge the magical world in "Jug of Silver." The narrator explains that the poor people live "down by the silk mill," and in cold weather they "[huddle] together in the dark at night and [tell] tales to keep their minds off the cold" (157). He also notes the smell of "silk-mill girls" at the drugstore on Christmas Eve because they have scented themselves for the occasion. Poverty not only marginalizes these people but also renders them largely invisible to the town—until Appleseed arrives. Though Appleseed is not one of the silk-mill kids, his poverty provides a visual reminder of class discrepancies. Appleseed, a poor farm boy whose family lives three miles from town, does not have twenty-five cents to spend. He must walk to the store every day, and his outfit—a shapeless red sweater, blue denim britches, and oversized shoes—suggests that he will continue to grow into this poor, working-class identity, not escape it. He wants to win the money in order to buy his sister a new set of teeth. He believes (along with his sister) that she will strike it rich in Hollywood as long as she appears beautiful: "Middy's gonna be a big lady in the picture shows. They make lotsa money . . . and then we ain't gonna never eat another collard green as long as we live" (156). Here Capote links the promises of Hollywood (the silver screen) with the silver jug. Both provide the illusion of an escape from poverty (either temporary or permanent) and from working- and/or middle-class life through sudden wealth.

Winning the jug of silver does not change Appleseed's life, however. He disappears from the town as inexplicably as he arrived, and his sister never becomes a movie star. For Capote, the promises of Hollywood make most Americans complacent about poverty and economic inequity. Society marginalizes the poor in part by perpetuating the fantasy that everyone can have access to riches and fame. Capote recognizes that fairy tales, fiction, and film typically provide happy, idealized endings, but he resists this outcome in "Jug": "That's not what happened [Middy does not become a star], so why should you lie?" (162). Narratives of easy fortune have damaging personal consequences. Appleseed's obsession over winning the jug, for instance, takes a physical toll, and Mr. Hamurabi responds to the boy's noticeable deterioration by viewing such false hopes as destructive: "Hope of this kind is a cruel thing to give anybody, and I'm damned sorry I was ever a party to it" (156). Through Hamurabi, Capote further questions America's prosperity myth. While there is much truth to Mr. Marshall's view that hope and disappointment characterize life, he here ignores the link to consumer culture. The disappointments and hopes in "Jug of Silver" are perpetuated by businesses and a popular culture that encourages nostalgic portraits of childhood.

Ultimately Capote invites the reader to recognize the harmfulness of such mythology.

First published in the November 1946 issue of *Harper's Bazaar* and included in *The Best American Short Stories 1947*, "Headless Hawk" too presents the social alienation that comes with isolation. Like "Children on Their Birthdays" and "Shut a Final Door," "Headless Hawk" begins with the ending, and its circular structure reinforces the protagonist's sense of entrapment. Vincent Waters wrestles with his own aimlessness and disconnection from the world. He views himself as "a poet who had never written poetry, a painter who had never painted, a lover who had never loved (absolutely)" (181), and this failure to act makes his job at an art gallery suitable. He does not create things; he merely displays the artistic accomplishments of others. One day an oddly dressed southern girl, D. J., enters the gallery with a painting to sell, and Vincent feels an immediate attraction. Comparing her to the carnival freaks he admired as a child, he recognizes "a little something wrong, broken" about her and admits that he typically falls in love with such people: "Strange, though, that this quality, having stimulated an attraction, should, in his case, regularly end it by destroying it" (179). The cyclical nature of his personal relationships (from desire to dissolution) parallels his stagnant professional life. Both lead him nowhere and reveal aspects of his personality that are self-destructive. After inviting D. J. to live with him, Vincent gradually learns of her obsession with an enigmatic figure named Mr. Destronelli, her history at a psychiatric hospital, her bisexuality, and her insatiable appetite for film. He calls her "crazy" at one point and locks her out of his apartment. D. J. continues to follow him, however, and Capote gives the sense that Victor—much like Mrs. Miller in "Miriam"—will not be able to escape the haunting of this double figure.

The imagery in D. J.'s painting not only captures the anxiety created by World War II but also reveals Capote's critique of isolationism. Her painting depicts "a headless figure in a monklike robe reclined complacently on top a tacky vaudeville trunk; in one hand she held a fuming blue candle, in the other a miniature gold cage, and her severed head lay bleeding at her feet: it was the girl's, this head, but here her hair was long. . . . The wings of a hawk, headless, scarlet-breasted, copper-clawed, curtained the background like a nightfall sky" (179–80). Neither religion (monk's robe) nor popular culture (the vaudeville trunk) provided much solace for a traumatized world during and immediately after the war. The savage violence of the recent past still hung overhead with outspread wings, and many Americans felt that war and economic depression could erupt again at any moment. Furthermore the type of violence possible through mass exterminations and the atomic age operated with a blind indifference to the human cost.

Vincent ignores the social implications of these images and instead views them as a statement about his own "secret" self, particularly his lack of direction (180). As suggested by the vaudeville trunk, the theatrical elements of this painting make Vincent characterize himself as "an actor unemployed"— as someone performing a role only for himself. This type of isolation makes him callous and indifferent to the pain of others. By identifying with the hawk, which typically soars high above the earth in search of prey and uses its keen visual ability to hunt effectively, Victor recognizes the ways in which he too is a hunter. He seeks out strange, broken individuals for relationships, including his cousin, the "poor, beautiful, stupid Lucille"; Connie, the deaf girl who wanted to become an actress; the romantic Gordon with his "kinky yellow hair"; and Allen, who "thought it was to be forever" (186). He brings these people into his grip and then destroys them through emotional and literal abandonment: "Was it true [Gordon] had shot himself?" Victor's identification with a *headless* hawk (one without sight) reveals his lack of perspective about himself and the consequences of his actions. This lack of vision gets reinforced through the blurred images that Victor sees of himself and D. J. At the antique store, for instance, "he saw [D. J.'s] greenness distorted wavy through double glass" (176). A candelabra of blue candles casts a "delirious light" throughout his apartment, and in a mirrored door he observes himself and D. J. as "pale and incomplete" in their "rippled reflection" (183, 184).

Vincent's limited sight extends to his other senses as well—most notably sound—and this detail reinforces Capote's message about a character's disconnection from the outside world. When Vincent hears his umbrella tapping against the pavement, it reminds him of Morse code (a crucial form of communication for the military in World War II), and yet its meaning remains indecipherable to him. This noise, like the "trick car horn hooting 'My Country, 'Tis of Thee'" and the "U.S.A. music pouring from jukeboxes," becomes part of the city's cacophonous sounds (177). For Capote, these details reinforce his portrait of Vincent as removed from American culture more broadly. Patriotic tunes and distinctively American music fail to resonate because he has become too locked within himself to care about outside events. Ultimately his relationship with D. J. pulls him deeper into an isolated, withdrawn space. It encourages greater disengagement from the social and political. He abandons his friends and loses his desire and ability to read the newspaper: "His eyes concentrated on the paper's headlines—but what did the damn thing say?" (176); and after D. J. first spends the night, "he thought of the *Tribune* and the *Times* waiting outside the door, but they, this morning, held no charms; it was best lying here beside her in the warm bed, sipping tea, listening to the rain" (185). Whatever engagement Vincent had with the outside world during the war has ended, and he retreats to the closed-off spaces of his apartment and the art gallery.

Capote also crafts D. J. as a type of doppelganger for Vincent to illustrate postwar Americans as haunted by a recent history that they are desperate to escape. In many instances D. J. assumes a ghostlike presence in Vincent's life. After their first encounter in the art gallery, she vanishes for months and then appears as an apparition in a carriage: "There was a single occupant, and this passenger, whose face he could not see, was a girl with chopped fawn-colored hair" (181). Weeks later he recognizes her amid a crowd of spectators watching two female dancers: "her eyes were clear-black. First terror, then puzzlement replaced the dead lost look" (183). By the end of the story, she follows Vincent like a phantom. Just as many Americans were still reeling from images and accounts of the massive destruction and loss of life during the war, Vincent is also being haunted by the past. His resistance and inability to read newspapers, for instance, suggest that modern life has contributed to these feelings of dread. Likewise he dreams of apologizing to his former lovers: "Gordon, forgive me, I never meant . . ." (189).

Both D. J. and Vincent escape the pain of personal and arguably social history through popular entertainment. Capote establishes a number of parallels between the characters. Both are bisexual, stalkers, and painters (though Vincent does not act on his desire to create art) who share an insularity that blinds them to the outside world. They also rely on popular culture such as funhouses and films to escape everyday anxieties. Though Vincent expresses frustration with D. J.'s daily obsession for movies, he admits to a similar passion: "There had been in his own life a certain time of limbo when he'd gone to the movies every day, often sitting through several repeats of the same film; it was in its way like religion, for there, watching the shifting patterns of black and white, he knew a release of conscience similar to the kind a man must find in confession to his father" (188). Vincent, like much of the country, felt in a state of limbo throughout the first half of the 1940s—caught between hope and fear, security and vulnerability. Religion (as explicitly referenced here and alluded to through the monk's robe) failed to provide comfort for many, which explains its absence in the story. D. J. notes, for instance, that she does not hear any church bells on Sunday morning (185). Vincent and D. J. have responded by turning toward popular entertainment instead, and while it seems to offer an emotional/psychological/spiritual outlet, it fails to provide lasting comfort.

Although D. J. is not a figment of Vincent's imagination (as Miriam is for Mrs. Miller), Capote does use her to introduce a bogeyman figure, Mr. Destronelli, as an image for destructive social and personal forces. D. J. explains to Vincent that Mr. Destronelli "looks like you, like me, like almost anybody" (184); "*sometimes he is something very different: a hawk, a child, a butterfly*" (194). He can assume different names, such as Dr. Gum at the psychiatric hospital, but ultimately he is connected with death: "*so I knew he was going to murder me. And he will. He will*" (194). On one level Mr. Destronelli represents the threat that outside forces pose to the individual in the form of mortality and the loss of innocence. The hawk image links him with the violent, predatory dangers of the world, while the association with children serves as a reminder of lost innocence and vulnerability. Mr. Destronelli's depiction as a butterfly implies transformation as well. The United States had certainly changed as a result of its experiences with war. Violent dangers became a part of everyday life, and in a sense the country lost its innocence. D. J.'s innocence has been shattered by the heartbreak of Miss Martha Lovejoy Hall's marriage, and she responds to this profound loss by withdrawing so far into herself that she cannot function in society. She is institutionalized, and after running away from the hospital, she becomes homeless—unable to let go of her past or to connect with others. This decision to turn inward reflects a broader attempt in America to retreat to prewar innocence through consumer culture and popular entertainment.

"My Side of the Matter" returns to the issue of gossip and male anxiety about female power in its portrait of another isolated figure. The narrator, a sixteen-year-old boy who gets married after a four-day courtship, finds himself with a pregnant wife who insists on moving back to a small Alabama town to be with her spinster aunts. Gossip in this story is about power and control, and the narrator uses it to assert his masculinity in an all-female space. Capote's humor comes in part from the contrast between the narrator's biases and the facts that he unintentionally reveals about himself concerning his own laziness, racism, and misogyny. His own fear of gossip underscores its power: "I know what is being said about me and you can take my side or theirs. . . . I just want the citizens of the U.S.A. to know the facts, that's all" (196). Many of the "facts" he provides about his aunts come from gossip, such as Aunt Olivia-Ann's "morbid crush on Gary Cooper" (200) and her ability to frighten the piano teacher to the point that "he tore out of this house one afternoon like old Adolf Hitler was on his tail" (201).

The narrator happily perpetuates mistruths in order to counteract the ways that Aunt Olivia-Ann and Aunt Eunice have emasculated him since his arrival. They immediately question his manhood: "He's not any sort of man whatsoever. . . . Why, he isn't even of the male sex" (198). Such sentiments continue unabated as the sisters criticize his lack of employment, his laziness around the house, and his unwillingness to help Marge during her pregnancy: "'How can a girl have a baby with a girl?' says Olivia-Ann, which was a calculated attack on my manhood" (199). The narrator's story responds to this emasculation by demeaning the sisters in as many ways as possible. He feels threatened by their money and their influence over residents of the small town. He claims at one moment that no one will speak out against them for fear of retribution. His paranoia reflects widespread fears about female power in the 1940s. He depicts them as physical grotesques ("Eunice is this big old fat thing with a behind that must weight a tenth of a ton" [197]), animals (Olivia-Ann's voice reminds him of "the mating call of a jackass" [199]), and not fully white. He notes that a photograph of Eunice and Olivia-Ann's father suggests that he "has black blood in him from somewhere" (202). Language enables the narrator to degrade them in the most powerful way possible—associating them with animals and African Americans. With his own wife he gets physical, slapping her when she gets too sassy: "I provided her with a couple of good slaps and put a stop to that" (201). He relies on physical and verbal aggression to reinforce patriarchal hierarchies. As the critic Blake Allmendinger has argued, the narrator "Sylvester creates a history for himself and other characters building a sexual hierarchy that subordinates women and defines people by establishing their patriarchal roots" (285).

This anxiety about female power in the story culminates in violence and isolation. When Olivia-Ann and Eunice's servant, Bluebell, refers to him as trash, he becomes enraged ("Naturally that coal-black nigger made me so mad" [204]) and breaks a silk parasol on her head. The sisters then attack the narrator. At one point Olivia-Ann gives him "this terrific knee punch" to the groin and starts singing: "Mine eyes have seen the glory of the coming of the Lord; He is trampling out the vintage where the grapes of wrath are stored" (204). She has, in a sense, crushed his grapes, and he accordingly decides to escape these women by barricading himself in the parlor with a box of Sweet Love candy (205).

Conclusion

Most critics have interpreted the dark, foreboding elements of Capote's work in psychological terms, arguing that Capote's primary interest rests in self-exploration and the inner world of his isolated, often fragmented characters. Indeed self-exploration is often a tortured and painful process for Capote's characters, but placing his works in the context of the 1940s provides an important additional framework for understanding his fiction. The shift between the horrific and the humorous in *A Tree of Night and Other Stories* reflects truths about contemporary struggles in American culture to feel safe in a climate of fear, to assert individuality amid conformity, and to find happiness within the self when consumer goods promised the good life. Additionally this critical approach offers a way to reconcile the division that critics have traditionally employed for interpreting Capote's works as alternating between "the dark and the sunny, the terrifying and the amusing" (Clarke 86). Instead we can view Capote as an incisive commentator on American culture and a writer deeply engaged with the social milieu. His collection emerges as a rich portrait of the anxieties and uncertainties that consumed the nation at the time. Even the internal structure of the collection —alternating between stories of anxious uncertainty and black comedy that builds toward and moves away from "Miriam"—reflects the mood of the era. Read within its historical context, *A Tree of Night and Other Stories* becomes a very different kind of collection. It captures the zeitgeist of the era, aligning itself with the short fiction of Eudora Welty, Carson McCullers, and Flannery O'Connor in its social and cultural commentary. In addition it provides greater insight into Capote's explicit references to World War II, communism, the Cold War, and gender hierarchies.

CHAPTER 3

Other Voices, Other Rooms

The photograph on the book jacket of Truman Capote's first novel, *Other Voices, Other Rooms* (1948), shows the author reclining on a Victorian couch and staring provocatively at the viewer.[1] In one hand he holds a cigarette, while the other rests on his crotch. Many reviewers found this image as distasteful as the book itself. *Time* characterized *Other Voices, Other Rooms* as "calculated to make the flesh crawl. . . . But for all the novel's gifted invention and imagery, the distasteful trappings of its homosexual theme overhang it like Spanish moss"; and the *New York Times Book Review* concluded that "the story of Joel Knox did not need to be told" (quoted in Clarke 155). These responses capture some of the pervasive concerns about homosexuality at the time. In the same year Alfred Kinsey released *Sexual Behavior in the Human Male*, which reported (among other things) that most men masturbated, nearly 50 percent had engaged in extramarital affairs, some experimented with bestiality, and 37 percent "had reached orgasm through at least one homosexual act" (Fraterrigo 41).[2] The House Un-American Activities Committee launched an investigation into Alger Hiss in 1948 as well, and rumors soon characterized Hiss's accuser, a former Communist and admitted homosexual, as a jilted gay lover. *Other Voices, Other Rooms*, which immediately landed on the *New York Times* best-seller list, contributed to this turmoil.

The novel is a coming-of-age story about a teenager who discovers and learns to accept his homosexuality. Since his mother's death, Joel Harrison Knox has been staying with his aunt, but he decides to leave after receiving an unexpected invitation to live with his estranged father in Skully's Landing. The nearest town to the Landing is populated by disabled and

freakish people, and the family members waiting for Joel—his stepmother
Amy and effeminate older cousin Randolph—have unusual bodies as well.
A faint mustache grows on Amy's upper lip, and her gloved hand thumps
like wood against solid objects. Randolph's feminine features, crooked nose,
golden hair, and pudgy body dovetail with his penchant for dressing as an
eighteenth-century countess. The strangeness of these characters—particularly those who blur gender boundaries—heightens Joel's discomfort with
his own body and sexuality. From the outset he worries that his father, Ed
Sansom, will reject him for not being "taller and stronger and handsomer
and smarter-looking" (51–52), but his fantasies about finding a masculine
role model are shattered soon after he arrives. Sansom, the former manager
of a prizefighter named Pepe Alvarez, became paralyzed after Randolph accidentally shot him. Grief and guilt have consumed Randolph ever since. When
Joel tries to leave town after going to the circus, he catches pneumonia, and
Randolph nurses him back to health. Joel's delirious state enables him to
recognize his burgeoning affection for Randolph.

In the closing moments of the novel, Joel sees Randolph dressed as a lady
and goes to him. This decision to embrace his own homosexuality, however,
seems to necessitate Joel's isolation from others. His friendship with neighbor Idabel Thompkins, a tomboy who discovers her own same-sex desire in
the novel, ends when her family sends her away to live with other relatives.
Likewise his deep affection for Missouri ("Zoo") Fever, a young African
American woman who works for Amy and Randolph, does not last either.
Her experiences with spousal abuse and rape position her too solidly in the
real world for Joel. He wants to be protected from the social realities of racial
and sexual violence, not exposed to them, so he chooses instead to live with
Randolph.

Freak shows, one of the most popular forms of entertainment in America
between 1840 and 1940, play an integral role in the novel. Acts of gender/
sexual ambiguity and racist depictions of nonwhites were staples on the
sideshow stage, and both appear in *Other Voices, Other Rooms* to indict the
ways society relegated same-sex desire and African Americans to the realm
of the freakish. For white gays and lesbians in the novel, homosexuality
transforms them into spectacles—figures to be mocked and ostracized by
mainstream America: "So fierce is the world's ridicule," Randolph explains
to Joel, that "we cannot speak or show our tenderness" (147–48). Just as
the book condemns these cultural practices, it also links homophobia with
the plight of African Americans. The damaged black body provides a visual
reminder of the degrading racial hierarchies and brutal violence that African
Americans have endured throughout U.S. history. Capote once claimed that

he "had more empathy with [African Americans] than [with] anyone else."
In many respects this comment suggests that he viewed homosexuals and African Americans as sharing similar experiences. In the same interview, Capote
elaborates on his ongoing concern with racial injustice: "Most of the time,
the relationships between white people and colored people in the South were
kind. But then there would be that moment when you saw them stepping
off the sidewalk for us to pass—I just couldn't accept that at all. Couldn't
believe it, almost. A little circus used to come to town. All the white children
would ride on the merry-go-round, while the colored children just watched. I
couldn't stand it. I never wanted to ride" (Steinem 103). Capote's protagonist
in *Other Voices, Other Rooms* witnesses a similar scene of racial segregation at the circus, hears racist epithets, and learns about Zoo's experiences
with sexual violence. Not only does he view numerous characters in terms
of freak-show performers, but he also encounters a dwarf who explicitly
equates homosexuality with being a freak. Freakishness thus emerges as a
central image for social marginalization, and it becomes part of the dreamlike texture in *Other Voices, Other Rooms* that exposes brutal inequities at
the heart of American society and rejects the silence surrounding violence
against black women and homophobia.

Freak Shows and Bodies on Display

First appearing in museums and then as part of circuses and world's fairs,
freak shows traveled throughout the United States between the 1840s and
1940s. For the price of admission (which usually ranged from ten cents to a
dollar), one could stare at alligator men, dog-faced boys, tattooed princesses,
midgets, the severely disabled, nonwhites, and anyone whose body could
be presented as strange and unusual. P. T. Barnum[3] and other freak-show
entrepreneurs used a variety of techniques, such as staging, costuming, and
spiel, to transform performers into freaks. Typically these displays relied on
juxtaposition and context to exaggerate differences: placing dwarfs next to
giants; fabricating marriages between fat ladies and skeleton men; dressing
nonwhites as exotic cannibals and wild men from Fiji, Africa, and South
America; and asking audiences to guess about (and in some cases pay extra
to "discover") the true sex of bearded ladies and hermaphrodites. Other com-
ponents of these shows further reinforced the performers' status as freaks.
Dwarfs and midgets, such as Charles Stratton ("General Tom Thumb") and
Leopold Kahn ("Admiral Dot"), assumed elevated titles. Giants wore hats
to enhance their height, and exotic exhibits dressed in scanty clothing, carried spears, and appeared with primitive backdrops. Freaks participated in
stage performances as well, acting out poorly written parodies and giving

renditions of popular plays. Tom Thumb,[4] for example, sang, danced, and did numerous impersonations. Siamese twins Chang and Eng performed acrobatics, including flips and other feats of physical strength.[5] All of these characteristics ritualized the encounters with the freaks and established what audiences expected to see.

The freak represented what the audience was not—the Other, someone excluded from mainstream society for being different—and in this way s/he reaffirmed the cultural superiority of the onlooker. This presentation of freakishness helped place conformity at the center of middle-class values, equating the unusual body with extreme individualism. As Rosemarie Garland Thomson has explained, "The spectator enthusiastically invested his dime in the freak show not only to confirm his own superiority, but also to safely focus an identificatory longing upon these creatures who embodied freedom's elusive and threatening promise of not being like everybody else" (*Extraordinary Bodies,* 69). To some extent this paradox between individuality and conformity in American society was mitigated by the freak, whose body made physical difference the clear basis for exclusion. Not surprisingly, the success of freak shows was contingent on their ability to maintain the distance between viewer and freak, to simultaneously challenge and reinforce binaries about gender (male and female), race (white and nonwhite), and bodies (able and disabled).[6]

Two of the most popular freak exhibits featured sexual ambiguity and nonwhites. The former played with questions of authenticity ("Is it a man or a woman?") that generated a great deal of public curiosity. Bearded ladies, for example, wore elegant gowns and took great pride in the length of their beards. Madame Jane Devere's beard, for instance, in 1884 measured fourteen inches, which her manager deemed a world record.[7] Although audiences wanted to know the true gender of bearded ladies, this question occurred in the context of exhibits that never explicitly challenged conventional gender roles. Bearded ladies were presented as the embodiment of Victorian womanhood. They claimed to be devoted wives and posed for photographs with their husbands. Some even gave birth. Likewise hermaphrodites, or half-and-halfs, appeared to be divided in two (with a male right side and a female left side, for instance), clearly displaying characteristics of each gender. This gender division was signaled most clearly by body hair, makeup, and clothing—though the female side of a hermaphrodite often displayed a breast. Like most freak exhibits, bearded ladies and hermaphrodites reinforced the idea that difference was visible, that ambiguity could not go undetected, and in this way these performers sent comforting messages to heterosexual audiences.

Ethnological or exotic exhibits reinforced existing racial hierarchies by presenting degrading images of nonwhites. The "exotic" origins of these exhibits were reinforced through staging (which often included rocks, shrubbery, and sticks), costumes, and routines that tended to feature crawling, growling, and other animalistic behaviors. Although freak-show managers primarily relied on African American performers, they worked tirelessly to obfuscate their ethnicity. Instead these performers appeared as "Congo, the Ape Man" or "The Wild Dancing South African Bushman." Barnum's notorious "What Is It?" offers an early example of this offensive legerdemain. First presented in 1860, Henry Johnson, a mentally retarded African American with microcephaly, was cast as a mysterious man-animal hybrid billed with the headline "What Is It?"[8] Many of Barnum's promotional images featured Johnson standing alone, and his isolation along with an exotic backdrop maintained the distance between viewer and spectacle. Any possible threat that Johnson could pose to onlookers was further mitigated by advertisements that referred to him as a docile and harmless "man-monkey."[9] As this example illustrates, freak shows used negative images of blackness to draw crowds. Whether those on display were actually from South Africa, the Congo, or New Jersey, they were presented as culturally inferior, socially barbaric, and non-American.

Although freaks played an integral role in circuses during their golden age (1870–1920), they gradually became less enticing for the public in this context. Instead of featuring one performer, circuses presented "ten-in-ones," allowing patrons to see ten exhibits for the price of one. Freaks were placed in separate tents from the big tops (hence the term "sideshow"), and this distinction further changed the atmosphere surrounding these exhibits. Inside a museum such as Barnum's, freaks had some respectability; they were integrated into a whole and displayed under the guise of learning and scientific study. But on the fairgrounds, the freak show gradually seemed dirtier and more difficult to justify. One even had to buy a separate ticket to see it. This contributed to its waning popularity, and by the 1940s the sideshow had become a distasteful and dying form of entertainment.[10]

Freakishness in *Other Voices, Other Rooms*

By framing the novel with two freak shows (one figurative, one literal), Capote taps into the declining reputation of the freak show both to reinforce Joel's view of same-sex desire as freakish and to critique the social marginalization of homosexuals and African Americans. In order to perceive himself as normal (that is, heterosexual), Joel needs to view Skully's Landing and its inhabitants in terms of a carnival sideshow. Amy and Randolph, for example, "were fused like Siamese twins: they seemed a kind of freak animal, half-man half-woman" (120). Little Sunshine is described as an ugly, bad-smelling, toothless hermit who brews magic potions, and Jesus Fever has a face "like a withered apple, and almost destroyed; . . . his sickle-curved posture made him look as though his back were broken: a sad little brokeback dwarf crippled with age" (29). As a matter of fact, the bodies of almost every character in the novel are deformed or disabled in some way—with the exception of Joel's. Only gradually does Joel seem to transform into something freakish as he becomes increasingly aware of his homosexuality. When he first looks into the mirror at his father's house, he sees only a distorted version of himself: "it was like the comedy mirrors in carnival houses; he swayed shapelessly in its distorted depth" (50). Later his unusual reflection gets associated with sexual identity, and shortly after this, he perceives his new haircut as disfiguring: "it made him in silhouette resemble those idiots with huge world-globe heads" (116). The farther away he drifts from conventional masculinity and heterosexuality, the more deformed his body appears to him, and Capote uses this self-loathing to illustrate one of the more insidious aspects of homophobia: it prevents many homosexuals from being able to envision their own sexuality as healthy and normal.

Capote primarily examines the problematic link between freakishness and homosexuality through Idabel and Randolph. The young girl gets introduced as a wild, feisty troublemaker whose clothing and tomboyish behavior make her a freak in the eyes of the townspeople: "Well, it wasn't no revelation to me cause I always knew she was a freak, no ma'am, never saw that Idabel Thompkins in a dress yet" (21). Clothes typically provide a visible sign of one's gendered identity, but Capote presents Idabel's garments as a form of protest. She refuses to wear a dress even if it means being banned from Miss Roberta's store, for instance, and her wild behavior consistently challenges gender norms. She yells, hurls rocks, spits, and throws punches. Among her family members she feels closest to her gay uncle, who is "so afraid of girls he won't look at one; he says I'm not a girl; I do love my Uncle August: we're like brothers" (130). Idabel signals her inchoate sexuality through boyish outfits, physical toughness, and her brotherly relationship with Uncle August. These efforts reject the pervading view of gender as a natural expression of one's sexuality. It is not surprising that these displays of unconventionality threaten the townspeople, who associate her body and behavior with freakishness. In an attempt at ridicule, her twin sister, Florabel, points out Idabel's deformed, blackened thumb, and this moment makes clear that Florabel reads the damaged body as another sign of her sister's social deviance.

Like most freak show audiences, Joel aligns himself with the crowd at first. He accepts Florabel's and the community's view of Idabel as a freak in order to feel normal—to "go away to a school where everybody was like everybody else" (110–11). He recognizes his effeminacy as deviating from the norm, and he fears that his feminized body—like Idabel's clothes and brash behavior—will make him a freak as well. In another example, Zoo Fever tells Joel the story of Randolph's mother, Angela Lee: "Honey, a mighty peculiar thing happened to that old lady, happen just before she die: she grew a beard; it just commence pouring out her face, real sure enough hair; a yeller color, it was, and strong as wire. Me, I used to shave her, and her paralyzed from head to toe, her skin like a dead man's" (124). Angela Lee's inadvertent transformation into a bearded lady becomes an image for Randolph's—and possibly her own—aberrant sexuality. Her body challenges a dualistic understanding of gender, and it suggests that Randolph's flamboyant homosexuality can be read on his mother's aging body as well. Randolph is not merely gay; he cross-dresses, becoming a "queer lady" who gazes out an upstairs window and wears hair like "a wig of a character from history: a towering pale pompadour with fat dribbling curls" (67). Like Idabel, he communicates his sexuality through outward signs such as clothing, which ultimately make him less threatening to the townspeople. Being able to "see" homosexuality leaves the categories of normal/abnormal and self/freak intact. It enables them to consider their own damaged bodies (such as the one-armed barber and Miss Roberta with hairy arms, a pronounced wart, dirty fingernails, and enormous breasts) as normal.

In the context of a society that needs to equate same-sex desire with freakishness, the only models for homosexual happiness (through Idabel and Randolph) come at the expense of being labeled a freak. Thus Capote suggests that sexual self-discovery for gays and lesbians cannot be understood apart from the social costs of coming out. In her frustration with being labeled a freak, Idabel convinces Joel to run away with her the night of the circus, and there she meets Miss Wisteria: "At the 10 cents Tent, they saw [her]. . . . They did not quite believe she was a midget, though Miss Wisteria herself claimed to be twenty-five years old" (191). Idabel's infatuation soon becomes clear to Joel: "Then a queer thing happened: Idabel, borrowing the lipstick, painted an awkward clownish line across her mouth, and Miss Wisteria, clapping her little hands, shrieked with a kind of sassy pleasure. . . . But as she continued to fawn over tiny yellow-haired Miss Wisteria it came to him that Idabel was in love" (192–93). Ironically, Miss Wisteria attributes Idabel's behavior to freakishness: "Poor child, is it that she believes she is a freak, too?" (195). Idabel's happiness helps open Joel up to the possibility of same-sex love, but for Idabel, that love is short-lived. Miss Wisteria abandons her to flirt with Joel, and Idabel's family eventually punishes her (for breaking her sister's nose, for attempting to run away, and arguably for defying social norms) by sending her to live with distant relatives. Her same-sex desire comes at a severe personal cost.

Likewise Capote uses Randolph's experiences as a gay man—along with his isolation in the Landing—to condemn the kind of anger and rage often directed at those living openly gay lives. When Randolph eventually rejects heterosexuality, he does so for an abusive, unrequited love affair. Before he meets Pepe, Randolph's marriage to Dolores was strained by her repeated fantasies about killing him. She kept a dream book/diary in which she wrote about Randolph "fleeing before her, or hiding in the shadow," and "she'd murdered in Madrid a lover she called L., and [Randolph] knew . . . that when she found R. . . . she would kill him, too" (144). Part of this rage came from her awareness of Randolph's sexuality. He had been able to hide it from her and himself until meeting Pepe. As he recalls to Joel, "Strange how long it takes us to discover ourselves. . . . The brain may take advice, but not the heart, and love, having no geography, knows no boundaries: weight and sink it deep, no matter, it will rise and find the surface: and why not? Any love is natural and beautiful that lies within a person's nature; only hypocrites would hold a man responsible for what he loves" (147). Randolph expresses the novel's central theme about sexuality as a true expression of the self, as something that does not adhere to social norms. As a result the persecution of someone on the basis of sexuality is immoral. Randolph's philosophy, however, does not protect him from the prejudices of others. He realizes that Samson and Pepe loathe him, and one evening a drunken Pepe urinates on Randolph's art, calls him hurtful names, and breaks his nose (149). His sexuality makes Randolph a target for abuse, which he accepts. Pepe eventually runs off with Dolores, and Randolph shoots Ed in a delusional rage. Ever since then Randolph has been sending letters to Pepe around the world, care of the postmaster: "Oh, I know that I will never have an answer. But it gives me something to believe in. And that is peace" (154).Ultimately Randolph hopes to find peace by seducing Joel and trapping him in the insular world of the Landing.

Of course Capote presents Randolph and Idabel as offering problematic models for living a homosexual life—Idabel gets exiled by her family, and Randolph exiles himself. The moment Joel accepts his homosexuality certainly raises questions about the extent to which Joel has come into his own. A teenager being seduced by an older man is far from ideal, and this option seems no better than the family life he had with Aunt Ellen. Joel is ultimately choosing the artificial world of Randolph, who has been manipulating him from the start: Randolph wrote the letter claiming to be Joel's father, sabotaged the boy's correspondence with his aunt, and took him to the abandoned Cloud Hotel just before his aunt's visit. Furthermore all of Joel's models for same-sex desire involve gender inversion (as illustrated by Idabel's boyish clothes and Randolph's gowns). But what about homosexual love that is not manifested by cross-dressing? That is mutual? Perhaps the absence of these models is best explained by Capote's use of freakishness. Freak-show imagery exposes the damaging impact of a social structure that provides few— if any—positive models for homosexual happiness. Joel's relationship with Randolph enables him to break free from the heterosexual imperatives to marry a woman and have a family, but at the cost of being perceived as freakish. Capote argues, however, that it is the hypocrisy of social attitudes that transforms homosexuality into something freakish. Post–World War II America needed the queer body to be seen as a kind of spectacle—as an unattractive alternative to heterosexuality—because the American Dream was so closely linked with images of the nuclear family. In this way the intersection of freakishness and same-sex desire in *Other Voices, Other Rooms* reveals the debilitating impact of heterosexual imperatives on everyone, regardless of sexual preferences. By choosing a young adult poised to make his own choices about sexuality, Capote gives heterosexual imperatives an insidious overtone. They make sexuality an issue of social control, a way of preserving white, middle-class hierarchies; sexual choice is not about personal freedom.

Capote uses the exploitation of the black body to illustrate another set of hateful ideologies underlying freakishness in American culture. Along with the other characters depicted as freakish in and around Skully's Landing, Joel views African Americans in terms of ethnological, freak-show exhibits. This perspective highlights the way that both this entertainment and the cultural notion of freakishness helped solidify widely held prejudices—even within people (such as Joel) who were susceptible to other forms of discrimination. Joel's racism contributes to a divisive culture that marginalizes both African Americans and homosexuals, and Capote is critical of Joel's inability to recognize this connection. Specifically, Joel likens all of the African American characters to freak-show performers. Jesus Fever, for example, is "a sad little brokeback dwarf crippled with age" (29), and the "bullet-headed" hermit Little Sunshine is toothless and has "a blue cataract in one eye" (95). Dwarfism and disability were commonly exploited traits on the sideshow stage. The shape of Little Sunshine's head also suggests that he suffered from microcephaly, "a condition associated with mental retardation and characterized by a very small, pointed head and small overall stature," and African Americans with this disability were frequently staged as "missing links" (Bogdan 111–12). Capote makes the connection between blackness and freak shows most explicit through Joel's offensive description of Zoo: "She was slant eyed, and darker than the charred stove; her crooked hair stood straight on end, . . . and her lips were thick and purple. The length of her neck was something to ponder upon, for she was almost a freak, a human giraffe, and Joel recalled photos, which he'd scissored once from the pages of *National Geographic,* of curious African ladies with countless silver chokers stretching their necks to improbable heights" (54–55). Joel views her body entirely in terms of the racial stereotypes associated with freak shows. Zoo becomes an animal-human hybrid here—much like Barnum's "What Is It?"—and the reference to African ladies with silver chokers further casts her in the exotic mode.

Capote includes this moment to reinforce his point about the dangerous power of freakishness. It makes a spectacle out of difference and transforms people into types, enabling their disenfranchisement and persecution. Capote's reference to *National Geographic* also alludes to the historical connection between freak shows and medical science. Throughout this entertainment's history, showmen relied heavily on the medical field to promote and advertise exhibits. Scientists often lent their names to these publicity efforts to gain access to people with disabilities and to promote their own careers. Yet medical science capitalized on the extraordinary body as well through hospital amphitheaters, textbooks, and museum exhibits such as embalmed bodies and other preserved remains.[11] Capote highlights science's contribution to widely held prejudices to raise questions about the kind of scientific judgments being made about race.

Violating the Black Body: Rape and the Early Civil Rights Movement

While Capote uses Zoo's classification as a subhuman-exotic freak to illustrate one dimension of southern racism, he also expresses concern about the way it tacitly encouraged the abuse of black women. Men repeatedly inflict violence on Zoo's body. Not only does her sexual assault remain unpunished at the end of the novel, but it becomes clear that no one outside of Skully's Landing will ever hear about it. Even Joel, who views Zoo as a mother figure and friend, reacts by "[plugging] his ears; what Zoo said was ugly, he was sick-sorry she'd ever come back, she ought to be punished" (216). This callous response reflects Joel's ongoing desire to cling to a fantasy world that silences the personal costs and social implications of sexual abuse. Capote, however, confronts the reader with the horrifying details of Zoo's story not merely to condemn the practitioners of such acts but to express moral outrage over white America's willful blindness to the problem of sexualized violence against black women. Throughout the Jim Crow era, sexual assault frequently served as a tool for terrorism. As McGuire notes, "[W]hite men abducted and assaulted black women with alarming regularity. White men lured black women and girls away from home with promises of steady work and better wages; attacked them on the job; abducted them at gunpoint while traveling to or from home, work, or church; raped them as a form of retribution or to enforce rules of racial and economic hierarchy; sexually humiliated and assaulted them on streetcars and buses, in taxicabs and trains, and in other public spaces" (xviii). Just as Zoo's experiences exemplify such practices, *Other Voices, Other Rooms* also interrogates the broader ways that male aggression functioned as a mechanism for affirming patriarchal power. Both white and black men torment Zoo; as such, physical abuse reflects a culture of violence that disproportionately harms black women.

On September 3, 1944, a few months after Capote returned to Monroeville, Alabama, and began writing *Other Voices, Other Rooms,* a rape in the nearby town of Abbeville started to receive national attention.[12] Recy Taylor, a sharecropper and twenty-four-year-old wife and mother of three, was walking home from a late-night church service when she was approached by a green Chevrolet. Several men armed with knives and guns pulled her into the vehicle and took her to a grove of pecan trees a few miles away. After being dragged from the car and forced to disrobe, she was raped six times, blindfolded, and dumped alongside the highway. Her description of the car helped police track down its owner, Hugo Wilson, whom she subsequently identified as one of the rapists. While being questioned by police, Wilson named the other men with him that night in the car. He claimed they "all had intercourse with her" but insisted that she was a prostitute who received payment. The sheriff released Wilson and decided not to arrest anyone.[13]

Reports of the incident, however, quickly spread across the state. Churches, pool halls, and other social gathering places for African Americans buzzed with the news. It soon caught the attention of Rosa Parks, an investigator with the NAACP whose work for the organization focused on cases of sexual violence against black women. She had read countless letters from rape victims and fervently believed this issue needed to play a central role in civil rights activism. Parks launched an inquiry into Taylor's rape, traveling to Abbeville to interview her and later returning to Montgomery to help organize a defense campaign. These efforts generated a great deal of media attention. On October 28, 1944, the *Pittsburg Courier,* the most influential black newspaper in the country with weekly sales topping two hundred thousand copies, ran its first article about the Taylor case. This newspaper "made the rape of Recy Taylor a national example of Southern injustice" (McGuire

17), and soon afterward letters from African American soldiers flooded the office of the governor of Alabama, Chauncey Sparks. Many railed against the double standard of asking African Americans to fight against fascism abroad while denying justice to blacks at home. Some even demanded a new trial.

The "Abbeville Affair," as it was dubbed, began to compromise the U.S. war effort by tarnishing the image of American democracy abroad.[14] It also brought unwanted publicity to the state. Eventually Governor Sparks agreed to launch an investigation, but these efforts proved fruitless. His investigators did discover new evidence, including contradictory statements from the assailants about the incident, but a jury of white men issued no new indictments in February 1945. Although the efforts of Rosa Parks and the NAACP failed to achieve justice for Taylor, her case—along with the massive migration of African Americans at the time, the political pressure that curtailed employment discrimination in federal industry, and the desegregation of the military in 1948[15]—helped strengthen ties in the black community across the country and set the stage for the civil rights movement. As McGuire has argued, "The 1955 Montgomery bus boycott, often heralded as the opening scene of the civil rights movement, was in many ways the last act of a decades-long struggle to protect black women, like Taylor, from sexualized violence and rape" (xvii). It seems likely that Taylor's rape inspired Capote to incorporate a similar incident in the novel. Capote, a voracious reader of news and fiction, spent much of his career as a journalist, and he was most certainly aware of the national controversy brewing around him. Despite the clear allusion to Taylor in the novel, the brutal sexual assault of Missouri "Zoo" Fever initially seems so out of place in the dreamlike narrative of Joel Harrison Knox that most literary critics have not addressed it. Placed within the historical context of 1940s Alabama, however, Zoo's experiences draw attention to the ongoing use of rape as a tool for oppressing black women and expose the unjust social hierarchies perpetuating such violence.

Dreaming of Snow: Rape and the Sexual Politics of *Other Voices, Other Rooms*

Capote initially presents Zoo's departure from the South as a response to Jim Crow laws. She lives at the Landing to care for her ailing grandfather, Jesus Fever, but as soon as he dies, she plans to leave for "some swell city up north like Washington, D.C." (56). Her desire to move north places her among the millions of African Americans who had been leaving the rural South since the 1890s to escape segregation, racial violence, and limited economic opportunities.[16] The fictional region surrounding the Landing offers all of these challenges for blacks. The narrator describes the jail in Noon City, for example, as not as not having housed "a white criminal in over four years"

(17), but Joel later notices "a young Negro [watching a woman] sadly from the isolation of the jail" (189). Law enforcement punishes African Americans disproportionately even as it allows "the most dangerous types of cutthroats . . . [to] run free and wild" (17).

Joel also witnesses segregation at the carnival, which prohibits African Americans from using the merry-go-round. This particular ride suggests that blacks are denied an entire range of pleasures that whites regularly—and merrily—enjoy. Furthermore on the Landing, Amy's explicit racism reminds Zoo of her place in the social hierarchy: "Niggers! Angela Lee warned me time and again, said never trust a nigger: their minds and hair are full of kinks in equal measure" (167). For Amy, the inferiority of nonwhites could be read on the body, and she links Zoo's decision to go north (without saying a word or making one final breakfast) with racist stereotypes about her hair. Even though the epithet "nigger" is not used by most of the characters, Joel does mock Zoo's intellectual limitations, and Randolph endorses the idea that African Americans belong to a lower social class. When Randolph learns about her journey to Washington, D.C., he tells Joel, "Missouri Fever will discover that all she has deserted is her proper place in a rather general puzzle" (168). Capote condemns these attitudes in part through Randolph's art. When Randolph explains that the feathers assembled on the cardboard simulate a living bird, Joel states, "What good is a bird that can't fly? . . . The other one, the real one, it could fly. But this one can't do anything . . . except maybe look like it was alive" (169). This metaphor suggests that Capote finds fault with laws (such as segregation) and a cultural climate that limit individual freedom. These things rob people of their authenticity and vitality, reducing them to lifeless objects.

In addition to these racist practices and attitudes, Capote also anchors Zoo's abuse in the history of slavery, highlighting white America's ongoing investment in racial hierarchies that disenfranchise African Americans. In the closing moments of the book, for example, the rape-ravaged Zoo tries to uproot a rusted slave-bell from the garden: "Zoo, crouched near the broken columns, was tugging at the slave-bell, trying, it seemed, to uproot it, and Amy, her hair disarranged and dirt streaking her face like war paint, paced back and forth, directing Zoo's efforts" (228). This is an image of both exploitation—through the reliance on black labor—and violence. Amy's war paint and pacing cast her as a kind of plantation overseer, and through this description, Capote suggests that the threat of violence tends to characterize white America's relationship with blacks. Interestingly, Amy hopes to sell this rusted bell as an antique, but the bell, like Southern racism itself, appears intractable. It cannot be moved because it is not yet a relic. It continues to reflect contemporary race relations: "As soon as [Amy] was gone, Zoo spit vindictively on the bell, and give it such a kick it overturned with a mighty bong" (229). Her anger and gestures of protest are futile, however. For Zoo, the bell offers another painful reminder of the loss of her social and sexual freedom. Her return to the Landing as a servant reveals a surrendering on her part. She no longer fantasizes about escaping or living in the North. She has accepted her place in the social hierarchy, as Randolph predicted.

A second allusion to slavery reinforces Capote's concern over the reluctance among many whites to acknowledge and respond to racial injustice. When Joel and Randolph arrive at the Cloud Hotel, their mule, John Brown, climbs a staircase before jumping to his death: "Then, as if insane with terror, he came at a gallop, and lunged, splintering the balcony's rail. Joel primed himself for a crash which never came; when he looked again, the mule, hung to a beam by the rope-reins twisted about his neck, was swinging in mid-air, and his big lamplike eyes, lit by the torch's blaze, were golden with death's impossible face, the figure in the fire" (226). The name directly refers to the white militant who orchestrated the 1859 raid on the federal arsenal in Harper's Ferry, Virginia. John Brown believed fervently in the abolitionist movement. He participated in the Underground Railroad, protected many runaway slaves, and killed several whites who held pro-slavery views. The Harper's Ferry raid, in which five African Americans and sixteen whites stormed the arsenal with the intent of arming slaves, ended with Brown's swift capture. He was then tried for treason and hanged. The mule's death thus signifies disengagement. White characters in the novel do not fight for black civil rights, and even Joel turns his back on social and political issues. He refuses to look at the hanging mule as he leaves the hotel, choosing instead to return to the insular world of the Landing. Capote presents this choice as irresponsible. The more Joel embraces Randolph's insularity the more emotionally detached he becomes from Zoo—refusing to listen to the story of her rape or to offer any empathy.

Capote further explores the consequences of racial hierarchies through Zoo's victimization at the hands of both black and white men. Shortly after meeting Joel, Zoo alludes to the cruelty of her former husband: "[O]ne time there was this mean buzzard name of Keg, but he did a crime to me and landed himself on the chain gang, which is sweet justice considerin the low-down kinda trash he was. I'm only a girl of fourteen when he did this bad thing to me" (56). Capote subsequently reveals that Keg Brown cut Zoo's throat from ear to ear, leaving a snake-like scar across her neck. Keg's punishment, however, changes little, for Zoo lives in perpetual fear of his return: "'And who knows but what Keg's done runaway from the chain gang? Joel, honey, latch the door. [. . .] Someday he gonna come back here lookin for to slice me up. I knows it as good as anythin'" (157; 158). Keg's motives are never explicitly revealed, but they can be understood, in part, as a response to his own powerlessness in white society. Capote implies as much by linking Keg with the African American who participates in Zoo's subsequent assault. Specifically, Zoo's white rapists are accompanied by a black man who rides in the back of the pick-up truck with a mound of watermelons. At one level, this racist imagery implies a profound anxiety among working-class whites who seek out and perpetuate degrading images of African Americans. His position in the truck and the fact that he is ordered to bring the rifle reinforce his subservient status. On another level, his complicity reveals a desire to assert a higher social position and modicum of power by contributing to Zoo's debasement. Even though he may have few options at this moment as a black man in the South, Zoo does not detect any hesitation, empathy, or remorse on his part: "'That mean nigger look a whole lot like Keg, an he put that rifle up side my ear'" (215). The reference to her former husband connects the two acts of violence, suggesting that both men lashed out against Zoo to some extent as a response to their own position in white society. Last, Capote links sexual violence with Zoo's "longin for city life" (57), which she first mentions when discussing Keg. Zoo dreams of walking through hip-deep snow and watching it fall from the sky (57), and this gives D.C. some of its appeal. Snow equalizes everything. It covers the ground, temporarily erasing the landscape, and in this way it becomes a metaphor for equality and forgetting. As a black woman, Zoo wants to leave behind the racist hierarchies of the South as well as her experience with spousal abuse. To some extent, she needs to forget these histories in order to achieve freedom, and she sees Washington, DC as a snow-covered refuge. This place should ensure her right to control her own body and to make her own choices. These hopes typify what America (as symbolized by Washington, DC) promised its citizens—social and personal liberty. Yet, as Zoo's story suggests, these promises were routinely and violently denied to African American women.

Zoo's violent rape on this trip, however, serves as a reminder of the ways race and sexuality intersect to oppress black women. Exhausted from carrying a quilt filled with her belongings and from walking for an entire day, Zoo decides to rest by the roadside. She is gazing at the stars overhead and nursing her blistered feet when several men in a red truck stop. The driver, an older man with a cigar, then pushes her into a ditch, tears open her dress, and invites the three boys with him to rape her. Meanwhile the African American man, who had been in the back of the truck "squatting on top of a mountain of watermelons" (215), now stands guard with a rifle to prevent her from screaming and trying to escape. When the white boys finish, they ask the driver to take a turn, but he refuses, claiming that he does not like to be watched. His refusal causes the others to laugh. In response he "[squats] impotent at her side like a bereaved lover . . . and '[pushes] that cigar in [her] belly'" (216). Zoo notes that one of the boys wore a pair of sailor's pants and a soldier's shirt, and this detail—like her decision to go to DC—points to the paradox of American democracy, which presented itself during and after World War II as a model for those struggling against oppression around the globe. Yet the discrimination against and abuses of African American women undercut such claims. Instead of protecting her, this soldier/sailor participates in her assault, and here Capote depicts the government (represented by this military figure) as tacitly endorsing racial and sexual abuses. Zoo has been used as a tool for white labor, as a sexual object, and now an as outlet for white rage when the impotent driver figuratively rapes her with his cigar. His burning of her flesh brands her the victim of male power.

Together these incidents make a broader statement about subjugation in American culture. Zoo occupies the lowest rung of the social ladder, and her repeated violation at the hands of white men, white women (Amy), and black men keeps her in this place. For the historian Darlene Clark Hine, "[T]he fundamental tensions between black women and the rest of the society —especially white men, white women, and to a lesser extent, black men— involved a multifaceted struggle to determine who would control black women's productive and reproductive capacities and their sexuality" (41). Zoo tries to take control of her sexuality by leaving the South, but she learns that these oppressive structures are not regional, but national. Her status as a black woman will always prevent her from achieving personal freedom.

Separate Rooms: Conclusion

Capote draws a connection between Joel and Zoo's freakishness in *Other Voices, Other Rooms* to highlight one of the problematic ways that society demonizes difference—through popular entertainment. Freak shows helped reinforce widely held prejudices by transforming race and sexuality into spectacles. It was not uncommon among sideshows, for instance, to charge customers extra to "see" the true gender of a hermaphrodite or a bearded lady, and these behind-the-curtain strip acts offered another layer of violation to the exchange. Freak-show performers were not only stared at, mocked, and in some cases prodded or groped while onstage, but they could also be unclothed to provide additional amusement for the viewer. These exhibits may have raised provocative questions about gender and sexuality, but they ultimately labeled anything other than heterosexuality as freakish. Capote illustrates the social appeal of this message through the community of the Landing and Noon City. The townspeople readily view unconventional expressions of gender and sexuality in terms of freakishness, and as a result homosexual characters—such as Joel and Idabel—feel a profound sense of marginalization. Likewise ethnological or exotic exhibits played into pervasive racial stereotypes. The presentation of nonwhites as culturally and socially inferior helped justify practices such as segregation, which none of the white characters questions or challenges in the novel. In the case of female ethnic exhibits, freak shows also made it easier for audiences to view black women as objects to use and violate.

Capote also implies a connection between Zoo and Joel by casting Joel as a rape victim of sorts. When Idabel—the girl who befriends Joel at the Landing—wrestles him to the ground after he tries to kiss her, a shard from her sunglasses cuts his buttock during the assault (as if he were losing his virginity): "'Please stop, I'm bleeding.' Idabel was astride him, and her strong hands locked his wrists to the ground. She brought her red, angry face close to his: 'Give up?'" (135). Joel's submission to Idabel's strength, his position on the ground beneath her, and the loss of blood evoke a rape. He experiences a figurative loss here, and his determination to find social acceptance through heterosexuality is shattered. For Capote, however, Zoo's actual rape and torture reveal prejudice to be far more insidious than homophobia in America. Even though Joel identifies with Zoo, he does *not* want to be marked like her: "Maybe she was like him, and the world had a grudge against her, too. But christamighty he didn't want to end up with a scar like that" (72). The distinction is an important one, for Capote recognizes that whiteness gives Joel access to power and privileges that African Americans do not have in the United States. He recognizes that the social and personal costs for black women are far greater than those for gay white men.

So where does Capote's novel leave us? Joel and Randolph retreat to a room removed from broader social concerns. Randolph's position as a white man of some means insulates him from most homophobic persecution, just as it facilitates a disengagement from sociopolitical issues. Joel's decision to enter this space signals a similar disconnect. He abandons his affection for Zoo and Idabel, focusing instead on himself, and while Capote does not condemn this choice outright, he certainly presents it as problematic. Joel is the victim of a predatory older man, and his isolation from others has already robbed him of empathy—his abandonment of Zoo and Idabel being the most notable examples. In the end, any shared sense of marginalization between Joel and Zoo (between homosexuals and African Americans) is fleeting, and it certainly does not build a coalition for civil rights. The groups remain separate from each other, in large part, because both heterosexual and homosexual whites still rely on the exploitation of black labor in the South. Racism, therefore, seems less surmountable than homophobia, and the white and black characters in the novel resign themselves to this. Perhaps lifting the shameful silence around rape is a step in the right direction. *Other Voices, Other Rooms*—like news reports about Recy Taylor's rape and other victims of sexual abuse—draws attention to the culture of violence inflicted on African American women. In this way it tries to undermine the silence surrounding this issue. Silence is a form of indifference, a tool for perpetuating social injustices, and even though Joel is not ready to "hear" Zoo's story, Capote forces his readers to listen.

CHAPTER 4

The Grass Harp

As children in rural Alabama, Truman Capote and Nelle Harper Lee often escaped to the tree house in her backyard, climbing up the chocolate-colored bark and disappearing for hours at a time. This place, Clarke notes, "became their fortress against the world, a leafy refuge where they read and acted out scenes from their favorite books" (22). The young Capote needed respite not only from town bullies but also from lingering doubts about the affection of his parents, who had left him with Lillie Mae's relatives in the summer of 1930. As a result Jennie, Callie, and Nanny Rumbley ("Sook") Faulk became the boy's family for the next two years; along with Harper Lee's tree house, they would inspire a number of his works, including *The Grass Harp* (1951).

Though *The Grass Harp* begins as a nostalgic meditation on self-discovery and love, it gradually becomes a cautionary tale about the dangers of social conformity and materialism. The narrative opens with the protagonist, Collin Fenwick, recalling his teenage years with the Talbo family. Verena, a composite of Jennie and Callie Faulk, is matriarch of the house and arguably of the town. Her successful businesses have made her its wealthiest inhabitant, and she has clearly used this money to influence local politics. Dolly, "a delicate happening" (11) and clear stand-in for Sook, possesses a childlike innocence, a quality Capote emphasizes through her passion for the color pink and sweets. Her closest friend, Catherine Creek, claims to be Indian (instead of African American), has no teeth (rendering her speech virtually indecipherable), and possesses a truculent nature (as illustrated by her fearless resistance to whites). She lives in a shed on the property, making Capote's homage to Anna unmistakable.[1] The central conflict involves Dolly's dropsy cure, an enigmatic gypsy medicine that she brews once a year in the backyard and sells to mail-order customers throughout the state. Once Verena real-izes its potential profitability, she decides to mass-market the product. She purchases an abandoned factory, gets involved with a shady business partner named Morris Ritz, and demands that Dolly disclose her secret formula in order to begin production. Dolly refuses, and later that night she runs away with Collin and Catherine to take up residence in a nearby tree house on the outskirts of town. This setting links their arboreal retreat to the central image of the novel: the grass harp. To get to the tree, the group must walk through the high Indian grasses that sing in the wind—grasses that remember the lives of the dead and whisper their stories like notes strummed on a harp. Two others join their escapade: a tough, free-spirited teenager named Riley Henderson; and the philosophical Charlie Cool, a retired judge.

The tree becomes a place where the group abandons social mores; they smoke, drink, and tell stories late into the night. Most important, they reveal hidden truths about themselves here. It becomes a space where, as Judge Cool explains, "five fools in a tree [are] free to find out who [they] truly are" (41). Meanwhile, Morris Ritz proves to be a con man, stealing thousands of dollars from Verena and skipping town. After discovering the extent of her losses, Verena commands the sheriff to remove the tree dwellers by force. When the police and an armed posse approach the tree at the end of the novel, the ensuing melee concludes with someone shooting Riley, shattering his shoulder and rendering him temporarily unconscious. The remaining mavericks descend from the chinaberry tree and resume a mundane existence in town. Dolly gives up her burgeoning romance with Judge Cool to reclaim her pink room and dies shortly thereafter from a stroke. Riley, who has previously admitted his emotional detachment from girls, gets married and becomes a prominent figure in the community. Collin abandons his deepen-ing affection for Riley and leaves town to pursue a law degree. From his adult reflections on his childhood, however, it seems clear that his place in the establishment has brought him neither happiness nor a sense of belonging.

Like many Jazz Age expatriates, Capote often wrote his best work about American life when he was overseas; he composed this novel between June 1950 and May 1951 in Taormina, Sicily. He may have been thousands of miles away from his beloved New York, but he never lost touch with happen-ings at home. He corresponded daily with friends and read several U.S. news-papers every afternoon.[2] Despite the charming humor of *The Grass Harp*, Capote admitted to his editor at Random House that there was something painful about writing it: "Satisfying as, in that sense, it is, it keeps me in a painful emotional state: memories are always breaking my heart. I cry—it is very odd, I seem to have no control over myself or what I am doing"(quoted in Clarke 219). Some of the pain must have stemmed from memories of his childhood abandonment. Even after Lillie Mae sent for him in 1932 to join her in New York, she continued a pattern of emotional abuse.[3]

At the same time, Capote's nostalgic impulse to revisit his childhood through *The Grass Harp,* instead of continuing with his novel about contemporary New York life,[4] can be seen as a reaction against the cultural climate of the Cold War in 1950. A closer look at his correspondence from this period reveals Capote's anxieties about the growing tensions over territorial control and political influence in Europe. On July 6, 1950, less than two weeks after the start of the Korean War, Capote wrote to his friend Andrew Lyndon: "Simply can't work this morning: across the hill they are having some sort of military maneuvers—much bullet fire etc. When it began we thought it was the Russians. And so have been thinking about the Russians ever since. No one here seems to feel there is going to be a big war; actually, they don't care—are really apathetic. We get our news here so late; I have no idea what is happening. Oh, the thought of a wartime America! I hope you will have the good sense to stay out of uniform this time."[5] In fact fears about another global conflict worried Capote throughout his time in Sicily, impacting his work on *The Grass Harp;* a few months later he complained, "What with war at the window and a river of lava at the door, it has been impossible to concentrate. . . . I suppose by this time the Russians have reached Messina: we never see any news except week-old issues of *Time.* I wonder really what we should do. I hate at this point to think of coming home."[6] While this notion of Russian-occupied Messina reflects Capote's cynical humor about American hysteria at the time, it also stems from legitimate fears regarding the Cold War. Capote repeatedly fretted about leaving Italy early: "Actually I don't think the war is going to start searing a path through Europe for another year or two, but even so I guess it is foolhardy to stay here beyond the spring."[7] These reservations about coming home might be attributed in part to the cultural climate in the United States. The maniacal efforts of McCarthyism to persecute Communists at home included vicious, public attacks on homosexuality, and these attitudes were undoubtedly an affront to Capote's identity.

This is not to suggest that Capote viewed himself as a political activist; he frequently described himself as apolitical. In a 1967 interview with Gloria Steinem, for example, Capote stated, "I'm not a political person at all. Everything with me is extremely personal. Vietnam involves me emotionally, but not politically" (103). Yet such statements were typically followed by

sociocultural criticism on his part. In this case Capote went on to condemn
segregation and to recount his childhood experiences with African Americans. Such mixed messages were quite common from a man who made an
art out of contradicting himself and misrepresenting his life and work. As he
once remarked, "I don't care what anybody says about me as long as it isn't
true" (Inge 178). Certainly Capote did not want to be a political writer at
a time when producing such work was dangerous in America (the jailing of
Hollywood screenwriters began in 1950), but an overt political agenda also
ran counter to his professional goals. He wanted to reach the widest possible
audience. He wanted to be famous. Nevertheless his art reveals an acute
eye for the zeitgeist of the period, and the popularity of *The Grass Harp*
suggests that the text resonated with a nostalgic desire among Americans to
climb into a tree high above the pervasive fears and realities of the Cold War.
Placed in the historical context of 1950, this enchanting coming-of-age story
becomes something far more radical in its call for social reform.

Fear of another world war and economic depression intensified in post–
World War II America with what appeared to be the rising Communist
threat. The Soviet Union tested an atomic bomb on September 3, 1949, an
event that made the prospect of a nuclear conflict seem inevitable for most.[8]
As Elaine Tyler May notes, a 1950 poll showed that more than 60 percent
of Americans believed that the United States should use atomic weapons
in a future war. Furthermore, "53 percent believed there was a good or
fair chance that their community would be bombed in the next war, and
nearly three-fourths assumed that American cities would be bombed. Most
agreed that since Russia now had the bomb, the likelihood of another war
increased" (May 25).Senator Joseph R. McCarthy only made matters worse
in a February 9, 1950, speech to the Republican Women's Club in Wheeling, West Virginia, in which he accused 205 State Department employees
of being Communists. Not much time passed before a political cartoonist
for the *Washington Post* labeled McCarthy's reckless fear mongering "Mc-
Carthyism" (Doherty 14); this term would inextricably link the senator's
name to the hysteria surrounding the Communist threat in the aftermath of
World War II. In June of that same year Julius Rosenberg was arrested for
espionage, and by the end of the month President Harry S. Truman had sent
troops to Korea, beginning a proxy war with the Soviets that lasted three
years and killed 2.5 million people. This conflict remained at the forefront
of public consciousness through daily newspaper reports, radio broadcasts,
newsreels, and televised news (Doherty 7).

Capote, like most Americans at the time, followed this news with increasing angst, and as an openly gay man he must have been particularly

concerned by the overt link between homosexuality and communism. In the wake of the Alger Hiss affair (in which the man accusing him of espionage was widely characterized as his jilted gay lover) and the shocking findings of the Kinsey report on male sexuality, the vilification of homosexuals was not surprising. When placed against this backdrop, the nostalgic sentiment and pastoral setting of *The Grass Harp* carry a complex sociocultural critique. Nostalgia comes from discontent, from a desire to escape the crises of the present by imagining another time as better. The seeming idealization of the past and rural life in *The Grass Harp* can therefore be read as capturing this Cold War–era disillusionment; it tapped into a yearning among Americans to establish a stable identity in a past undisturbed by the threat of nuclear weapons and homosexuality. Despite the novel's failure to provide an alternate way of achieving lasting happiness in the present, it does highlight the dangers of conformity in its call for reform. It points to the corrosive nature of rumor and innuendo, portrays human sexuality as complex, and argues for the importance of civil rights and social acceptance. In these ways Capote uses the characters' ultimate capitulation to the establishment to condemn the conformist, homophobic values of 1950 America and the methods used to enforce them.

The Homosexual Menace: "Perversion," Subversion, and the Lavender Scare

"If you want to be against McCarthy, boys," the Wisconsin senator once told two reporters, "you've got to be a Communist or a cocksucker" (quoted in Halberstam 54). This comment stemmed from the belief, as he explained in his 1952 monograph *McCarthyism: The Fight for America*, that "espionage agents often have been successful in extorting information from [homosexuals] by threatening to expose their abnormal habits. . . . In addition to the security question, it should be noted that individuals who are morally weak and perverted . . . certainly detract from the prestige of this nation" (14–15). Ironically enough, McCarthy has been given too much credit for McCarthyism and its demonization of homosexuality. His hearings into Communist subversion tend to be associated with the House Un-American Activities Committee (HUAC); but McCarthy, who chaired the Senate Permanent Subcommittee on Investigations, did not play a formal role in these congressional investigations. Nor did he participate in hearings that targeted homosexuals. As a middle-aged, unmarried man, he most likely recused himself to prevent any questions about his own sexuality.[9] Regardless of the reason, the attention given to McCarthy (in most historical studies of the era and in the popular imagination) has tended, as David K. Johnson argues, "to keep the antigay purges in the shadows" (4).

The formation of HUAC in 1938 gave the government a powerful mechanism for enforcing social and political conformity, and the committee wasted no time questioning the patriotic loyalty of over fourteen hundred groups and people—including newspapers, labor unions, the Boy Scouts, Shirley Temple, and homosexuals (Miller and Nowak 25). Nine years later HUAC turned its attention to the subversive content of film and television, and its members questioned dozens of Hollywood writers, directors, actors, and producers. When they posed what became known as the sixty-four-dollar question to Ring Lardner, Jr. ("Are you now, or have you ever been, a member of the Communist Party?"), for instance, he replied, "I could answer it, but if I did, I would hate myself in the morning" (Doherty 22). Yet another important question emerged during the congressional investigations of the postwar era: "Information has come to the attention of the Civil Service Commission that you are a homosexual. What comment do you care to make?" (Johnson 5). This implied link between communism and homosexuality became increasingly explicit, and by the time Capote was writing *The Grass Harp*, most Americans viewed both groups as dangerous threats to the country.

The State Department played a prominent role in the public's perception of homosexuals as security risks. In 1947 the Senate Appropriations Committee passed a bill giving the secretary of state power to dismiss any government employee in the name of national security. Based on the committee's recommendations, the State Department began issuing annual security checks for its workforce to target two groups: 1) Communists (and others committing espionage); and 2) people with a history of "habitual drunkenness, sexual perversion, moral turpitude, financial irresponsibility or criminal record."[10] The latter, primarily aimed at homosexuals, inspired other government agencies to follow suit. Such practices and news about the people who lost their jobs received considerable attention in the national media.[11] Between 1947 and 1950, 574 federal employees were accused of sexual perversion; 420 lost their jobs, through either resignation or termination; 121 of them worked for the State Department.[12] Likewise the homosexual scandal surrounding HUAC's 1948 investigation of Alger Hiss,[13] a former State Department employee, reinforced the impression that a sinister connection existed between homosexuals and Communists.

While McCarthy did not spearhead the demonization of homosexuals, he certainly encouraged it. His inflammatory accusations in Wheeling, West Virginia, required some kind of response from the State Department, and Deputy Undersecretary John Peurifoy's subsequent remarks stoked the fire. He rejected the claim that Communists worked in the State Department but admitted that 91 homosexuals—all considered security risks—were forced out. Suddenly McCarthy's "list" achieved validity (at least for the public), and it had the effect of starting the "Lavender Scare"—a heated national debate about homosexuality and a concerted political effort to remove thousands of gays and lesbians from government service. As Johnson explains in *The Lavender Scare: The Cold War Persecution of Gays and Lesbians in the Federal Government,* Peurifoy's revelation, along with McCarthy's initial claims, "unleashed a flurry of newspaper columns, constituent mail, public debate, and congressional investigations throughout 1950 about the presence of homosexuals in government and their connections to Communists" (18). Although McCarthy continued to make exaggerated, false, and uninformed claims about these connections, he was not the only one with a flair for misinformation and shameless self-promotion. Just a few weeks after Peurifoy's admission, Roy Blick, a lieutenant in the Washington, D.C., vice squad, testified before a congressional committee that 5,000 homosexuals lived in the nation's capital and 3,750 of them held government jobs. A media frenzy followed these baseless allegations as journalists, politicians, and other public figures repeated these numbers and further amplified the supposed threat posed by homosexuals.[14] By the summer of 1950 the climate in the country was such that many people would have agreed with the sentiments of Senator Kenneth Wherry, who stated in a July interview with the *New York Post,* "You can't hardly separate homosexuals from subversives. . . . Mind you, I don't say every homosexual is a subversive, and I don't say every subversive is a homosexual. But a man of low morality is a menace in the government, whatever he is, and they are all tied up together" (quoted in Terry 341).

The brewing scandal led to a Senate subcommittee investigation "into the employment by the Government of homosexuals and other sex perverts"; their findings were published in December 1950. The committee, chaired by Senator Clyde Hoey, concluded that homosexuals should be excluded from government service for their questionable morality, which allows gays and lesbians to indulge in perverted sexual acts; for their ability to "entice normal individuals to engage in perverted practices"; and for their susceptibility to blackmail ("Employment" 221, 244).[15] The committee could find almost no evidence to support this claim, so they relied heavily on Alfred Kinsey's *Sexual Behavior in the Human Male* (1948) to justify their position. Based on over five thousand interviews, Kinsey's study revealed that 46 percent of men had engaged in homosexual behavior and that 37 percent had achieved orgasm through homosexual contact, a number that increased to 50 percent for men who did not marry before the age of thirty-five (Reumann 21, 165).

Not only were these statistics receiving renewed attention in the wake of Peurifoy's and Blick's comments, but also several months earlier Kinsey had testified before the California Subcommittee on Sex Crimes that homosexuality could not be cured through psychiatric therapy (Terry 327). Many conservatives interpreted Kinsey's data as evidence that homosexuality posed a threat to traditional American values as embodied by the nuclear family. In the context of the Senate subcommittee's report, these data were being manipulated yet again to argue that homosexuality presented an immediate danger to American institutions. The report, along with public perception that the State Department was a hotbed of sexual perversion, led to the government's aggressive persecution of homosexuals, persecution that John D'Emilio describes as a tightening "web of oppression" that included FBI surveillance, mail tampering, discharges from the military, and, of course, dismissals (60).

The feverish antihomosexual campaigns of 1950 cast gays as fundamentally disloyal, immoral, criminal, and un-American. Even the language used to justify their legal persecution—such as the term "pervert"—helped encourage a sweeping denigration of homosexuals in American culture. These campaigns also issued a tacit mandate for conformity. Trustworthy citizens, in other words, got married, had children, and lived an outwardly conventional (heterosexual) lifestyle. In this environment homosexuals had no choice but to live in secret. "To escape the status of pariah," May explains, "many gay men and lesbians locked themselves in the stifling closet of conformity, hiding their sexual identities and passing as heterosexuals. As one lesbian recalled, 'It has never been easy to be a lesbian in this country, but the 1950s was surely the worst decade in which to love your own sex'" (13). It is not difficult to understand why in this oppressive climate Capote might feel overcome by nostalgia for a time and place (small-town America) that he could construct as potentially accepting. On one level, Capote achieves his critique of contemporary America through the novel's assault on conformity, its condemnation of the legal system, and the portrayal of all sexuality as natural. On another level, the characters' acquiescence to the conforming establishment contains a damning message as well. Each of these characters resists the social trends being enforced in 1950, but Capote suggests that such a resistance cannot last. The nostalgia of the novel proves to be as illusory as the acceptance of sexual and racial difference in contemporary America. At one moment Collin weeps at the thought that "so little, once it has changed, changes back" (60), and Capote's ultimate fear—and the warning offered by the novel—is that the changing national attitude about homosexuality could be irrevocable.

Gossip, Sexuality, and Conformity in *The Grass Harp*

Capote announces his indictment of the hearsay characterizing the start of the McCarthy era through the role of gossip in *The Grass Harp*. Early in the book Collin claims that "anyone could have told you the facts" (26), but these "facts" mostly come from suppositions that get repeated often enough to be accepted as truth. In his account of the day that Riley saved his sisters from being drowned by their mother, for instance, Collin states, "It was said that Riley broke the door down with a hatchet, which seems a tall order for a boy of nine or ten, whatever he was" (26). The passive construction of this sentence casts doubt on the veracity of the story and raises questions about all of the anecdotes in the book. The biography of Judge Cool's wife includes the caveat "all that I repeat comes second-hand" (35), and Maude announces that Collin has a reputation for "fibbing" (54). Capote's point in part is that people's private lives are private and that to know the complete truth is impossible. He also suggests that no story, no claim can be understood apart from the biases of the teller.

Two types of gossip emerge as particularly dangerous in *The Grass Harp*: the kind associated with public exposure/persecution and the kind encouraging self-suppression. The threat of public exposure certainly haunts Judge Cool, whose sons care far more about taking possession of their father's house than about his well-being. After reading the judge's mail (a common practice of the government for suspected "perverts" in the 1950s), the sons discover his correspondence with a young girl and conclude that he is sexually attracted to children. Capote juxtaposes this conclusion (based solely on these letters) with the judge's version of events; the contrast highlights the problem of using such "evidence" to ascertain the desires and behaviors of others. The judge explains to his tree-house confidants that five years earlier he came across a children's magazine with a listing of potential pen pals. Posing as a fifteen-year-old boy, he began corresponding with a teenage girl in Alaska named Heather Falls, and he relished the nostalgia evoked by their rapport: "To be growing up again and have a sweetheart in Alaska—well, it was fun for an old man sitting alone listening to the noise of a clock" (42). After the girl fell in love with someone else, which pained the judge, she sent him a gold nugget as a gift for his acceptance into law school. He still carries this trinket with him, but the experience has been tarnished by his sons' feeling that "they know something shameful about" him (42). Capote points out that the sons do not talk to their father about the matter; the judge happens to overhear them discussing it with their wives: "They think it all a sign of . . ."

(43). He can articulate neither the words "sexual perversion" (a term readily applied to homosexuals and pedophiles during the Cold War) nor the depth of his hurt by these accusations.[16] Supposition has replaced real communication and understanding here, and the judge, not wanting to justify himself to his sons or to face the humiliation of such an accusation, hides away first in a tree and later in a boardinghouse. Truth is trumped by accusation in this climate, and the mere suggestion of aberrant sexuality, Capote suggests, has the power to diminish, terrorize, and marginalize.

In the judge's case, these accusations remain private since he chooses to abandon his home, but Capote also portrays a character who is publically victimized by rumor. Sister Ida Honey, an evangelist who operates a traveling show with her fifteen children, clearly rejects conventional notions of domesticity and marriage, choosing instead to have a variety of sexual partners because she enjoys being pregnant. When she comes to town, Reverend Buster immediately capitalizes on her marginal status by spreading rumors about her. He claims that Sister Ida is known "throughout six states as an infamous trollop" (66), but his tale has little effect. After witnessing the popularity and profitability of her show, he becomes enraged and tells Verena that Sister Ida called Dolly "an infidel, an enemy of Jesus" (67). This accusation secures Verena's influence and pressures the sheriff to run Ida's family out of town—after Reverend Buster steals her money, of course. Though several townspeople defend Sister Ida, their voices are powerless against the legal system (sheriff/future Senator), business interests (Verena), and religion (Reverend Buster). Collin even points out that "everybody had a grand time [at Sister Ida's show] except Reverend and Mrs. Buster" (66). Capote thus satirizes both religious hypocrisy and the way influential public figures can use gossip for personal or ideological gain. Once again Capote contrasts the reverend's lies with an alternate vision of Sister Ida and her children. The subsequent description of the hungry children as impoverished, lovingly devoted to their mother, and deeply appreciative of Judge Cool's feast makes the reverend and the other forms of oppressive authority appear callous and criminal. Capote explicitly gives voice to the dangers of this kind of supposition through Dolly—the central figure of the narrator's and most of the characters' devotion. At the end of the novel, she condemns the accusations and violent behavior of the town: "'I don't think you can accuse me of conniving with anyone. . . . Especially not with bullies who,' she a little lost control, 'steal from children and drag old women into jail. I can't set much store by a name that endorses such methods. It ought to be a mockery'" (81).

Gossip has the power to enforce sexual self-suppression as well, which Capote presents as one of the more insidious consequences of McCarthy-era

persecution. Not surprisingly, given the highly public vilification of homosexuality in 1950, the first instance of gossip in the novel involves Verena's
ambiguous sexuality. Collin's father, an irresponsible salesman who resents
Verena's wealth, spreads rumors about her being a hermaphrodite: "One of
the stories he spread, that Verena was a morphodyte, has never stopped going around" (10). Such rumors can do little to change her privileged status,
but they do reflect the town's ongoing need to characterize aberrant behavior
as freakish. The townspeople learn of her intimate relationships with Maudie
Laura Murphy and later Morris Ritz, but most of their speculation about
Verena proves false. The gossipers at the pool hall assume that Verena is
carrying on an affair with Morris at the abandoned cannery, but it turns out
that the two of them are merely examining the property as a potential investment. She later explains that her love for Morris was not sexual: "We were
kindred spirits" (84), sharing a similar passion for making money. The real
love of her life appears to be Maudie, who breaks Verena's heart by marrying
a liquor salesman and moving to the Grand Canyon. Verena spends countless nights looking at photos of her, crying, and pacing her bedroom with the
lights off. Even at the end of the novel, Verena still dreams of visiting Maudie
out West, but it seems clear that she will never make the trip. She cannot act
on her same-sex desires, in part because she worries about public perception.
In a moment of weakness, she blames Dolly for her loneliness and emotional
paralysis: "Has it not struck you that I never ask anyone into this house?
. . . I'm ashamed to" (22–23). Capote suggests, however, that Verena is actually afraid of falling in love with another woman: "Men were afraid of her,
and she herself seemed to be afraid of women" (12). Her fear comes from
the destructive predicament that the town has created for homosexuals and
lesbians. Gossip may not cause her active persecution, but it does contribute
to the ways in which she suppresses her own desires and identity.

Capote also links the most effeminate man in the text with the kind of
gossip that leads to self-suppression. Everyone in town refers to the barber,
Amos Legrand, as "old sis," and he addresses all of his customers (men and
women) as "honey." Since Amos's ability to talk easily with folks of all ages
makes him likable, Collin assures readers that the term "old sis" was never
intended as an insult: "they didn't mean any harm; most people enjoyed
Amos and really wished him well" (63). Of course their kindness is predicated on Amos's sexuality remaining private, which may explain his decision
to live in a boardinghouse surrounded by old women who dote on him. In
this context his private life remains above suspicion. He might come across
as homosexual, but he does not seem to have outlets for acting on same-sex
desire. This kind of sexual repression was not uncommon in the South at the

time. As the historian Pete Daniel explains in *Lost Revolutions: The South in the 1950s:*

> The rural nature of the South, its class system, and segregation created a distinct gay and lesbian culture. As in other parts of the country, most southerners accepted neighbors and friends whom they might have labeled as "sissies" or "old maids." Rural and small-town people might have whispered or giggled about "queers," but they seldom took public action. As long as people played a role in the community and were discreet about their sexual preferences, they could live "normal" lives. . . . Although most southerners considered them perverts and thought they were damned, southern lesbians and gays offered neighbors enough ambiguity to guarantee their acceptance and security. (155)

Amos's treatment reflects the culture of gossip and conditioned acceptance surrounding southern gay life. He is ridiculed through the name "sis" (or sissy), but he is not actively persecuted because his sexuality remains invisible to the community. Interestingly, Capote makes Amos the biggest town gossip, and in many ways his position as storyteller gives him some control over his own sexual narrative. He can direct the town's attention toward others and away from himself. Like Verena's wealth and political influence, Amos's gossiping protects him from unwanted scrutiny.

Capote depicts the narrator as a victim of homophobic culture as well. Throughout the novel no one discusses sex or sexuality openly. Judge Cool cannot say the words "sexual perversion." Collin avoids the term "masturbation" (but not the act). Even Sister Ida skips over the details of her affair with her sister's husband. In this climate it is not surprising that the characters lack a vocabulary for same-sex desire and that Collin can only hint at his romantic feelings for Riley Henderson: "I longed for him to be my friend!" (27); "Riley beckoned for me to come with him" (47); "I'd yearned so much for a ride in Riley's car" (57); "I crossed an admiring heart" (48). Part of Collin's attraction comes from his desire to be a conventional boy: "I longed to tell him that he was all I wanted to be" (44). A capable fisher, hunter, mechanic, and carpenter, Riley embodies the traits of a stereotypical man. He spends time with town floozies, driving them around town in his red sports car. He is tough and intimidating, whereas Collin is emotional and hypersensitive. When Riley urinates on his shoe as a joke, for example, Collin gets angry, but all is forgiven when Riley throws his arm over his shoulder: "the moment, at least, when there began in him an affectionate feeling for me that supported my own for him" (47–48). Since he grows up in a predominantly heterosexual culture, Collin's attempts to romance Maude Riordan make sense, but his lackluster efforts seem motivated more by a desire to imitate Riley than any genuine attachment for her. He "*imagined* for a while that [he] was in love with her" (52, emphasis mine), but this qualified statement comes after he realizes that she "was heartset on Riley" (52).

He wants so much to be like Riley (and to be liked by him) that he seeks affection from the girls who fawn over Riley. Such a reading resonates with Eve Kosofsky Sedgwick's notion that homosocial desire tends to triangulate a man's desire for another man through mutual affection for a woman.[17] Riley and Collin cannot openly express their affection for each other, so they find an outlet through Riordan. Like other potentially gay figures in town, Collin also does not have a social model for acting on same-sex desire. Unlike Joel Knox in *Other Voices, Other Rooms,* whose uncle provides a viable, albeit questionable, model for same-sex desire, Collin remains part of a culture that criminalizes and marginalizes homosexuality—a culture that gives gay men and women little choice but to be secretive. The nostalgia in this novel, therefore, expresses a longing for, as Garson states, not only "the irretrievability lost world of childhood" (*Truman Capote,* 33) but also for a time when the freedom of choice seemed possible. As Dolly explains, "It's what I want, a choice. To know I could've had another life, all made of my own decisions. That would be making my peace, and truly" (68). The absence of personal freedom has the effect of encouraging self-suppression and rendering gay culture invisible, and Capote presents this situation as one of the more destructive aspects of homosexual persecution in the early 1950s.

Riley appears conflicted about his sexuality as well, and Capote uses this character to present the drive for material and social success in America as antithetical to living an openly gay life. Collin observes Riley's conservative attitude toward gender and sexuality when Sister Ida's fifteen children (of all ages and genders) bathe in the creek: "It's only now, seeing the kind of man he turned out to be, that I understand the paradox of his primness: he wanted so to be respectable that the defections of others somehow seemed to him backsliding on his own part" (72). These defections clearly include sexuality, and his embarrassment over nakedness—along with his disapproval of Sister Ida's promiscuity—suggests a discomfort with his own sexual identity. Riley, however, cannot entertain this notion because he views any type of nonconformity as threatening his dreams of social success. In the confines of the tree house (as a space for outcasts and unconventional behavior), Riley admits that he has "no feelings [for girls]—except for [his] sisters, which is different" (43), and he considers women "bitches, by and large" (58). He goes on to describe his emotional aloofness for his recent girlfriend, whom he has been dating for one year: "You said before about the one person in the

world. Why couldn't I think of her like that? It's what I want, I'm no good
by myself. Maybe, if I could care for somebody that way, I'd make plans and
carry them out: buy that stretch of land past Parson's Place and build houses
on it—I could do it if I got quiet" (44). Riley's restlessness can be attributed
to his discomfort with heterosexual romance, but given his professional aspirations, Capote suggests that he too has little choice in the matter.

The intense pressure on young Americans to get married and become
home owners in the 1950s made any alternative risky. "Individuals who
chose personal paths that did not include marriage and parenthood," May
has argued, "risked being perceived as perverted, immoral, unpatriotic, and
pathological. Neighbors shunned them as if they were dangerous; the government investigated them as security risks. Their chances of living free of
stigma or harassment were slim" (92). The nuclear family, in other words,
provided a form of protection, promising personal fulfillment and offering an
image of patriotic solidarity. After the community in the tree disbands, Riley
marries Maude and becomes a suburban contractor in the mold of William J.
Levitt, who applied Ford's assembly-line principles to suburban development
and started Levittown in 1946 (in Hempstead, Long Island).[18] Riley becomes
part of the suburban growth industry and everything it represented in 1950:
the white, heterosexual American family. As Levitt himself remarked in
1948, "No man who owns his own house and lot can be a Communist. He
has too much to do" (quoted in Jackson 231). Capote presents this kind of
materialistic drive and investment in suburban culture as a disabling force in
America: it prevents people from considering any alternative way of achieving personal happiness.

Capote reinforces his critique of 1950s conformist America through the
novel's central message about social acceptance and love. While Judge Cool
fears that there "may be no place for any of us" (37), the tree house offers a
temporary escape from the social pressure to fit in. Situated on the outskirts
of town, it literally elevates its occupants above the community's petty griev-
ances and myopic attitudes. It gives them a perspective that the rest of the
townspeople lack. As the judge explains, "But, ah, the energy we spend hiding from one another, afraid as we are of being identified. But here we are,
identified: five fools in a tree. A great piece of luck provided we know how
to use it: no longer any need to worry about the picture we present—free to
find out who we truly are" (41). Capote suggests that greater self-awareness
is essential for both social tolerance and love, an awareness that can be
achieved only apart from concerns about appearances ("the picture we present"). Not surprisingly, the tree house provides a freedom from conformity
that enables the characters to articulate a philosophy of inclusiveness. Collin

provides the most succinct version of this when he muses, "No matter what passions compose them, all private worlds are good, they are never vulgar places" (51).

Of course this celebration of private worlds is common in Capote's fiction of the 1940s and 1950s. In *Other Voices, Other Rooms,* for example, Randolph explains that "any love is natural and beautiful that lies within a person's nature; only hypocrites would hold a man responsible for what he loves" (147). Likewise, Holly Golightly makes a similar claim in *Breakfast at Tiffany's.* In all of these works, the notion of emotional and psychological honesty is connected with sexuality;[19] yet society prevents the characters in *The Grass Harp* from breaking free of conformity. There is no place for them outside the tree house. The only alternative, which many gay Americans had to accept in the 1950s, is offered by the African American character Catherine, whose race severely limits her civil rights: "People ought to keep more things to themselves. The deepdown ownself part of you, that's the good part: what's left of a human being that goes around speaking his privates?" (45). Her belief that private worlds should remain private reflects a social reality that heterosexual white characters in the novel never have to face—the actual dangers of being visibly different. Collin even notes that the sheriff would have shot Catherine if he had understood some of her remarks, and "many of the white people in town would have said he did right" (32). In this respect, Catherine's attempts to pass as Indian parallel Collin's attempts to pass as heterosexual.[20] *The Grass Harp* suggests, however, that these efforts are inauthentic and problematic. They ultimately lead to disillusionment and isolation.

The pressure to conform in the text comes from a range of sources—gossip, the threat of violence, and pervading social attitudes—that work together powerfully to suppress difference, just as they did in American culture at the time. At one point the maternal Mrs. County (the baker's wife and a mother) tries to persuade Collin and Dolly to resume their previous lives: "You people should go home, Dolly ought to make her peace with Verena: that's what she's always done, and you can't turn around at her time of life. Also it sets a poor example for the town, two sisters quarreling. Leading citizens have to behave themselves; otherwise the entire place goes to pieces" (60–61). The townspeople value the appearance of normalcy to such an extent that any image of discontent or nonconformity must be quelled. Thus the sheriff's hand always remains poised on his pistol and the town is willing to use violence to bring Dolly and the others back into the fold. No wonder Riley Henderson retreats to marriage and suburbia. His capitulation, like the judge's and Collin's, reinforces Capote's social and cultural critique. After

Dolly and Collin return home, Mrs. County expresses relief: "Ha ha, guess we can laugh about all that foolishness now" (89). In a book filled with rich humor, her laughter rings false here. The pressures of conformity are too great to allow Dolly and the others what they most desire: the freedom to follow their own passions. Sadly Capote's characters do not get this choice, and in the context of 1950, neither did gay Americans.

Laws, Violence, and Conformity

The Grass Harp also condemns laws shaped by politics—as opposed to ethical principles—and this message rejects the fear mongering and public persecution of homosexuality that characterized McCarthyism. Early in the novel Sheriff Candle uses the law to justify Dolly's eviction from the tree, but Capote presents the police as agents for the most influential and moneyed figures in town—namely Verena, whose wealth enables the sheriff (and future senator) to get elected to office, and the reverend. In fact Capote consistently links politics and political figures with corruption. When Judge Cool returns to Europe after the death of his wife, for example, he is perceived as a political liability: "Politicians like Meiself Tallsap and his gang had come into power: those boys couldn't afford to have Charlie Cool sitting in the courthouse" (36). Ideological difference is something to be feared in the world of the novel, and his removal, which does not serve the community, is necessitated by the threat Judge Cool represents to the prevailing political agenda. On a more mundane level, Collin points out that Riley buys his sports car from a politician in New Orleans who was "bound for the penitentiary" (58), but even this humorous detail raises questions about the degree to which the public should trust the actions (and accusations) of politicians. In these ways Capote depicts small-town America as succumbing to the same types of political pressures and prejudices facing the country as a whole. Thus the characters' choice to live in a tree becomes an act of political as well as social resistance.

Capote attacks the ethical failings of the legal system as well, and he first expresses these concerns through Judge Cool, who explains to the tree dwellers that "the law doesn't admit differences" (41). The judge uses antimiscegenation laws as an example, and after describing the love affair between a white fisherman and an African American girl, he notes that the couple could not have gotten married legally despite their desire to do so. The man would have been arrested and subsequently convicted by the judge. This legal outcome flies in the face of his—and arguably the novel's—philosophy about love: "[the African American girl] was to [him] what no one has been to me, the one person in the world—from whom nothing is held back" (41). The law here impedes human happiness. It encourages secrecy as opposed to honesty (holding nothing back), and it creates barriers between people by labeling the desire to love someone of another race—or by extension the same gender—as criminal.[21] Such laws make the judge question his participation in the system: "I sometimes imagine all those whom I've called guilty have passed the real guilt on to me: it's partly that that makes me want once before I die to be right on the right side" (41). For Capote, the guilty are those who enforce unethical laws—especially those who recognize their immorality—and the judge's wish to be both morally right *and* on the right side of an issue points to the corruption at the heart of the American legal system.

Most of the violence in the novel involves the enforcement of unethical laws, and this aggression stems from a social response to the fear of nonconformity. The visible presence of guns disrupts the pastoral setting of the text. The sheriff immediately gets associated with his gun: "Sheriff Candle slouched forward, his hand cocked on his pistol. He stared at us with puckered eyes, as if he were gazing straight into the sun" (31). Of course the narrator is mocking his performance here, but in many respects the sheriff (who represents the law) is blind to the meaning and value of nonconformist behavior. He does not care to understand the motivations of the tree dwellers or the social problems that have contributed to their choice. He just wants to force them back into socially acceptable modes. This moment also foreshadows the disproportionate use of force that will characterize his response to the tree dwellers. Catherine's dress gets torn down the middle when the sheriff's posse drags her through the grass to jail, and some of the men return with shotguns to arrest the remaining tree dwellers. Very little suggests the need for guns. Three elderly women and two teenage boys are sitting in a tree, not robbing a bank, but they symbolize a much greater social problem in American culture.

Difference challenges the status quo and existing hierarchies, which the townspeople desperately want to preserve. In fact most of them try to convince Dolly to return home. Mrs. Buster (the reverend's wife) rails, "I say shame on you. How can you have come so far from God as to sit up in a tree like a drunken Indian—sucking cigarettes like a common . . . floozy while your sister lies in misery flat on her back" (32). Her racism and moral condemnation of sexuality reflect mainstream values that she threatens to maintain through force. After an empty orangeade jar accidentally falls on her head, she threatens Dolly: "You may imagine you're getting away with something. But let me tell you there will be retribution—not in heaven, right here on earth" (34). The most explicit act of violence is Riley's shooting.

After Big Eddie shoots him during the melee, he slinks away from Verena's wrath, grateful that the boy is alive. No one in the town claims to have wanted violence, yet they brought the guns to prompt it. Here Capote points to a need for a greater awareness about the consequences of using the law and the threat of violence. It can cause lasting harm, and the literal injury to Riley can be viewed as a metaphor for the real damage being done to gay Americans in 1950. Interestingly enough, violence works here. The shooting disbands the tree dwellers, and it seems to convince Riley to abandon his restlessness for living a clichéd 1950s life as a family man who builds suburban houses. This might point to Capote's larger fear that the methods of persecution so rampant while he was writing the book were, indeed, working.

This historical context may also explain some of Capote's feelings of sadness while writing the novel. The short-lived nature of the tree house and the characters' capitulation to larger, communal forces suggest Capote's pessimism, which can often amount to nothing more than an implicit endorsement of the status quo. The same is true for the characters' philosophy about private worlds since retreating to a private realm tends to depoliticize issues. Such a retreat can place them outside the boundaries of public debate. However, such a reading fails to acknowledge the real terror that many Americans felt during the Cold War. It is my contention that Capote uses the nostalgia of the novel to create a yearning in his readers for a space that can make inclusiveness a lasting possibility instead of something ephemeral. Ripping the characters from the tree house shatters the pastoral atmosphere of the book; likewise this moment rips readers out of complacency. *The Grass Harp* may not provide a concrete map for achieving greater civil rights for homosexuals and nonwhites, but it does capture a troubling moment in U.S. history, a moment characterized by fear and paralysis and by an inability among marginalized groups to voice the failure of American democracy to treat its citizens with dignity, respect, and equality. It is, for Capote, a moment that demands interrogation and social change.

CHAPTER 5

The Muses Are Heard

When Capote received an invitation to accompany the Everyman Opera Company to the Soviet Union, he jumped at the opportunity. No American theatrical group had performed in Russia for decades, and Cold War tensions promised to generate significant international interest in the event. Of course suspicions ran high on both sides. The State Department worried about the ways Soviet propaganda might use this revival of George Gershwin's *Porgy and Bess* to highlight U.S. hypocrisy over racial discrimination. The Russian Ministry of Culture, on the other hand, orchestrated the trip to limit access to some of the socioeconomic hardships of Soviet life. Nevertheless the opera company and its entourage boarded a train for Leningrad on December 19, 1955. Capote crafted his experiences into *The Muses Are Heard,* which first appeared in two consecutive issues of the *New Yorker* and then as a book in 1956.[1] The title alludes to the metaphor used by a senior Russian official to describe the cultural exchange between the two countries: "When the cannons are heard, the muses are silent; when the cannons are silent, the muses are heard" (60). In many respects Capote took this declaration as his central argument for art's potential to drown out the embattled rhetoric and practices of the Cold War.

Capote begins part 1 ("When the Cannons Are Silent") with a State Department briefing two days before the company's departure from East Berlin. This forum enabled the troupe to raise questions about everything from the quality of tap water to the limits placed on personal freedom: "We heard they were going to trail us. And open our letters" (9). As soon as they boarded the Blue Express, they caught their first glimpse of the cultural differences between the United States and the Union of Soviet Socialist Republics. Men

and women (regardless of ethnicity) were required to share sleeping compartments, endure without a range of amenities (including a dining car),
remain on the train at station stops (unless they wanted to be escorted back
inside by "pale flat-faced" soldiers [43]), and adjust to subzero temperatures.
The company also encountered forthright Russian workers such as the dis-
gruntled tea maker and a member of the Ministry of Culture who had yet to
marry because his "stipend [was] not yet equal to the aspiration" (77). At the
Russian border and in Brest Litovsk, the Americans got a more detailed look
at life behind the Iron Curtain. Women performed hard labor, "swinging
picks, shoveling snow, pausing only to blow their noses into naked, raw-red
hands" (56), and every kiosk sold the same items including "hairy slabs of
raw bacon slipped between thick slices of grime-colored bread" (62). Their
arrival in Leningrad concludes the first part.

In part 2 ("The Muses Are Heard"), Capote traces the company's experiences leading up to and including the performance of *Porgy and Bess*
on December 26, 1955.[2] The section opens with their accommodations at
the Astoria Hotel, which lacked the niceties associated with "Western ideas
of a deluxe establishment" (88). Prior to the performance, members of the
company attended a ballet at the Mariinsky theater, went shopping in the
government-owned stores on Nevsky Prospekt, and toured the Hermitage.
Capote also became acquainted with a Russian man who drunkenly confessed his attraction to the director's assistant. The night of the performance
proved challenging. An array of exhausting speeches and introductions
preceded the opera; when the curtain finally rose, the audience struggled to
follow the first act because the program notes had not been copied. They
warmed up to the second act, but the production did not elicit the response
many had hoped it would. Although Capote remains uneasy about the politics shaping the opera's reception among journalists and officials, he presents
art itself—whether through *Porgy and Bess* or his own book—as offering an
invaluable opportunity to promote mutual understanding and to mitigate
Cold War tensions.

The Muses Are Heard has not received much critical attention because
most scholars view it primarily as a stepping stone to *In Cold Blood*. This
connection makes sense on a number of levels. First, Capote described his approach to both books in similar terms. As he explained to Pati Hill in 1957,

> Actually, I don't consider the style of this book, *The Muses Are Heard*, as
> markedly different from my fictional style. Perhaps the content, the fact
> that it is about real events, makes it seem so. After all, *Muses* is straight
> reporting, and in reporting one is occupied with literalness and surfaces,

with implication without comment—one can't achieve immediate depths the way one may in fiction. However, one of the reasons I've wanted to do reportage was to prove that I could apply my style to the realities of journalism. But I believe my fictional method is equally detached—emotionality makes me lose writing control: I have to exhaust the emotion before I feel clinical enough to analyze and project it, and as far as I'm concerned that's one of the laws of achieving true technique. If my fiction seems more personal it is because it depends on the artist's most personal and revealing area: his imagination.[3]

Capote not only viewed a kinship between journalism and his "equally detached" approach to fiction, but he also saw this style of reportage as fruitful ground for literary innovation—innovation that clearly shaped *In Cold Blood*. Second, *The Muses Are Heard* gave Capote the opportunity to develop an extended work that fused journalistic and fictional techniques. This hybrid style, as suggested in the interview, combines literal reporting with the nuance of fiction.

This latter dimension in *The Muses Are Heard*, however, has largely been overlooked. For starters, Capote fictionalized a number of elements in the text. He changed the order of events, glued together different episodes, invented scenes such as the material in Brest Litovsk, and even created composite characters.[4] These details reveal *Muses* to be far more than mere reportage, and they invite closer scrutiny—particularly in regard to Cold War and racial politics. When Capote left for the Soviet Union, McCarthyism had reached a fevered pitch in America. HUAC's ongoing assault on the Communist threat had included investigations into everyone from State Department officials such as Alger Hiss to the television star Lucille Ball in 1953. Around the same time Julius and Ethel Rosenberg were executed for conspiracy to commit espionage, and in 1954 Senator Joseph McCarthy turned his attention to a possible Communist infiltration of the U.S. Army. Likewise many segregationists began using accusations of Communist subversion against groups advocating equal rights.

The performances of *Porgy and Bess* in the Soviet Union enabled Capote to write about the troubling intersection between Communist fears and racial discrimination in America. As Capote remarked after the trip, "Everybody in the West seemed to be so fantastically naïve about Russia . . . as though it were different from any other country. Well, it basically isn't, because human nature is what it is" (quoted in Clarke 305).[5] His notion of human nature provides a central key for understanding *The Muses Are Heard*. By humanizing Russians and African Americans, he challenges the demonization of

Communists in the McCarthy era and the racial ideologies that justified segregation and discrimination. Capote's narrative also links mythmaking (as manifested through gossip and propaganda) with racism to suggest that U.S. fears of the Other were constructed from falsehoods to serve a political agenda. For Capote, art offers a solution to this problem. Just as it humanizes people from different cultures, political perspectives, and ethnicities, it also has the power to bridge cultural differences and, as suggested by the title, to lessen the possibilities of war.

Demonizing the Other: McCarthyism and Civil Rights

Although the term "McCarthyism" has become shorthand for the anti-Communist hysteria of the 1950s, a number of incidents set the stage for the fear-mongering that McCarthy championed throughout much of that decade. HUAC, which formed in 1938, had investigated over 1,400 groups and individuals before turning its attention to Hollywood in 1947. In the same year President Truman required federal employees to sign loyalty oaths, issuing an Executive Order to protect "the United States against infiltration of disloyal persons into the ranks of its employees" (quoted in Miller and Nowak 26). This security program investigated 6.6 million people between 1947 and 1952; although it discovered no cases of espionage, "about 500 persons were dismissed in dubious cases of 'questionable loyalty'" (26). In 1949 China became a Communist country, and the Soviet Union tested its first atomic weapon. One year later, shortly after the conviction of Alger Hiss for perjury, the British government arrested the atomic scientist Klaus Fuchs, who confessed to spying for the Soviet Union during his time at the Los Alamos Laboratory in New Mexico. The American public was still reeling from this news when McCarthy gave his speech accusing 205 State Department employees of being Communists. McCarthy, who subsequently chaired the Senate Permanent Subcommittee on Investigations from 1953 to 1954, never played an active role on HUAC, but he crafted a public image that inextricably linked his name with Communist persecution. He even titled his 1952 manifesto on the Communist threat *McCarthyism: The Fight for America*. Just like the sixty-four-dollar question that became a benchmark of so many government hearings ("Are you now, or have you ever been, a member of the Communist Party?"), McCarthy's highly visible assault on communism exacerbated Cold War fears in the United States. His inflammatory rhetoric gave the impression that threats to American democracy lurked everywhere—even in the house next door. This climate of fear reached epic proportions by the middle of the decade. In 1954 a national poll revealed that "a whopping 78 percent thought reporting to the FBI neighbors or acquaintances they suspected of being Communists a good idea" (Altschuler 7).

McCarthyism also fueled a hysteria that empowered the persecution of any perceived social, cultural, or political threat; it is not surprising that legislators and other influential groups in the South used this "Red Scare" to thwart efforts toward African American civil rights. Despite the racism found in some television programming, such as *Amos 'n' Andy* (which debuted in 1951), many variety shows provided powerful forums for promoting social equality. Ed Sullivan's *Toast of the Town,* for instance, was praised by leading African American newspapers for presenting blacks and whites on the same stage without bias. As the historian Thomas Doherty has explained, "More multicolored than monochromatic, and more multicultural in spirit than most of the nation, television in the 1950s ran far ahead of the tolerance curve" (73).

Many television stations in the South vehemently objected to this message of integration. In 1956 state legislators in Louisiana even accused the television industry of using "the communist technique of brainwashing for racial integration by bringing into private homes in the state harmful programs designed to affect the minds and attitudes of juveniles" (quoted in Doherty 73). Such accusations did little to alter these broadcasts, which had already been sold to sponsors, but they did reflect attempts within the government to link communism with racial integration. When the Senate's Internal Security Subcommittee launched a 1954 hearing on Communist activity in the South, for example, the investigation primarily targeted whites who were critical of segregation. One organization in particular, the Southern Conference Education Fund (SCEF), came under particularly intense scrutiny (and persecution). The SCEF used education as a means to eliminate "racial discrimination and segregation, and to promote in all possible ways greater understanding and friendship between people of diverse cultural backgrounds," and it actively promoted the desegregation of schools and hospitals in the South.[6] As the historian John Salmond explains, "by 1953 it was probably the most important southern proponent and publicist of the integrationist cause" (434–45). Not surprisingly, numerous people testified before the subcommittee that the SCEF was promoting communism in the South. Likewise political figures and pamphleteers commonly referred to desegregation as a "communistic disease."[7] One 1955 pamphlet even argued that Communist Russia promoted desegregation in the South as a means for encouraging miscegenation, which would produce "an ignorant, weak, easily conquered race" (quoted in Bacon 94). Such inflammatory statements contributed to the resurgence of the

Ku Klux Klan, which conducted approximately 530 acts of racial violence in the second half of the 1950s (Miller and Nowak 37). As these examples illustrate, racism and anticommunism often coexisted in powerful ways in southern politics.

The reckless use of Cold War paranoia to justify racial discrimination did little to slow African American activism, and the bus boycott in Montgomery, Alabama, soon became a national rallying cry for civil rights. Prior to the boycott, African Americans were routinely abused: shortchanged, thrown off buses for demanding correct change, ignored at stops, and humiliated by the process of buying tickets in the front of the bus—which then required them to exit and reenter in the rear. Montgomery's bus system, which was unique in the state of Alabama, also gave drivers discretionary power over "no-man's-land," the few rows between the clearly marked white and black sections. Drivers could order the blacks in these seats to move for white customers. This is where Rosa Parks—a veteran activist who had been secretary of the NAACP for twelve years and an important member of the Women's Political Council—was sitting on December 1, 1955. On this day the driver ordered the four African Americans in Parks's row to move for a single white passenger, since whites would never be expected to sit next to blacks. Though the three men moved reluctantly, Parks refused. The driver then had her arrested for violating the city's segregation laws.[8] The day after her arrest, community leaders, inspired in part by Parks's plea for them to do something about the abuses of black women in the city, decided to have a one-day bus boycott in protest. The boycott continued, and religious leaders and activists quickly organized the Montgomery Improvement Association to oversee its progress. They also elected the newcomer Martin Luther King Jr. as president. He would become the public face for the actions and demands of the black community, which were quite modest at the outset.[9] The boycott ended after 381 days, not because the revenue for Montgomery buses dropped a crippling 80 percent but because of a civil lawsuit filed by four African American women: Mary Louise Smith, Aurelia Browder, Susie McDonald, and Claudette Colvin. These women had been arrested for refusing to surrender their bus seats to white passengers nine months prior to Rosa Parks. In Browder v. Gayle (the mayor of Montgomery), a district court ruled that the city's segregation law for buses violated the Fourteenth Amendment. The Supreme Court upheld this decision on December 17, 1956, and on that day Martin Luther King Jr. and numerous other African Americans rode in the front seats of several Montgomery buses.

The desegregation of public transportation was a logical extension of Brown v. Board of Education in 1954, a unanimous Supreme Court decision that ended segregation in public schools for being both unconstitutional and psychologically harmful. As Chief Justice Warren explained, separating black pupils "from others of similar age and qualifications solely because of their race generates a feeling of inferiority as to their status in the community that may affect their hearts and minds in a way unlikely ever to be undone" (quoted in Thernstrom and Thernstrom 101). The court based its decision in part on economic data that showed southern states spending twice as much to educate whites as blacks overall. These statistics were even more damning in regard to children and university students. The South allocated four times more financial support for white children, and white colleges received ten times more funding than black institutions. The determination in Brown v. Board that separate was *not* equal created immediate legal shockwaves. According to Thernstrom and Thernstrom, "Other decisions quickly followed giving blacks access to public beaches and bathhouses, municipal golf courses, and other facilities. Furthermore, just six days before Rosa Parks defied the Montgomery ordinance, the Interstate Commerce Commission . . . had outlawed racial segregation on all trains and buses traveling across state lines, and in the waiting rooms of the stations they used" (110).

Many people were reluctant to follow these laws, however. One of the most dramatic acts of defiance occurred in September 1957 when the governor of Little Rock, Arkansas, Orval Faubus, called out the National Guard to prevent nine African American students from attending Central High School. The families of these children had sued for the right to attend an integrated school, which made the governor's actions a violation of a federal court order. Although Faubus claimed that the students needed protection, there was no evidence of any danger. However, his public grandstanding on the issue, which was politically motivated to win reelection, did inspire a mob of segregationists to gather at the high school. Their actions prevented these nine students (out of a student body of two thousand) from entering. Television coverage quickly made the event a national issue. After Faubus ignored President Eisenhower's advice to use the National Guard to escort the students to class, Eisenhower had to act. He federalized the Arkansas National Guard, ordering them to return to their barracks, and sent one thousand paratroopers from the 101st Airborne Division to the high school. A number of soldiers remained in Little Rock for the entire year, but when the soldiers were not around, the students experienced verbal and physical abuse. As Pete Daniel notes, "The nine black students faced open hatred, guarded violence, and studied indifference" (274). Only one of the nine graduated, but on that day Martin Luther King Jr. sat in attendance to watch him receive his diploma along with four hundred other students.

Cannon Fire: Propaganda and Cold War Paranoia in *The Muses Are Heard*

Capote first undermines Cold War fears in *The Muses Are Heard* by casting them largely as products of propaganda. The embassy briefing in part I offers one example of government efforts to exacerbate anxieties about the Communist threat. In Capote's hands, these officials function as fear mongers who consistently undermine anything that might encourage a more accepting view of Russian culture. One official admitted that "there are some nice Russians. Very nice people. But they have a bad government. . . . You must always bear in mind that their system of government is basically hostile to our own" (6–7). This emphasis on Communist Russia as fundamentally hostel to the United States would shape the entire briefing, which went on to highlight Russian hostility toward personal freedom, privacy, and transparency (such as not being provided with information about travel visas, hotel accommodations, and their daily schedule). Likewise when a cast member asked about being invited into someone's home, the same official encouraged him to accept but immediately added, "From what I understand . . . , your hosts plan an extensive program of entertainment. Something every minute. Enough to wear you out" (7). This caveat not only presented the Russian government as invested in preventing any unscripted encounters but also tacitly discouraged the Americans from seeking them out. Capote, however, quickly raises doubts about these criticisms of the Soviet Union. He notes the officials' admission that "the Embassy has never been bothered with that problem [of socializing with Russians]. We're never invited *any*where" (7); and when asked if the company's "letters would be censored, their hotel rooms wired and the walls encrusted with concealed cameras" (5), they responded that troupe members should expect their privacy to be violated: "Again, it's the sort of thing you should assume. Of course, no one really *knows*" (10). This lack of certainty—from the company's travel itinerary to possible surveillance—and the fact that embassy officials remained largely insulated from Russian culture undermine the legitimacy of the fears presented here.

Capote further criticizes the embassy's perspective by having a cast member refer to the rumors of surveillance as "myth talk": "There's been so much myth talk around here. We've heard we're going to be trailed all the time" (8). In effect Capote aligns propaganda with mythmaking and Mrs. Ira Gershwin's gossip: "It can't be true! After all, *where* are we going to gossip? Unless we simply stand in the bathroom and keep flushing" (5). Mrs. Gershwin objected to Soviet surveillance not on political or ideological grounds but because it threatened to curtail her own ability to myth talk. By linking these three discourses (propaganda, mythmaking, and gossip), Capote suggests that they all share a similar goal: spreading untruths and exaggeration. The U.S. officials thus emerge as nothing more than mouthpieces for government propaganda, spreading McCarthy-era paranoia and gossip to amplify the Communist threat. In the closing moments of the briefing, Capote responds to the final warning ("I suppose you realize that we're being monitored right now") by adding that "any evidence, at least in the shape of mysterious strangers, was not apparent" (12).

Capote challenges Cold War myths through his depiction of surveillance as well. When the opera company arrived in Leningrad, the Hotel Astoria appeared to confirm everyone's worst fears about Communist Russia as invasive and antithetical to personal freedoms. Hotel employees sat at desks in the lobby, "simplifying their task of keeping tabs on the comings and goings of the guests," and dormitory matrons monitored each floor from "dawn to dawn, never allowing anyone to leave his room without giving him the key, and constantly, like human punch-clocks, recording ins and outs in a bulky ledger" (88). Despite this element of watchfulness, the guests had free rein to come and go. Capote and the director's assistant, for instance, explored the neighborhood of St. Isaac's Square within minutes of their arrival. The biggest risk was the bitter cold weather and their sense of direction. When they got lost, they needed to rely on the kindness of several locals to guide them back to the heated hotel. One of the American journalists on the trip later searched Capote's room for listening devices: "Leonard Lyons . . . was convinced the Astoria's rooms were wired for sound, which was not remarkable, considering that two American diplomats from the Moscow Embassy had told them at a briefing in Berlin that, during their Russian visit, they should 'assume' their rooms would be wired and their letters opened" (98). Capote's reference to the briefing again reinforces the U.S. government's role in generating fear. The embassy warnings kept everyone uneasy even though, as Capote points out, there was little evidence to support such concerns.

In another example, Capote began to notice someone following them: "He always stood at the rear, a chunky man with a crooked nose. He was bundled in a black coat and astrakhan cap and half his face was hidden behind the kind of windshield dark glasses skiers wear" (112). The ominous, threatening description of "Ski-Glasses," the man who seemed to lurk around every street corner, gets undercut when Capote accidentally leaves his hat box in a courtyard. Ski-Glasses retrieved the item for him, but "before [Capote] could think to say thank you, he'd tipped his cap and walked away" (114). This seemingly sinister figure had been hired to assist and protect the group. Mrs. Gershwin cheerfully remarked that it was "simply adorable of them to take such good care of us. . . . Isn't it a comfort to know you can't *lose* anything in Russia?" (114–15). What do get lost or dismantled over the course of the trip, however, are the group's anxieties and misperceptions about Russian culture, and Capote uses this type of anecdote to take the reader on a similar journey.

Capote also attacks McCarthy-era biases by emphasizing the commonalities between American and Russian cultures. Early in the narrative several travelers noticed similarities in the geographies of the two countries: "'Know what this reminds me of,' said Ira Wolfert, pointing a pipe at the severe landscape. 'Parts of America. The West.' Sartorius nodded. 'Wyoming in the winter'" (52). The most significant parallels, however, involved people. The company's first encounter with Russians occurred while boarding the Blue Express in East Berlin: "they [officers and sleeping-car attendants] managed to preserve a stony uninterest despite the bold attentions of those Americans who approached and stared at them as though amazed, and rather peeved, to discover Russians had two eyes correctly located" (33). On one level, their shock humorously reveals the extent to which Russians had been "othered" in American media. On another level, this moment suggests a frustration with this misrepresentation. It was the company's first glimpse at the gap between propaganda and reality, and most subsequent encounters would continue to deconstruct their cultural biases. Once aboard the train, for instance, the paternalistic tea maker in car 2 felt quite comfortable complaining about his working conditions: "He said his feet hurt him, his back hurt him, that he always had a headache from overwork . . . and considered himself underpaid. . . . Lyons paused in his notetaking and said, 'I didn't know they were allowed to complain like this. The way it sounds, I get the impression, this guy is a discontent'" (45). Again, his surprise stemmed from the juxtaposition between his assumptions about Soviet culture and the actual experiences of this man who, like most people at one time or another, felt underappreciated and undervalued at his job.

Another example occurred at the Brest Litovsk train station when a Norwegian businessman remarked "that Americans are the only people who remind me of Russians. . . . Americans are so generous. Energetic. And underneath all that brag they have such a wishing to be loved, they want to be petted, like dogs and children, and told that they are just as good and even better than the rest of us. . . . But they simply won't believe it. They go right on feeling inferior and far away. Alone. Like Russians. Precisely" (67).

Capote uses this fictionalized moment to reinforce his message about the importance of commonality over divisiveness. Here generosity and energy get presented as defining characteristics for both cultures. Throughout the text Capote provides numerous instances of these apparent similarities. The author himself certainly benefited from the social generosity of people such as Stefan Orlov, a passionately opinionated man who loved dancing and drinking, and the cast member playing Strawberry Woman experienced a spiritual generosity at the Baptist Evangelical Church in Leningrad: "I've been going to church since I can walk, but I never felt Jesus like I felt Jesus today. . . . [When] it came time to go . . . , they stood up, the whole congregation. They took out white handkerchiefs and waved them in the air. And they sang, 'God Be With You Till We Meet Again'" (149). As the observations of the Norwegian businessman and the Strawberry Woman reveal, both cultures share similar emotional, psychological, and spiritual needs. For Capote, this recognition is a starting point for the kind of mutual understanding that transcends propaganda.

Although Capote mentions the impact of Soviet propaganda on its citizens (most notably through his discussion of the exhibit at Kazin Cathedral), he primarily presents his experiences as a way to challenge readers to reject cultural biases. Capote holds the same fears as the rest of the opera company at the outset of the journey. His concerns about surveillance get projected onto Ski-Glasses and a watchful chauffeur—who does nothing more than yawn at him in passing. Most dramatically, while waiting to meet Orlov for drinks, Capote witnesses a beating that becomes a metaphor for his own fears: "four men in black had a fifth man backed against the cathedral wall. They were pounding him with their fists, pushing him forward and hitting him with the full weight of their bodies" (118). Capote tries to help the beaten man, but Orlov intervenes, pulling Capote into his car and warning him not to get involved in the affairs of others. These details seem to cast Leningrad as a place of limited freedom and inexplicable danger. These incidents, however, are soon juxtaposed with Capote and Orlov's rollicking night of drinking. Even the bars that initially seem menacing have a camaraderie that Capote soon admires. All of his initial impressions get overturned. Ski-Glasses helps him; Orlov becomes a sincere, somewhat sentimental figure; and the rowdy bar patrons are harmless guys having a good time. In this way he deconstructs his own stereotypes and anxieties. As Capote moves from fear to acceptance, anxiety to comfort, he invites the reader to do the same. Ultimately he suggests that Cold War propaganda and all of its potentially dangerous consequences can best be mitigated by recognizing a shared humanity.

The Racial Politics of *The Muses Are Heard*

Capote also applies this message about shared humanity to the issue of race in the United States. Just as he questioned the country's fear about Communist culture, Capote wanted to challenge white fears about black civil rights. Specifically he desired to give segregationists a way to accept integration by exposing the hypocritical link between Cold War politics and racist ideologies. Not wanting to alienate white readers invested in various forms of discrimination, Capote assumed the role of an objective reporter to foreground the volatile politics of the trip. During the Embassy briefing, one actor referred to "the big problem": "now what do we say when they ask us the political stuff? I'm speaking of the Negro situation" (10); and another cast member quickly seconded these concerns: "How do we handle it? Should we answer the way it is? Tell the truth? Or do you want us to gloss over it?" (11). The official's response drew on the kind of antisegregationist rhetoric that often linked integration with Communist subversion in the South: "Believe me, sir, the Russians know as much about the Negro situation as you do. And they don't give a damn one way or another. Except for statements, propaganda, anything they can turn to their own interests. I think you ought to keep in mind that any interviews you give will be picked up by the American press and reprinted in your home-town newspapers" (11). In other words, criticizing U.S. race relations could be used by Communists as a political weapon, and it could be perceived as unpatriotic by some Americans—an act with potentially dangerous consequences for Americans.

Capote included the official's veiled threat here to expose the double standard imposed on African Americans, who lived in a country demanding patriotic allegiance while denying them equal rights. When the issue of racism threatened to ignite tempers at the briefing, however, the situation was defused by the comments of a female cast member: "'We all know there's discrimination back home,' she said in a shy voice to which everyone listened respectfully. 'But in the last eight years Negroes have made a lot of progress. We've come a long way and that's the truth. We can point with pride to our scientists, artists. If we did that (in Russia), it might do a lot of good'" (11–12). Capote presents her celebration of African American achievement as quelling the group's concerns, but it seems more likely that he wanted to use a different voice to criticize segregation—the voice of Soviet propaganda: "the situation of the American Negro as depicted in *Porgy and Bess*, an exploited race at the mercy of ruthless Southern whites, poverty-pinched and segregated in the ghetto of Catfish Row, could not be more agreeably imagined if the Ministry of Culture had assigned one of their own writers to

the job" (20). By presenting segregation as a weakness in American culture
that could be exploited, Capote offers a palatable political argument for segregationists to reconsider racist policies and practices. It is an argument that
does not condemn southern white culture per se; instead it exploits Cold War
fears in much the same way some white segregationists vilified integration.

Through the persona of a reporter/eavesdropper, Capote also creates an
intimacy between the reader and the troupe that challenges racial stereotypes
and practices. According to the director, "The very presence of the Negro
cast, their affluent appearance, their so obviously unoppressed outspoken-
ness, their educated, even worldly manner . . . would impress on the Russian
people a different image of the American Negro from the stereotype that
continues to make Harriet Beecher Stowe one of the Soviet's best-selling authors" (21). Some of the political importance of *Porgy and Bess* would come
from the performers whose lives offstage might be able to undermine Soviet
stereotypes.

In many respects the director's observations reflected Capote's attempt
in *The Muses Are Heard* to provide an image of black life that challenged
American stereotypes. The integrated space on the Blue Express offers one
powerful example of this. The train, an emblem of public transportation,
evokes the long history of African American civil rights—from Homer
Plessy's arrest for sitting in a whites-only train car to Rosa Parks's refusal
to give up her seat on a Montgomery bus two weeks before the Everyman
Opera Company's trip. When the company learned that men and women,
black and white would be sharing sleeping cars onboard the train, however,
only the issue of gender was raised briefly: "So I'm afraid we'll have to do
as the Russians do. They always put boys and girls together" (28). Although
the integration of race and gender occurred by necessity here, it implausibly
went unremarked. This strategic silence points to one of the more radical
aspects of the book. By not referencing the implications of this arrangement
in the United States, Capote suggests that there is nothing remarkable, problematic, or dangerous about integration. These living quarters also enable
him to offer an intimate portrait of African Americans that highlights the
similarities between blacks and whites. Just as African Americans shared
the same Cold War anxieties as whites, they could also partake in the same
excesses. Capote repeatedly notes Mrs. Ira Gershwin's ostentatious displays
of wealth to poke fun at pretentious upper-class society: "Without discarding
her diamonds, Mrs. Gershwin had changed into slacks and a sweater" (44);
her "diamonded decorations made her look as though she were moving in
a spotlight" (163). Likewise two African American cast members engaged
in equally vainglorious displays: "Miss Thigpen, a concert artist before she

joined *Porgy and Bess* four years ago, is a small, plump woman, lavishly pow-
dered. She wears the highest heels, the tallest hats, and generous sprinklings
of Joy ('The World's Costliest Perfume')" (37). Earl Bruce Jackson, who affected "a chin goatee" and kept his hands "radiant with rings, diamonds, and
sapphires and rubies" (36), wanted to get married in Moscow to promote his
own career: "The first couple of Negro Americans married in Moscow. That's
front page. That's TV" (38).

Both Thigpen and Jackson shared Mrs. Gershwin's flair for displaying
socioeconomic success through jewelry and clothing. Ultimately the African
Americans in this text emerge as no different from the whites traveling with
them or many of the Russians they encounter. They all share similar desires,
needs, and pretensions. In fact Capote uses so few descriptions of skin color
that it becomes difficult at times to recall a character's ethnicity. For Capote,
the integrated train becomes a metaphor for viewing blacks and whites as
interconnected, as more similar than different, and by normalizing integration, Capote reveals the corrosive impact of segregation and discrimination.
It perpetuates myths and stereotypes that prevent whites from recognizing
their shared humanity with African Americans.

Conclusion: Muses and Forceful Happenings

Both the Everyman Opera Company and Capote's book capture the shared
humanity of people from different cultures, political perspectives, and ethnicities, illustrating art's potential for building community and lessening the
possibility of conflict. Capote first announces this theme in the title, which he
borrows from the Ministry of Culture official responsible for the *Porgy and
Bess* tour. Throughout the text, this official uses a cannon-muses metaphor
to explain the significance of this trip. Just as the weapons of war drown out
art's ability to promote global peace, propaganda and segregation function
as the cannon fire silencing tolerance and mutual understanding in the United
States. Capote offers art as the central tool for breaking through this silence,
however. In addition to the text of his own book, he presents the Peacock at
the Hermitage and jazz as powerful muses that offer a pathway for mitigat-
ing Cold War fears and racial intolerance.

Despite various grumblings among the group, Capote uses their visit to
the Hermitage as a tangible example of art that transcends political, ethnic,
and cultural differences. The museum tour culminates at the Peacock, an
eighteenth-century clock designed by James Cox as a gift for Catherine II.
As the guide explains, "When the hour strikes, we have here a forceful happening. . . . The peacock spreads her tail, and the rooster cackles. The owl
blinks her eyes, and the squirrel has a good munch" (137). Although one cast

member belittles the clock for lacking any utilitarian function and another dislikes museums for being mausoleums to mortality, the chiming clock turns out to be a forceful happening: "A gang of soldiers, part of another tour, approached The Peacock just as the hour chimed, and the soldiers, country boys with their heads shaved bald, their drab uniforms sagging in the seat like diapers, had the double enchantment of gaping at foreigners and watching the golden-eyed winkings of an owl, a peacock flash its bronze feathers in the wan light of the Winter Palace. The Americans and the soldiers crowded close to hear the rooster crow. Man and art, for a moment alive together, immune to old mortality" (138–39). Capote depicts the Russian soldiers not as threatening representatives of the Soviet military but as country boys who are childlike with wonder. At that moment the chiming clock creates a shared experience. Art is a reminder here not of death but of vitality. It embodies the possibilities for social and cultural community.

Likewise the impromptu jazz performance on Christmas Eve creates a similar moment of cultural exchange between East and West, black and white. The lackluster nightclub in the Astoria Hotel was filled with nearly catatonic patrons when the opera company arrived at two o'clock in the morning: "The Soviet habit of seating strangers together does not encourage uninhibited conversation, . . . [and most of the patrons] sat around bored and uncaring as castaways on a Pacific atoll" (142). Several cast members soon took the stage and started singing: "It was as though the castaways had sighted rescue on the horizon. Smiles broke out like an unfurling of flags" (143). Capote notes that some of the Russian band members had already been fans of jazz. One even owned a large record collection and considered himself a devotee of Dizzy Gillespie. This previous exposure to jazz established an immediate openness for playing together. The Russian and American musicians gave a joint performance that invigorated the apathetic crowd: "A Chinese cadet tapped his foot, Russians packed close to the bandstand, riveted by Lamar's scratchy voice, the drumbeat riding behind it. . . . Mrs. Breen, a smiling shepherd gazing at her flock, turned to Leonard Lyons. 'You see. We've broken through. Robert's done what the diplomats couldn't'" (143). Mrs. Breen's celebration of art encapsulates Capote's theme. Likewise the imagery in this passage reinforces the political implications of this exchange. For most readers at the time, his reference to castaways on a Pacific atoll would likely conjure up images of Bikini Atoll, the sight of over a dozen nuclear tests since 1946, including the detonation of a hydrogen bomb in 1954. Fears of the atomic age played a central role in Cold War tensions and 1950s propaganda, and Capote suggests that art can offer a way to move beyond such fears. It provides an access point for mutual understanding.

Finally, Capote uses *Porgy and Bess* as an example of art as an emissary for overcoming cultural differences. At first the audience was puzzled by the opera. They did not applaud after "Summertime" or most of the other famous numbers of act 1, which Capote largely attributes to a desire among Russian audiences to understand: "fearful of missing the essential phrase, the significant clue that would unmask the mysteries confronting them, they listened and watched with the brooding intentness of students in a lecture hall" (170). In many respects Capote portrays the audience as "students" or learners of both the show and American culture. Their reception warms as soon as they recognize the love story between Porgy and Bess. After "Bess, You Is My Woman Now," they "deluged the performers with applause that was brief but heavy like tropic rain" (171), and this moment and the song by a street peddler were situations "the Russians could grasp" (176). The commonality of human experience through love and work resonated even as aspects of African American culture and elements of Gershwin's music remained elusive. In the words of Capote's Russian companion Orlov, "And in the summer, that's what you'll hear: young people whistling along the river. They won't forget" (178). Capote gets a glimpse of this after the show as he hears three Russian friends singing, "There's a boat leavin' soon for New York, come with me, that's where we belong, sister" (178).

By crafting *The Muses Are Heard* as an intimate narrative, Capote invites readers to share in the opera company's experiences. The author's ability to move beyond fear and propaganda-shaped prejudices takes readers on a similar journey. Like the art of *Porgy and Bess*, it provides an opportunity for his audiences to challenge their own biases about Soviet and African American cultures even if elements of each remain mystifying. Capote certainly recognizes that responses to *Porgy and Bess*—like those to his book—are subjective: "'What really happened.' There is no absolute truth in these matters, only opinion, and as I attempted to formulate my own . . . , I stretched on the bed and switched out the light" (164). But he offers both as a starting point for moving beyond political intransigence and overcoming cultural prejudice. He just hopes that the cannons will be silent long enough for this message to be heard.

CHAPTER 6

Breakfast at Tiffany's

JERRY: [*Breakfast at Tiffany's*] is kinda old, isn't it?
GEORGE: [The book club] wanted to read a Truman Capote book.
JERRY: Oh, sure . . . Truman Capote.
GEORGE: He's a great writer.
JERRY: Oh, yeah.
GEORGE: Did you ever read anything by him?
JERRY: No. You?
GEORGE: Nah.

Seinfeld, "The Couch" (1994)

When George Costanza (Jason Alexander) joins a book club to impress a woman, he assumes that reading Truman Capote's *Breakfast at Tiffany's*—at only "ninety pages"—will be a breeze. He soon realizes that he has trouble concentrating on anything unrelated to sports and decides to track down a copy of the film instead. At the end of this *Seinfeld* episode, the book club meets, and George disagrees with his would-be-girlfriend's interpretation of female independence in the novel: "After all, [Holly] did get together with George Peppard. I mean, Fred." To which she replies, "George . . . Fred's gay." This humorous exchange certainly pokes fun at the ways popular culture often appropriates literature. It replaces complexity (in this case regarding sexuality) with the conventional, and it encourages passive consumption (watching a film) over intellectual engagement. In short, it cultivates aliteracy—a willingness to accept Capote's "greatness" as a writer without actually reading his works. George not only goes to great lengths to avoid reading, but he also wants to be entertained during the screening of the film, asking for dimmed lights, popcorn, grape juice, and a seat on the couch closest to the television. These trimmings provide a physical comfort that parallels the reassurances offered by a happy Hollywood ending. The substitution of the film for the book also speaks to the tremendous popularity of the 1961 adaptation starring Audrey Hepburn. In many respects George's preference for Hepburn's Holly reflects a choice that continues in the American cultural imagination. Our investment in the film's message about the redemptive power of heterosexual love and monogamy persists, and we do not seem to want anything—not even the book—to challenge them.

This *Seinfeld* episode offers a clever counterpoint to the ways that *Breakfast at Tiffany's* has become a cultural shorthand for true love and glamorous New York nightlife.[1] Most popular allusions to the work either celebrate the film's message of idealized romance or lament its failed promise. The 1994 song "Breakfast at Tiffany's" by Deep Blue Something, for example, does both in response to a disintegrating romantic relationship. The couple in the song has only a vague recollection of the movie, but the singer clings to the hope that this shared experience might somehow resuscitate their love. Likewise in the pilot episode of *Sex and the City*, Carrie Bradshaw (Sarah Jessica Parker) bemoans the romantic difficulties facing single women in New York City: "Welcome to the age of un-innocence. No one has breakfast at Tiffany's, and no one has affairs to remember. Instead we have breakfast at 7 A.M., and affairs we try to forget as quickly as possible." Although she claims that true love has "fled the co-op," this sentiment does not prevent her and her friends from pursuing the happy ending of Hepburn's Holly for the next six years. Whether it serves as an image for finding personal contentment through love or as an excuse to make Tiffany's a destination spot for every tour bus in Manhattan, *Breakfast at Tiffany's* continues to have a cultural capital far removed from the novel. Like Roland Barthes's notion of the face of Garbo, the image of Hepburn looking in the window of Tiffany's represents something beyond itself. It has become an idea that continues to inspire romantic fantasy.[2] Yet our investment in Hepburn's Holly, as well as the comforting messages of the film, has skewed our understanding of Capote's work and the era in which it was written—the 1950s. It has, in effect, robbed the book of its historical and social significance.

Much like Fitzgerald's *The Great Gatsby*, *Breakfast at Tiffany's* (1958) tells the retrospective story of a captivating, enigmatic, and morally problematic figure through the eyes of a nostalgic narrator. Both novels depict postwar escapism and a narcissistic youth culture that rejects middle-class values through late-night parties, drinking, and sexual freedom. The nameless narrator of *Breakfast at Tiffany's* first learns of Holly Golightly in 1943 when he rents the apartment above hers in an Upper East Side brownstone.

The card on her mailbox reads "Holly Golightly, Traveling," and this description announces the value she places on social and personal freedom: "After all," she offers by way of explanation, "how do I know where I'll be living tomorrow?" (42). Holly, he soon learns, earns money ("powder-room change") as an escort for wealthy men and as a messenger for the mobster Sally Tomato. She gets compensated one hundred dollars per week for visiting Sally in prison and relaying his "weather report" to a man posing as his lawyer. These messages, which seem innocuous to her, help Sally maintain control over his global narcotics business. Meanwhile, as the narrator gets glimpses into Holly's vibrant social life, he soon discovers that she is not who she appears to be. She has abandoned her husband, masked her southern accent, changed her name from Lulamae to Holly, and lost weight in an effort to remake her identity. This transformation has helped her access New York's high-end social scene, which she does in the hope of finding a wealthy husband. Beneath this facade, however, Holly possesses a refreshing frankness. She embraces the notion that women should enjoy sex and recognizes the complexity of human sexuality. She even admits to being "a bit of a dyke [herself]" (22) and argues that "a person ought to be able to marry men or women" (83).

Eventually Holly finds what she is looking for, or so it seems. She gets romantically involved with José Ybarra-Jaegar, a South American diplomat who aspires to become president of Brazil, and she soon becomes pregnant. Always a chameleon, Holly tries to reshape herself into a domestic housewife—staying at home, buying furniture, taking José's suits to the cleaners, and attempting to cook. The news of her brother's death in the war and the sudden publicity surrounding her involvement with Sally Tomato, however, shatter this illusion. Her arrest, which receives front-page coverage in the tabloids, threatens José's political career, and he flees to Brazil. Soon afterward Holly loses her baby during a horseback-riding incident in Central Park. She not only recognizes that this scandal and her abandonment by José have ruined her social currency in New York, but she also refuses to testify against Sally. Such an act would violate her moral code about emotional honesty. She decides instead to leave the country, abandoning her cat in Spanish Harlem and disappearing—never to be seen by the narrator or his friends again.

Although the narrator's relationship with Holly takes place in the early 1940s, he tells her story in 1957, and this span enables Capote to give Holly broader cultural significance. As he explained in a 1968 interview with Eric Norden, "So these girls are the authentic American geishas, and they're much more prevalent now than in 1943 or 1944. . . . The main reason I wrote about

Holly, outside of the fact that I liked her so much, was that she was such a symbol of all these girls who come to New York and spin in the sun for a moment like May flies and then disappear. I wanted to rescue one girl from that anonymity and preserve her for posterity" (141). For Capote, Holly symbolized the growing number of young women seeking social and sexual autonomy. Certainly a range of social changes was exacerbating conservative fears about female sexuality at the time. Forty-eight states overturned laws prohibiting the distribution of contraceptive devices in the 1950s, and as Glenn C. Altschuler notes, "The availability of condoms and penicillin were making promiscuity safe, accepted, and universal to the post–World War II generation" (67). Alfred Kinsey's best-selling study *Sexual Behavior in the Human Female* (1953) shocked readers by exposing the enormous "gulf between women's prescribed social and sexual roles and their actual desires and behaviors" (Reumann 87). According to his findings, nearly 50 percent of women engaged in premarital sex, and Kinsey believed that these experiences led to happier marriages.[3] In the same year, *Playboy* magazine hit the stands for the first time, and its celebration of bachelor life included a portrait of women as sharing a comparable sexual drive with men. The tasteful bachelor life, which was defined by consumption and sexual pleasure, was predicated on the "lovely, single, sexually available girl who had no intention of charting a course to the altar" (Fraterrigo 3). The pages of Playboy magazine, along with the Kinsey report, the popularity of Marilyn Monroe, and the music of Elvis Presley, fueled growing anxieties about female sexuality.

Capote's novel contributed to these concerns through its depiction of Holly's dynamic single life and her philosophy about sexuality. Holly takes pleasure in sex, enjoys material comforts, and is in no rush to the altar. In these ways she prefigures the single girl of Helen Gurley Brown's advice book *Sex and the Single Girl* (1962) and provides an ideal counterpart to *Playboy*. Brown's books and Hefner's magazine advised readers to cultivate a refined lifestyle and, in a sense, to reshape their identity. One of the characters in *Breakfast at Tiffany's* labels this quality in Holly as "phoniness," but Capote uses it to raise questions about the investment American culture places on outward appearances. These questions reflect on the novel's concerns about materialism as well. None of the wealthy characters finds personal or romantic fulfillment, which undercuts Holly's vision of Tiffany's as a place of stability and contentment. Financial security may be an essential ingredient for living an autonomous single life, but it does not seem to help women break free from the ideology of domesticity in America. They still seek meaning in men and marriage. When Holly fails to do both, she must flee the country, and Capote uses this moment to suggest that America denies a lasting place for people who reject or resist this ideology—particularly single women (who are single for too long) and homosexuals. In addition, placing *Breakfast at Tiffany's* in the context of the 1950s provides a valuable counterpoint to the film. Hepburn's Holly never strays far from middle-class values. Her pursuit of wealthy men is motivated by a desire to care for her brother, and her decision to accept her love for the narrator—to see marriage as a romantic possibility and not a cage—reinforces the very messages that Capote set out to question.

Playboy, Kinsey, and the Modern American Woman

When discussing his frustration with the film adaptation of *Breakfast at Tiffany's,* Capote complained that "Marilyn was my first choice to play the girl, Holly Golightly. . . . Holly had to have something touching about her . . . unfinished. Marilyn had that. . . . Audrey was not what I had in mind when I wrote that part" (Inge 317). Capote's desire for Marilyn Monroe to play the lead stemmed both from his friendship with her and his understanding of her cultural significance. She represented something entirely different from the wistful beauty and innocence of Audrey Hepburn in *Roman Holiday* (1953) and *Sabrina* (1954), for instance. Monroe could stand over a New York subway grate and bask in the fun of her fluttering white dress and exposed legs, but Hepburn could not. This image from *The Seven Year Itch* (1955) typifies what Monroe signified for so many Americans in the 1950s—the ability to take pleasure in one's body and sexuality without shame or guilt. Her photograph on the cover of *Playboy*'s first issue two years earlier communicates a similar message about sexuality. Her raised hand and open-mouthed smile imply a greeting, and her v-cut top, which exposes part of her breast, invites the viewer to see more inside the magazine.[4] For Hugh Hefner, Monroe was exactly the type of woman he wanted to associate with the playboy life—physically attractive, sexually available, and fun-loving.

Hefner followed the pattern of most young men after the war. He found work quickly, married his high-school sweetheart, and became a parent; like so many others, Hefner soon found this routine stultifying. As Elizabeth Fraterrigo notes, "He could not shake the gnawing sense that somehow he had missed out on something along the way" (18). This feeling inspired Hefner's interest in American sexual culture. He eagerly read Kinsey's 1948 report on male sexuality, and its depiction of the gap between private behavior and public image aligned with Hefner's perception of American culture. Furthermore he resented the importance placed on marriage as a bastion against immorality, the Communist threat, and the dangers of homosexuality. These attitudes shaped his vision for creating a men's magazine that would reject these notions and continue the conversation started by Kinsey. As the first editorial of *Playboy* explains, the magazine would fulfill "a publishing need only slightly less important than the one just taken care of by the Kinsey Report" (quoted in Fraterrigo 21).

Hefner struggled to find a name for the magazine that would reflect his central message about social class and hedonism. His original plan to christen the publication *Stag Party* ran into copyright difficulties,[5] but he soon settled on something far more evocative in its Jazz Age sensibility: *Playboy*.[6] On one level, *Playboy* sold an upper-class fantasy through its image of sophisticated, urban bachelors with the financial resources to enjoy themselves. Playboys lived a gallant lifestyle, and the magazine presented several essential characteristics for demonstrating this: wearing fashionable clothing, listening to jazz, owning (several) sports cars, making the perfect martini, and living in a tastefully decorated apartment. Of course these things were best enjoyed in the company of women who were not concerned with commitment, marriage, and family. On another level, the editorials, articles, advertisements, and photographs in *Playboy* inextricably linked consumerism and refinement with hedonistic pleasure. "Awareness of liquor, music, food, hi-fi equipment, fine art, even philosophy," Fraterrigo explains, "made the playboy a connoisseur, with its attendant meanings of refinement and sophistication. In turn, his connoisseurship was linked to seduction and sexual indulgence, and all were situated within the realm of the bachelor pad" (83). Money, sophistication, and a room of one's own, in other words, facilitated seduction. These images resonated with readers because, as David Lubin explains, *Playboy* democratized "its readers' aristocratic desires and pretensions" by suggesting that "any man, any regular guy . . . could achieve playboy status for the nugatory price of a newsstand copy" (51). By 1958 the magazine was outselling *Esquire,* and two years later it claimed a readership exceeding one million people.[7]

Playboy's depiction of women as sexual beings dovetailed with Kinsey's findings about female sexuality in the same year. Published in September 1953, *Sexual Behavior in the Human Female* sold 185,000 copies in ten days.[8] According to a *Newsweek* poll, coverage about the report "was ranked as equaled in public interest only by the possible advent of a third world war" (Reumann 94). Kinsey and his team of researchers conducted 5,940 interviews, and they found that 20 percent of married women had had illegal abortions, 50 percent had engaged in premarital sex, and 26 percent had admitted to having extramarital sex.[9] Additionally 28 percent of women experienced erotic encounters with other women, and 13 percent of these cases resulted in orgasm.[10] These findings not only exposed the gap between the prescribed social roles and private sexual behaviors of women, but they also raised questions about the morality of American culture. As the historian Miriam G. Reumann has argued, "Virtually all authorities who commented on female sexuality believed that women's behavior indicated the state of the nation's morality and culture and offered valuable clues to its future. Thus, the postwar years witnessed intense disputes over the evolving roles of American women" (90). These anxieties about national morality positioned women as guardians of a conservative domestic ideology. They were expected to be wives who preserved traditional gender roles and mothers who raised children to eschew extended bachelorhood, homosexuality, and communism. As May explains, "The family was the arena in which that adaptation was expected to occur; the home was the environment in which people could feel good about themselves. In this way, domestic containment and its therapeutic corollary undermined the potential for political activism and reinforced the chilling effects of anticommunism and the cold war consensus" (17). Certainly women played too crucial a role in establishing such an environment to be living adventurous single lives.

After almost a decade of *Playboy* magazine, a female counterpart to Hefner's bachelor finally emerged. In her 1962 book *Sex and the Single Girl,* Helen Gurley Brown celebrated singlehood for women in similar terms as *Playboy* did for men and offered advice on a range of topics, including fashion, physical fitness, home decor, cooking, kissing, makeup, and how to conduct an affair. Brown encouraged women to achieve financial independence and personal fulfillment through material goods and sexual pleasure outside the context of marriage. Even though Brown advocated female autonomy, she did not do so in ways that challenged gender inequality. As Fraterrigo notes, Brown "articulated a relationship between feminine identity, paid employment, and consumption that accepted women's limited career opportunities and constructed marriage to be the eventual goal, while placing sexuality and commodity consumption at the center of a prolonged stage of pleasure-oriented singlehood" (106). While the single girl sought physical and material pleasure, she did not question her ultimate position as a housewife and mother. In fact, Brown argued, the social and sexual experiences of the girl would make her a more desirable wife.

Playboy magazine communicated a similar message about marriage. Despite its more radical politics, *Playboy*'s critique of marriage and endorsement of premarital sex were tempered by the fact that it did not endorse endless bachelorhood. Hefner's magazine merely "promoted prolonged, commitment-free bachelorhood with the implication that delaying adult responsibility would ultimately strengthen marital bonds" (Fraterrigo 5).

These messages spoke to a generation of young men and women who were becoming sexually active. After approving birth control pills for treating miscarriages and menstrual disorders in 1957, for example, the FDA later, in May 1960, endorsed them as contraceptive devices. "By the end of 1961, some 408,000 American women were taking the Pill, by the end of 1962 the figure was 1,187,000, and by the end of 1963 it was 2.3 million and still rising" (Halberstam 605). Holly Golightly—along with Hefner's magazine and Kinsey's work—certainly prefigured the sexually active single girl of the 1960s and demonstrated that this figure had been a significant part of 1950s urban culture as well. Holly's attitudes about sex gave the lie to the sexual conservatism typified by sitcom moms such as June Cleaver, but her vibrant singlehood did not free her from other social constraints. She remained a victim of a socioeconomic hierarchy and domestic ideology that disempowered women by insisting on marriage and motherhood.

Pastures of the Sky: Holly Golightly and the Single Life

According to Capote, the publication of *Breakfast at Tiffany's* began the "Holly Golightly Sweepstakes" as several women, including Phoebe Pierce, Gloria Vanderbilt, Oona O'Neill, Carol Marcus, and Doris Lilly, claimed to be the inspiration for its heroine.[11] One Manhattan resident, Bonnie Golightly, even filed an eight-hundred-thousand-dollar lawsuit against Capote for libel and invasion of privacy. Capote never provided a name for his inspiration, but in a 1968 interview with *Playboy* magazine, he did give credit to "a German refugee who arrived in New York at the beginning of the War, when she was 17 years old. Very few people were aware of this, however, because she spoke English without any trace of an accent. She had an apartment in the brownstone where I lived and we became great friends" (Norden 142). In addition to his German neighbor and the wealthy friends with whom Capote dashed from one nightclub to another in the 1940s, it seems likely that Holly Golightly was also based on his mother. Clarke observes that "both Nina and Holly grew up in the rural South and longed for the glitter and glamour of New York, and they both changed their hillbilly names, Lillie Mae and Lulamae, to those they considered more sophisticated" (313). Both women also suffered from severe bouts of anxiety, fell in love with Latin American men, and believed they could remake themselves in order to find happiness. Thinking of Holly Golightly as a composite of these women gives her character the kind of cultural significance Capote seemed to be after when he claimed in the same interview that she was "a symbol of all these girls who come to New York . . . then disappear." She becomes any woman (an immigrant, a poor southern girl, a wealthy heiress) who desired social and sexual freedom in postwar America.

In *Breakfast at Tiffany's*, Capote critiques the culture of sexual repression in 1940s and 1950s America most explicitly through Holly's lifestyle, which is characterized by sexual freedom and a progressive attitude toward sex. Holly first meets the narrator after climbing through his bedroom window—an act that serves as a metaphor for her sexual temerity. She takes pride in being "very brazen" (18), and this quality makes her comfortable expressing her desires for men. Capote aligns Holly with the biblical Eve as well to signify her defiance of paternalistic authority. Soon after entering the narrator's apartment, she ravenously eats an apple, and this hunger represents her insatiable pursuit of "forbidden" knowledge (that is, unconventional behaviors). She abandons her first marriage and motherhood (the quintessential norms for women at the time) to taste personal freedom. Furthermore she cultivates male companionship like one might sample clothing: trying on different sizes until something fits well enough. When she invites the narrator over for a drink one night, he observes that all of the men in her apartment appeared somewhat disappointed: "Within the next quarter-hour a stag party had taken over the apartment, several of them in uniform. . . . Except for the lack of youth, the guests had no common theme, they seemed strangers among strangers; indeed, each face, on entering, had struggled to conceal dismay at seeing others there. It was as if the hostess had distributed her invitations while zigzagging through various bars; which was probably the case" (35). While the lack of commonality among these partygoers captures her scattershot approach to courtship, it also illustrates the public nature of her sexual identity. She goes from one bar to another inviting men to a party, and these activities suggest an openness about female sexuality that was largely absent in mainstream America at the time.

Capote also communicates his condemnation of sexual repression through Holly's progressive philosophy about sexuality. When her acquaintance and short-term roommate, Mag Wildwood, claims that she cannot remember her experiences with José in bed, Holly advises her to turn on the lights: "What's wrong with a decent look at a guy you like? Men are beautiful, a lot of them are. José is, and if you don't even want to *look* at him well, I'd say he's getting a pretty cold plate of macaroni" (50). Holly engages in sex with the lights on—openly and without shame—and she considers passion integral to any romantic relationship. In defense, Mag labels herself a conventional person with a "n-n-normal attitude," but Holly rejects this notion outright: "It may be normal, darling; but I'd rather be natural" (50). This exchange highlights the same gap that Kinsey's *Sexual Behavior in the Human Female* noted between public (normal) and private (natural) behavior in women. Similarly Capote condemns any construct that places social norms at odds with natural instincts. Not surprisingly, Mag's relationship with José falls apart, and she marries a wealthy homosexual man to secure her place in upper-class social circles.

Along with Holly's attitude about personal and sexual freedom, Capote uses her perspective on same-sex desire to condemn homophobia as well. Holly embraces the notion of sexuality as complex and fluid—a radical sentiment both in the context of homosexual persecution during the Cold War and in regard to the anxieties surrounding same-sex environments during World War II. As the scholar John D'Emilio has argued, the war created opportunities for gay culture to flourish in unprecedented ways:

> The war plucked millions of young men and women, whose sexual identities were just forming, out of their homes, out of towns and small cities, and away from the heterosexual environment of the family, and dropped them into sex-segregated situations—as GIs, as WACs and WAVES, in same-sex roominghouses for women workers who had relocated to find employment. Wartime society freed millions of the young from the settings where heterosexuality was normally encouraged. For men and women who were already gay, the war provided the opportunity to meet persons like themselves, while others were able to act on erotic desires they might otherwise have denied. World War II was something of a nationwide "coming out" experience for homosexuals and lesbians. (65–66)

D'Emilio notes that heterosexual norms privileged the nuclear family in ways that both marginalized gay culture and fueled bigotry. Holly's endorsement of gay marriage recognizes the need within American culture to make homosexuality visible. As she explains to the narrator, "I'd settle for Garbo any day. Why not? A person ought to be able to marry men or women or—listen, if you came to me and said you wanted to hitch up with Man o' War, I'd respect your feeling. No, I'm serious. Love should be allowed" (83). This notion that love cannot be circumscribed by social propriety and bigotry, that it is a natural expression of the self, is common to Capote's fiction, but Holly's argument for gay marriage moves the issue from the private to the public realm. Unlike the closed world of *Other Voices, Other Rooms* and the temporary space of the tree house in *The Grass Harp, Breakfast at Tiffany's* argues that homosexual relationships need a public/legal place in American society.

Capote captures some of the dangers of homophobic culture through gay characters who repress their own sexuality. The novel opens with a description of the matronly Joe Bell, the bartender who befriended the narrator and Holly Golightly in the early 1940s. Bell not only tends to his bowl of flowers with meticulous care, weeps at Holly's departure, listens to the soap serial "Our Gal Sunday," and operates what appears to be a gay bar,[12] but he also suppresses his own desires: "Not that I don't think about that side of things (sex). . . . It's a peculiar fact—but, the older I grow, that side of things seems to be on my mind more and more. I don't remember thinking about it so much even when I was a youngster and it's every other minute. Maybe the older you grow and the less easy it is to put thought into action, maybe that's why it gets all locked up in your head and becomes a burden. Whenever I read in the paper about an old man disgracing himself, I know it's because of this burden. But . . . I'll never disgrace myself" (9–10). Sexual desire has been a lifelong burden for Joe. At the age of sixty-seven, he still cannot stop himself from thinking about sex. He is comforted only by the knowledge that he can prevent himself from acting on these urges, insisting that he will never "disgrace" himself. For Joe, sex is shameful, and this attitude makes his platonic relationship with Holly so appealing: it does not involve sexual temptation. Although Joe serves drinks at a gay bar, the anonymity of the place and its one-way mirrors symbolize his efforts to hide his own sexuality. Likewise the millionaire Rusty Trawler fears the social stigma associated with homosexuality to such an extent that he gets married repeatedly. As Holly explains to the narrator, "Use your head. Can't you see it's just that Rusty feels safer in diapers than he would in a skirt? . . . I told him to grow up and face the issue, settle down and play house with a nice fatherly truck driver" (42). Holly's infantilizing characterization of Rusty parallels his physical description in the book as "a middle-aged child who never shed its baby fat" (35). These moments suggest that maturity requires an awareness and acceptance of one's sexuality.

Capote presents the narrator as sharing a similar discomfort with his own sexuality and its potential social consequences. Even though the narrator remains largely quiet about his homosexuality, Holly immediately recognizes it. Later in the novel she even refers to him as "Maude" (103), a slang term for a homosexual. The closest the narrator comes to expressing same-sex desire happens through a description of José: "I was charmed. He'd been put together with care, his brown head and bullfighter's figure had an exactness, a perfection, like an apple, an orange, something nature had made just right" (47). Although the narrator views José's body as something beautiful and natural, he does not feel the same way about his own desire for him. Once again Capote uses Holly to criticize this type of sexual repression. She recognizes the narrator's closeted homosexuality and repeatedly tries to force him to acknowledge it—through nicknames such as Maude, criticisms of Rusty's closeted sexuality, and her belief that the narrator should be able to marry a "Man o' War."

Breakfast at Tiffany's also questions the value placed on social image in American culture. Most of the characters in the novel have created personae to advance personal and/or professional goals. After moving to Los Angeles, for example, Holly takes French lessons to disguise her southern accent, loses weight, colors her hair, and wears fashionable clothing—all of which are essential for making her a starlet. Even her dark sunglasses suggest an obfuscation on her part—an ongoing attempt to hide her true self behind a carefully constructed facade. Capote first signals the value Holly places on outward appearance through her name. By abandoning Lulamae for Holly (an abbreviation for Hollywood),[13] she identifies herself fully with a town/film industry that manufactures and sells fantasy. Holly too is selling a fabricated version of herself. Her last name (Golightly) further implies the ease with which she moves from one identity (one place) to another. As suggested by her unfurnished apartment and the word "traveling" on her Tiffany cards, she defines herself by movement, particularly the ability to pack up and go at a moment's notice. She even refuses to name her cat because that would imply permanence: "we don't belong to each other: he's an independent, and so am I" (39). For Holly, freedom is the ability to alter her identity when necessary, and owning (or being owned) is antithetical to that.

Similarly, Mag Wildwood has approached the construction of her own image with "scientific" precision. She does not completely abandon her Arkansas accent or downplay her stutter. Instead she exaggerates the latter to cultivate male interest: "Even the stutter, certainly genuine but still a bit laid on, had been turned to advantage. It was the master stroke, that stutter; for it contrived to make her banalities sound somehow original, and secondly, despite her tallness, her assurance, it served to inspire in male listeners a protective feeling" (44). Her affectations, like Holly's, are designed to enhance social standing by making her appear more elegant and, in this case, more intelligent than she really is. Capote does not place the blame on these characters entirely, though. He seems far more critical of the culture that encourages—even requires—superficial transformations for social acceptance. As Peter Krämer has argued, Holly represents the type of liberated women in the 1940s "who come from a foreign, provincial or lower class background and therefore *have* to reinvent themselves to gain entry into the social and economic elite" (61). This need for reinvention, however, casts doubt on the extent to which Holly and her ilk are liberated. They can act with abandon and pursue their own desires so long as they look and behave according to certain social standards. The need for Lulamae to become Holly, in other words, reveals a rigid class hierarchy in America that limits personal and social freedom to those who do not conform.

Much of this reinvention is motivated by material and consumer culture, which Capote presents as trapping women. Holly initially dreams of leaving Texas and crafting a new identity after thumbing through countless "show-off pictures" (69) in glossy magazines. Popular culture, whether in magazines or in Hollywood films, defines glamour and beauty in America, and for Holly it has instilled an insatiable desire to possess them. As her husband Doc Golightly explains, every day the images in those magazines drew her further and further away from the family farm. Not surprisingly, she views Tiffany's as the epitome of upper-class life: "nothing very bad could happen to you there, not with those kind men in their nice suits, and that lovely smell of silver and alligator wallets. If I could find a real life place that made me feel like Tiffany's, then I'd buy some furniture and give the cat a name" (40). This fantasy about Tiffany's contributes to Holly's characterization as someone constantly longing for things that are out of reach: she dreams of finding love but discards her love letters (V-letters) from servicemen; she seeks domestic stability but constantly misplaces her keys; she longs to reconnect with her brother, but he remains overseas in the army. Her desire to find a "real life place" like Tiffany's is also unattainable. Her admiration for the store comes in large part from a belief that wealth and all of its material trappings (nice suits, silver, alligator wallets) provide stability and security. Certainly Holly's experiences with poverty, starvation, and abandonment make this idealization understandable, but she cannot recognize the ways that consumer culture has influenced/shaped this fantasy. In reality Holly is surrounded by people who sacrifice their happiness for wealth (such as Mag Wildwood) and/or their social position (Rusty Trawler). When the narrator sees Holly at the prestigious 21 Club, for example, she sits "idly, publicly combing her hair" and with an expression that the narrator describes as "an unrealized yawn" (15). Even though she finds most wealthy men to be tiresome rats, the glamorization of material culture exerts a gravitational pull on her and, by extension, on any American who aspires to partake in upper-class life. Like Holly, who wants a list of the fifty richest men in Brazil before fleeing the country, many Americans share her blind pursuit of wealth and elite culture.

While the Holly types are trapped by certain social expectations, wives and mothers are victimized by the social roles expected of them as well. Capote links Holly with the other female visitors at Sing Sing to show how

their outward roles/appearances are driven by the needs of patriarchal culture: "It's sweet as hell," Holly tells the narrator about her visits. "The way
the women wear their prettiest everything, I mean the old ones and the really
poor ones too, they make the dearest effort to look nice and smell nice too,
and I love them for it" (23). Holly values this performance largely because
she shares a similar investment in image—both at the prison and in various
New York nightclubs. Like the poor women in the visiting room, Holly has
used similar trappings (for example, clothing and perfume) to project happiness and to please men. At the same time, these performances take a personal
toll: "It's different afterwards . . . I see them on the train. They sit so quiet
watching the river go by" (24). Capote implies that Holly's constant movement provides a way to escape the sadness and angst that come after "visiting
hours," so to speak. Her anxiety attacks ("the mean reds") are a reminder of
the limitations of any facade.

She may use face powder, mascara, and lipstick to steel herself for the bad
news of José's farewell letter ("thus armored, and after a displeased appraisal
of her manicure's shabby condition, she ripped open the letter and let her
eyes race through it while her stony small smile grew smaller and harder"
[99]), but these efforts offer only temporary solace. The loss of her pregnancy
and her brother cannot be painted over so easily. In some respects, leaving
the country is the only way to prevent others from seeing her pain. Thus
Capote portrays wives, mothers, and single girls such as Holly as continually
performing roles for men that limit personal freedom and individual identity.

To some extent the notion of emotional authenticity emerges in the novel
as a solution for both the culture of artifice and the mode of repression.
At one point Holly wonders about the morality of her sexual history with
eleven men: "Does that make me a whore? . . . Of course I haven't anything
against whores. Except this: some of them may have an honest tongue but
they all have dishonest hearts. I mean, you can't bang the guy and cash his
checks and at least not try to believe you love him. I never have" (82). While
Holly accepts money from men as an escort, she views sex and love as in-
extricable, which shapes her philosophy about emotional authenticity. Holly
can accept superficiality as long as she remains emotionally authentic, and
this philosophy directly challenges 1950s social norms that privileged social
propriety over openness. At the same time, Holly's frank talk about sex and
her ability to take pleasure in it repudiate sexual repression. "Love should
be allowed," she proclaims after endorsing gay marriage. Whether it involves
homosexuality or a woman's ability to pursue a man, Holly accepts sexuality
as a natural part of human identity, and in this way Capote has her voice the

central concern of the novel: the need within American culture to cultivate an attitude of inclusiveness and acceptance.

Conclusion: A Tale of Two Hollys

Capote did not like the 1961 adaptation of *Breakfast at Tiffany's*. As he remarked in an interview, "The book was really rather bitter, and Holly Golightly was *real*—a tough character, not an Audrey Hepburn type at all. The film became a mawkish valentine to New York City and Holly and, as a result, was thin and pretty, whereas it should have been rich and ugly" (Norden 160). By transforming Holly from a morally complex character to a good girl who just needs to be rescued by heterosexual love, the film abandons the moral and social complexity of the novel for something far more conventional. Even the studio's decision not to hire Marilyn Monroe to play Holly reflected, in part, their discomfort with the messages of Capote's novel. Certainly her reputation for struggling to memorize lines and delaying film schedules did not help. Monroe's sexualized public image would also make it impossible to recast Holly as the "good girl." Ironically these changes point to some of the rich ugliness Capote wanted to challenge.

By the time Capote sold the film rights to Paramount Pictures for sixty-five thousand dollars, he had enough experience with the industry to know the risks. His work on the film adaptation of *Beat the Devil* (directed by John Huston and starring Humphrey Bogart) showed him how little preserving the original text mattered. Huston, who had already rejected two versions of the script, hired Capote a few days before shooting. Capote had little choice but to improvise the dialogue, staying up every night to produce new pages for the actors. The end result of this wild experience reflects Capote's imagination and Huston's vision far more than those of the original novel by James Helvick. In short, Capote knew that anything could happen to his own novel. He also must have harbored some concerns about censorship when *Harper's Bazaar* rescinded on its agreement to publish the novel. They expressed concern about its sexually explicit content and Holly's immorality, but Capote refused to change a word. The magazine's response to the text did not bode well for the film adaptation either, which would need to modify aspects of the story for the Production Code Administration. In the end the 1961 film— despite setting the story in 1960 as opposed to 1943—neutralized the book's sociopolitical stance on sexuality in American culture. It became a conventional romantic comedy or, as one studio memo characterized it, a film about a woman who "is eventually able to love and accept the love of one man" (quoted in Krämer 62).

Many studio executives objected to the original treatment of *Breakfast at Tiffany's* because of the narrator's sexuality. According to a memo by the producer Richard Shepherd, "The young man he has written is petty and unattractive, borders on the effeminate, which we all detest" (quoted in Wasson 81–82). This sentiment reflects the kind of homophobia Capote had been challenging in his fiction since *Other Voices, Other Rooms,* and it highlights Hollywood's contribution to social attitudes about homosexuality as something shameful. The studio's subsequent decision to hire George Axelrod, who had written the film adaptation for his own play *The Seven Year Itch* a few years earlier, insured the suppression of the book's homosexual content. Axelrod would give the studio executives what they were looking for: a *heterosexual* romantic comedy. By recasting the narrator as heterosexual, Axelrod removed the most radical statements from the book—namely Holly's perspective on homosexual desire as natural and her support of gay marriage.

Capote's depiction of female sexuality posed a problem for the adaptation as well. In addition to removing Holly's illegitimate pregnancy and miscarriage, the executives and producers involved with the film recognized that her role as an escort for wealthy men—men who could afford her fifty-dollar trips to the powder room and another fifty dollars for cab fare—needed to be tempered. Axelrod found two ways to accomplish this. First, he made the narrator a "kept man." The money his wealthy lover spends on his apartment, clothing, and sexual encounters, placing crisp bills on the table before she leaves, positions *him* as the prostitute, not Holly. Axelrod thus created a dynamic in which both of the main characters need to redeem each other from their immoral lifestyles. Second, Axelrod's Holly not only is portrayed as rejecting her escorts sexually but also reminds the audience that her actions stem from a desperate need to care for her brother: "I need money, and I'll do whatever I have to do to get it." Her financial hardships and the burden of family, not greed or a longing for sexual freedom, have put her on the prowl for a wealthy husband. The narrator's closing speech to Holly, which was revised heavily by the director, Blake Edwards, presents Holly's dilemma as being afraid to love. When she decides to find her cat (which she does), place a ring on her fourth finger, and kiss Paul, she becomes the good girl who is motivated by heterosexual love, romance, and the desire for marriage, not money.

Aubrey Hepburn as a cultural figure also undercut Capote's more radical depictions of sexuality. As Krämer has argued, "Audrey Hepburn's celebrated style, respectability, and even nobility finally neutralized Holly's sexual transgressiveness; on or off screen Hepburn was hardly perceived as a sexual being at all" (63). She was, in effect, the anti–Marilyn Monroe. Nevertheless the studio did not want to take any chances. The film removed any reference to her illegitimate pregnancy, miscarriage, flight to Brazil, and disappearance in Africa. The censors made sure that the film only hinted at the sexual relationship between Holly and Paul—cutting a scene with the couple in bed, for instance. Furthermore Paramount launched a publicity campaign that emphasized Hepburn's marriage. One interview even noted that the actress was often found knitting a sweater for her husband on the set. To neutralize some of the more disconcerting aspects of the film (such as her abandonment of Doc and his children), the studio went to great lengths to present Hepburn's Holly as a "kook"—a lovable eccentric who is ultimately content with social norms (Wasson 178). Such efforts seemed to have worked. Something about Hepburn's Holly—with her elegant black evening gown, kooky behavior, and vulnerability—has persisted in the cultural imagination. Just as the *Seinfeld* episode suggests, the film continues to overshadow the book. It offers an affirming narrative of heterosexual love with a heroine who is ultimately endearing in her conventionality. Hepburn's Holly was—and arguably continues to be—appealing because she does not threaten gender hierarchies and sexual repression. She presents the conventional as fun-loving and glamorous. Although Capote was disappointed with such changes, the adaptation exposes some of the very anxieties about female sexuality and homosexuality that he set out to critique in the novel.

CHAPTER 7

In Cold Blood

On November 15, 1959, Dick Hickock and Perry Smith drove approximately four hundred miles to the small town of Holcomb, Kansas, and brutally murdered four members of the Clutter family. Armed with a hunting knife and a twelve-gauge shotgun, the two men entered the house through an unlocked door just after midnight. They were expecting to find a safe filled with thousands of dollars, but when Herb Clutter denied having one, they tied him up and gagged him. They did the same to his wife, Bonnie, his fifteen-year-old son, Kenyon, and his sixteen-year-old daughter, Nancy. Afterward they placed each of them in separate rooms and searched the house. When they found no more than forty dollars, Perry Smith slit Mr. Clutter's throat and shot him in the face. He then proceeded to execute the rest of the family. Each one died from a point-blank shotgun wound to the head.

The following day Truman Capote read an article in the *New York Times* about the crime. Both the horrifying details of the murders and the strangeness of the place appealed to him. Everything about Kansas—the landscape, dialect, social milieu, and customs—seemed foreign to Capote, and he was energized by the prospect of trying to capture this world in prose. He recognized that the case might never be solved, but that did not concern him at the time. He primarily wanted to write about the impact of these horrific killings on the town. As Clarke explains, Capote was less interested in the murders than in their potential "effect on that small and isolated community" (319). Six years later he completed his "nonfiction novel" *In Cold Blood: A True Account of a Multiple Murder and Its Consequences*.

The critical and popular success of *In Cold Blood* is a testament to both the artistry of the book and Capote's celebrity. For years he had been giving public readings and interviews promoting the book, and he did everything in his power to generate public interest. Capote's gifts for self-promotion shaped the critical response to *In Cold Blood*. Two assertions in particular continue to be the focal points of much debate. The first revolves around Capote's claim that he created a new literary form—the "nonfiction novel." As he once explained, "Journalism always moves along on a horizontal plane, telling a story, while fiction—good fiction—moves vertically, taking you deeper and deeper into character and events. By treating a real event with fictional techniques (something that cannot be done by a journalist until he *learns* to write good fiction), it's possible to make this kind of synthesis" (quoted in Clarke 357). Not surprisingly, the term "nonfiction novel" has been hotly debated since the book's publication.[1] Many scholars have demonstrated that Capote was participating in a long tradition of historical fiction and literary nonfiction, including works such as Theodore Dreiser's *An American Tragedy* (1925). Others consider *In Cold Blood* one of the first significant works of New Journalism, which included 1960s writers such as Tom Wolfe, Norman Mailer, and Hunter S. Thompson, but this label has also been contested.[2]

Second, scholars have scrutinized Capote's insistence on the factual accuracy of the book. Phillip K. Tompkins first challenged Capote's claims in his article "In Cold Fact," which appeared in the June 1966 issue of *Esquire*. Tompkins conducted interviews with many of Capote's sources, and he uncovered a wide range of discrepancies—including the claim that Perry Smith supposedly apologized moments before the execution. More than a decade later, Jack De Bellis compared the *New Yorker* publication of *In Cold Blood* with its release as a book ten weeks later, and he discovered that Capote "made nearly five-thousand changes, ranging from crucial matters of fact to the placement of a comma" (520). Most famously Capote (as he himself acknowledged) fictionalized the ending, adding the scene where Dewey encountered one of Nancy's former friends at the Garden City cemetery. Such concerns about accuracy resurfaced again during the 2012 auction of the original Kansas Bureau of Investigation case file and other notes from the Clutter crime. Numerous other critical frameworks, such as queer theory and Foucault's notion of panopticism,[3] have been applied to *In Cold Blood* as well, and the book has recently been read in the context of the gothic and horror traditions.[4]

Not long after Capote first arrived in Holcomb, he realized that this project would be much larger than the magazine article he originally envisioned. Between 1959 and 1965 it grew into a meditation on the impact of violence on a small community, an investigation into the psychology of two killers, a portrait of contemporary law enforcement, an indictment of capital punishment, and an examination of the pervasive fears defining 1950s America. This latter aspect has largely been ignored by critics, in part due to the extensive debates about the book's literary form and accuracy. The fact remains, however, that the crimes, pursuit, and arrest of these men occurred in 1959, and Capote conducted the majority of interviews about the impact of the murders in that year as well. Most of this material thus reflects attitudes shaped by the 1950s, not the 1960s. Furthermore viewing *In Cold Blood* as a work of and about the 1950s reveals Capote's concerns over the climate of violence and fear at the time. The author suggested as much in an interview shortly after the book's publication: "About 70 percent of the letters [I have received] think of the book as a reflection on American life—this collision between the desperate, ruthless, wandering, savage part of American life, and the other, which is insular and safe, more or less. It has struck them because there is something so awfully inevitable about what is going to happen. . . . Every illusion [Perry Smith would] ever have, well, they all evaporated, so that on that night he was so full of self-hatred and self-pity that I think he would have killed *some*body—perhaps not that night, or the next, or the next. You can't go through life without ever getting anything you want, ever" (Plimpton 67). Capote's response highlights several important aspects of *In Cold Blood*. First, these letters expressed profound fears about the tension between the prosperous and the disenfranchised in America. The "ruthless, wandering, savage part" presented a real threat to the country's prosperity myth. Poverty turned many people into wanderers and thieves who often resorted to violence, and Dick Hickock and Perry Smith provided an extreme case study on the impact of such deprivation. Additionally the sense of impending doom expressed in these letters reflected widely shared anxieties about the atomic age. At a time when the specter of nuclear war loomed large, Capote's depiction of the Clutter murders evoked these broader concerns about national safety and stability.

Numerous references squarely situate this text in 1950s Cold War culture. For example, Capote repeatedly notes that Eisenhower appointed Herb Clutter to the Farm Credit Board; the jailhouse snitch, Floyd Wells, learned of the Clutter murders while listening to a news broadcast about the U.S. space program; Alvin Dewey held a former position as an FBI agent working in cities throughout the country; Perry was a veteran of both World War II and the Korean War; and Dick even shook hands with President Truman in a hotel lobby. These details help anchor the text in the broader anxieties characterizing the era. Not long after HUAC began blacklisting and jailing writers, actors, and producers who refused to name individuals with current or former ties to Communist organizations, the hysteria of McCarthyism had firmly taken hold of the country. Anxiety, distrust, and paranoia cast a shadow over daily life, and the impact of these fears can be seen throughout *In Cold Blood*. For instance, Mrs. Myrtle Clare, the town postmistress, repeatedly expressed suspicion about her neighbors: "If it wasn't him [who killed the Clutters], maybe it was you. Or somebody across the street. All the neighbors are rattlesnakes. Varmints looking for a chance to slam the door in your face. It's the same the whole world over" (69). For Mrs. Clare, anyone could be a threat; anyone had the potential for violence. Capote uses her sentiments to capture the way such paranoia defined Cold War America.

These fears also stemmed from concerns about annihilation. The Soviet Union posed a significant military threat after its successful test of an atomic bomb in 1949. Families began building bomb shelters, and a majority of Americans feared that a nuclear war was imminent. A 1956 poll showed that nearly two-thirds of the public "believed that in the event of another war, the hydrogen bomb would be used against the United States" (May 25). Such statistics come as no surprise given the publicity surrounding atomic research at the time. The United States launched a series of thermonuclear tests called "Operation Castle" between March and May 1954, and these detonations announced the hydrogen bomb as part of America's military arsenal. These tests, many of which were televised, received considerable news coverage. The first nationally broadcast atomic explosion occurred on April 22, 1952, and about a year later the Atomic Energy Commission and the Federal Civil Defense Administration (FCDA) conducted another televised broadcast from Yucca Flat, Nevada, with Walter Cronkite and other news media in attendance at Ground Zero (two miles from the blast).[5] The terrifying realities of the atomic age inspired several groups and organizations, such as the FCDA, to offer advice on surviving a nuclear attack. These security preparations, which ranged from first-aid training, feeding drills, teaching schoolchildren to cover their eyes during a blast, and the construction of bomb shelters, only exacerbated popular fears. As May explains, "[These measures] intensified the nation's consciousness of the imminence of nuclear war, raising the specter of sudden carnage" (102). Not surprisingly by 1959 two out of three Americans considered nuclear war "the nation's most urgent problem" (26).

In some ways the Clutter murders served as a microcosm for these anxieties. It was a cataclysmic event for the town of Holcomb, and the unexpected brutality of it created shockwaves of damage. Local citizens began leaving on their lights throughout the night and locking their doors. Several residents moved away. In addition many who remained were irrevocably changed. One woman could no longer perceive the natural beauty of the landscape and instead compared the nighttime prairie wind to a bombing: "It's noisier than a bomb raid" (115). An anonymous caller theorized to Alvin Dewey that Herb Clutter killed his family and then himself "with a bomb. A hand grenade stuffed with buckshot" (101). A close friend of the Clutters, while sitting in front of a bonfire, thought about their deaths in terms of atomic annihilation: "How was it possible that such effort, such plain virtue, could overnight be reduced to this—smoke, thinning as it rose and was received by the big, annihilating sky?" (79). These images of explosive devastation make sense amid the ongoing arms race between the United States and the Soviet Union. As the critic Ilse Schrynemakers argues, the book "deals [not] with the failure of containment, but with the tensions specific to the atomic world. In its focus on the widespread psychological toll of one incident of apocalyptic-level violence, *In Cold Blood* grapples with a central preoccupation of the atomic age" (51).

The motif of invasion and annihilation emerges most extensively in Capote's portrait of the dangers posed by poverty and juvenile delinquency. Many sociologists in the 1950s viewed poverty as a breeding ground for violence among young men, and a debate about the causes and implications of juvenile delinquency raged throughout the decade. Dick and Perry, who had been delinquents themselves, became the logical extension of such behavior—adult criminals—and their crimes reflected broader social problems involving economic inequity and class. Poverty and adolescent delinquency, in other words, exposed the American Dream as a cruel myth. It gave lie to the material wealth and familial stability promised by the suburbs and small-town America. Ultimately, when understood in the context of the 1950s, the importance of *In Cold Blood* consists in its exposure of the myths of American prosperity and suburban harmony and the realization that such myths—because prosperity and harmony were unrealizable for so many—actually contributed to eruptions of violent, murderous rage.

Down and Out: Poverty, Delinquency, and Violence in *In Cold Blood*

In the 1950s television assumed a prominent place in American living rooms. TV dinners first appeared in 1954, and by 1956 most Americans spent more time in front of television than at work. Historians estimate that 81 percent of households owned televisions by the mid-1950s, and over fifty million televisions had been purchased in the United States by 1960. In addition to the ways that television sitcoms idealized white, middle-class suburbia, most programming—including the news—avoided the topic of poverty. This omission can partially be attributed to the widespread impression of America as the land of plenty. Nothing symbolized the country's affluence more than the rise of personal income, the acquisition of consumer goods, and the growth of home ownership. In fact personal income jumped an astonishing 293 percent between 1940 and 1955, and the United States was consuming "one-third of the world's goods and services by the middle of the 1950s" (Jones 22). Furthermore suburban populations doubled between 1950 and 1970—eighteen million moved to the suburbs in the decade of the 1950s alone—and "83 percent of the nation's growth during those years took place in the suburbs" (May 162). Such prosperity fueled arguments that America still provided its citizens with the opportunity to share in greater wealth and social mobility. While the influence of communism continued to spread worldwide, these images of prosperity were viewed by many as evidence of the superiority of America's free-market capitalism.

Yet poverty affected the lives of approximately forty to fifty million Americans in the 1950s. It had become such a significant problem that John F. Kennedy's first official act as president was to double food allocations to destitute families. As the historian Alice O'Connor notes, the 1950s actually "brought slower growth and two major recessions, leading working-class families to rely more heavily than ever on women's wages and welfare benefits to stay out of poverty" (101). She concludes that 25–30 percent of the population remained in poverty at any given point throughout the decade. Even though one could not find much evidence of these problems on television or in the average suburban neighborhood, the real dangers of economic inequity were receiving considerable attention in social science and before government committees—particularly in regard to male violence. Michael Harrington's study *The Other America: Poverty in the United States* (1962), for example, examines the factors contributing to the invisibility of the poor. He argues that poverty was hidden through segregation in slums and schools, through the mass production of affordable clothing that masked one's socioeconomic status, and through the absence of political influence and lobbying power. The text also explores the psychological and social impact of pervasive poverty. Scientific research at the end of the 1950s suggested that mental illness was higher among the poor, and Harrington concludes that such conditions were having serious ramifications: "the other America [the poor] feels differently than the rest of the nation. They tend to be hopeless and passive, yet prone to bursts of violence; they are lonely and isolated, often rigid and hostile. To be poor is not simply to be deprived of the material things of the world. It is to enter a fatal, futile universe, an America within America with a twisted spirit" (129). This language of two Americas resonates with Capote's depiction of the "savage" and "safe" elements colliding on the night of November 15, 1959. The Clutter murders offered a troubling example of the violence that could erupt from such prolonged deprivation.

In the context of the poverty problem in the 1950s and 1960s, Capote's choice to highlight Dick and Perry's economic hardships as one of the forces shaping their criminality raised troubling questions about this growing national problem. As the critic David Galloway has observed, the Hickock family "lived remorselessly near the subsistence level, a level below which they might fall at any moment (and did once when Mr. Hickock became ill and unable to work). Life for the Smiths was more erratic and more sordid: poverty, alcoholism, prostitution, and violence formed the background in which Perry Smith grew up" (160). Dick may have been somewhat better off than Perry, but poverty—and living near a subsistence level—shaped the lives of both men. In fact economic need influenced most of their choices, such as robbing homes and office buildings, stealing cars, breaking into the Clutter home, and recycling Coca-Cola bottles for cash. The promise of "good-paying jobs" remained elusive for these men. After a failed business venture with his father (setting up a lodge in Alaska), for instance, Perry simply moved from one low-paying job to another: "he washed dishes in an Omaha restaurant, pumped gas at a [sic] Oklahoma garage, worked a month on a ranch in Texas" (136). Eventually he recognized the dehumanizing impact of poverty on himself. From his temporary jail cell in the Finney County Courthouse, he watched the tomcats scavenge for food (that is, dead birds) on the grilles of parked cars and trucks. This daily ritual pained him when he realized that "most of my life, I've done what they're doing. The equivalent" (264).

Poverty inspired different emotions in each of the men, but these feelings were ultimately expressed through violence. For Dick, being poor fueled a savage envy and hatred of those with money: "Envy was constantly with him; the Enemy was anyone who was someone he wanted to be or had anything he wanted to have" (200). After noticing one wealthy man with a beautiful blonde "who resembled Marilyn Monroe," for example, he became enraged. The man appeared to be twenty-eight years old, Dick's age at the time, and he communicated an air of knowing about "money and power." Dick could not understand the disparity between wealth and poverty in America: "Why should that sonofabitch have everything, while I have nothing?" (201). Dick's rage was mitigated only by fantasies of violence, of lashing out at such "big-shot bastards": "With a knife in his hand, he, Dick, had power. Big-shot bastards like that had better be careful or he might 'open them up and let a little of their luck spill on the floor'" (201). At this moment Dick decided to leave, but the encounter helps explain his insistence that they "leave no witnesses" on the night of the Clutter robbery. From the outset Dick viewed the Clutters as embodiments of economic inequality and the unjust distribution of wealth in the United States.

For Perry, poverty evoked similar feelings of shame and rage at the most critical moment of the text—Mr. Clutter's murder. On the night of the crime, which Perry participated in because he "wanted the money as much as [Dick] did" (234), Perry was searching Nancy's room when he found a purse with a silver dollar. After the coin fell to the floor and rolled under a chair, Perry got on his knees to grab it: "I was just disgusted. Dick, and all his talk about a rich man's safe, and here I am crawling on my belly to steal a child's silver dollar. One dollar. And I'm crawling on my belly to get it" (240). This humiliation—lowering himself like a snake for a mere coin—quickly turned to murderous rage. Tellingly he recalled this moment just before cutting Mr. Clutter's throat: "I thought of that goddam dollar. Silver dollar. The shame. Disgust. . . . But I didn't realize what I'd done till I heard the sound. Like somebody drowning. Screaming under water" (244). Perry's comments about listening to Herb Clutter's gruesome death can also be understood metaphorically. For most of his life Perry had been drowning and screaming underwater, in large part as a result of his experiences with poverty. His violence stemmed not merely from being poor but from the tremendous gap between his unmitigated poverty and the myth of American prosperity. Films such as *Treasure of the Sierra Madre,* which he had watched eight times, and the prospecting adventures of his father in Alaska ("teaching his son to dream of gold, to hunt for it in the sandy beds of snow-white water streams" [133]) encouraged his unrealistic fantasies about wealth. Perry believed that anyone could strike it rich, and this belief fueled an obsession with buried treasure.

On one level, Capote uses Perry's preoccupation with maps and his perpetual movement (in the family truck as a child and various stolen cars with Dick) as images for this quest. Capote first introduces Perry to the reader when he was "[studying] a map spread on the counter before him—a Phillips 66 map of Mexico" (14), and this image casts Perry as a man continually searching for both treasure (whether buried gold or ten thousand dollars in a safe) and a place to be. His meandering journey, however, led nowhere. He found no gold in Alaska with his father or in Mexico with Dick, who blurted out at one point in frustration, "Wake up, little boy. There ain't no caskets of gold. No sunken ship" (124). Ultimately the two killers ended up back in Kansas—imprisoned and immobile. As one critic notes, the Clutter murders can be viewed as Perry's assault on the American Dream: "In striking down the Clutters, Perry is striking at the embodiment of the American Dream—not, however, because he disapproves of it, but because he cannot get in on it" (McAleer 211).Only at the Clutters' did Perry finally seem to realize that he would always be denied access to such wealth. In this way he also viewed the Clutters as a symbol: "And it wasn't because of anything the Clutters did. They never hurt me. Like other people. Like people have all my life. Maybe it's just that the Clutters were the ones who had to pay for it" (290). Whether or not they represented all of the people who had wronged Perry, the economic language in this passage—of payment due—suggests that the Clutters embodied the virtually insurmountable distance between poverty and prosperity as promised by the American Dream. Perry's rage therefore can be understood as stemming from his disillusionment over being deceived by America.

Though poverty remained invisible to most Americans in the 1950s, it played a role in public debates over juvenile delinquency and gang culture. Delinquent subculture became a heated topic in prominent journals, newspapers, publications by social scientists, religious sermons, films, radio programs, newsreels, comic books, and political hearings. By the time the Kefauver Committee on Juvenile Delinquency (named after Senator Estes Kefauver when he became chair in 1955) started conducting televised hearings into the matter, public panic over juvenile crime had reached a fevered pitch. One poll in 1959 even reported that "delinquency was viewed more seriously than open-air testing of atomic weapons or school segregation or political corruption" (Gilbert 63). This fear stemmed partially from the perception that youth crime in the 1950s was becoming increasingly violent—that it shared the type of disillusionment fueling Perry's homicidal rage. As James Gilbert argues in *A Cycle of Outrage: America's Reaction to the Juvenile Delinquent of the 1950s*, "By 1956 . . . well over one million kids 'came to the attention of the police annually.' . . . Many ever-younger criminals committed crimes against property. Car theft was the top juvenile crime. But startlingly often, the young also committed acts of inexplicable and pointless violence—rape, beatings, murders" (280). Even though mounting fears about adolescent crime were exacerbated by misleading statistics from the FBI (based on annual arrests) and the Children's Bureau (based on records of juvenile court cases), few people questioned these data. Instead the public wanted answers.

Popular concerns centered around two types of delinquents: the socioeconomic (or anomic) delinquent and the psychological delinquent. The sociologists Richard Cloward and Lloyd Ohlin labeled the first type anomic, borrowing and adapting the term "anomie" (meaning lawlessness or normlessness) from the nineteenth-century sociologist Emile Durkheim. As Cloward and Ohlin explain, "It is our view that pressures toward the formation of delinquent subcultures originate in marked discrepancies between culturally induced aspirations among lower-class youth and the possibilities of achieving them by legitimate means" (78). The gap between personal expectation and limited socioeconomic opportunities, in other words, often inspired this group to embrace a delinquent subculture. In *Delinquent Boys: The Culture of the Gang* (1955), Albert K. Cohen placed a similar emphasis on economic conditions. He attributed elements of delinquent subculture to the way conspicuous consumption functioned to establish social status in America: "Among those segments which have the least access to the legitimate channels of 'upward mobility' there develop strong feelings of deprivation and frustration of status and its symbols. Unable to attain their goals by lawful means, these disadvantaged segments of the population are under strong pressure to resort to crime, the only means available to them" (35). Delinquent subculture not only repudiated middle-class values, but it also legitimized aggression and violence as tools for expressing resentment against class hierarchies and a middle-class value system that marginalized the working class. Other researchers used psychoanalytic theory to understand the second type of delinquent. These individuals apparently suffered from stunted psychological growth as a result of an absent/ineffectual father and an overbearing mother. Talcott Parsons pioneered this approach in the late 1940s, and in "Psychoanalysis and the Social Structure" (1950), for example, he argued that the modern family's investment in the psychological socialization of children created problems for boys whose "intense relation to the mother and remoteness of the [breadwinning] father" instilled a need to assert "compulsive masculinity" into adolescence and beyond (344–45). This assertion of compulsive masculinity often took the form of aggressive behavior. Though Parsons's theories did not resonate much beyond the 1950s, "an important component of Parsons's theory did: the notion that weak and especially absent fathers produce problem sons" (Schryer 137). This belief comforted many Americans by situating the problem at home as opposed to blaming broader social issues such as poverty.

Throughout *In Cold Blood*, Capote includes several anecdotes about juvenile delinquency to situate this text within this broader narrative about transgressive youth culture. Perry came from a broken family that moved continually because of his parents' traveling show, and after his mother's death, he was shuffled from one abusive orphanage/foster home to another. It comes as little surprise that he was first arrested as a child—on his eighth birthday, in fact—for theft. He subsequently experienced "several confinements in institutions and children's detention centers" in his youth (184). Later in his life, Perry reflected on these early moments of delinquency with satisfaction: "Once, when he was a running-wild child in San Francisco, he and a 'Chink kid' (Tommy Chan? Tommy Lee?) had worked together as a 'purse-snatching team.' It amused Perry—cheered him up, to remember some of their escapades" (192). One robbery of an old woman, who fought like a "tiger" to hold onto her bag, involved knocking her down on the pavement. In many respects Perry was seduced by the delinquency culture around him. Not only had he and a Chinese boy worked together to orchestrate this purse-snatching scheme, but in 1955 (at the age of twenty-seven), Perry also burglarized an office building largely because a hitchhiker suggested the idea to him. He would be equally susceptible to Dick's invitation to help him with "the Perfect Score" in 1959 at the Clutter house (44). Ultimately, as the killers' biographies reveal, Perry and Dick became America's worst fears realized: juvenile delinquents turned career criminals. One of Perry's friends, a former inmate, even believed that "all crimes were only 'varieties of theft.' Murder included. When you kill a man you steal his life" (290). His attitude makes sense in the context of delinquency culture. Petty theft among young men was perceived as a mere stepping stone to more severe forms of criminality.

At the same time, Capote uses delinquency to comment on the violent milieu of American culture as well as on contemporary fears about annihilation. Capote mentions several murder cases at one point, including an African American soldier's dismembering of a prostitute, the bludgeoning of a young boy by an army corporal, the drowning of a nine-year-old girl by a hospital employee, and the strangulation of a fourteen-year-old by a laborer/pedophile (299). These passing, almost casual references (the list above appears parenthetically) highlight the commonality of violence in the 1950s. Violent crime was such a ubiquitous part of the landscape that it did not leave a lasting impression. Capote includes an excerpt from the *Garden City Telegram* to make this point explicitly: "Since the four members of the Clutter family were killed last fall, several other such multiple murders have occurred in various parts of the country. Just during the few days leading up to this trial, at least three mass murder cases broke into the headlines. As a result, this crime and trial are just one of many such cases people have read about and forgotten" (271–72). Capote then juxtaposes these "forgotten" crimes with several mass murders committed by teenagers. One inmate on death row, Lowell Lee Andrews, murdered his family when he was eighteen years old. In another example, George Ronald York and James Douglas Latham, who were eighteen and nineteen years old respectively, killed seven people in a "cross-country murder spree" (322). Both men shared a similar philosophy: "the world was hateful, and everybody in it would be better off dead. . . . There's no answer to it but meanness. That's all anybody understands—meanness" (323).

In the context of *In Cold Blood*, these juvenile crimes appear to be a logical (albeit extreme) outgrowth of the violence in American culture and a growing dissatisfaction with the status quo. These men, along with Dick Hickock and Perry Smith, were products of a social environment suffused with brutality and cruelty. The unexpected nature of these crimes also tapped into Cold War fears about annihilation—particularly the anxiety that devastation could come at any moment. York and Latham, for instance, killed two Georgia housewives who happened to ask them for directions at a gas station. The young men then led the women to a swamp and strangled them. Within the next ten days, some of their other victims included two men in a St. Louis suburb, a traveling salesman, a railroad worker, and a grandfather. For the latter, York and Latham had parked by the roadside with the hood of their car propped up, pretending to need assistance. The grandfather stopped to help, and as soon as he spoke, "York, at a distance of twenty feet, sent a bullet crashing through the old man's skull" (324). Like the other Cold War fears in the text, this capacity for savage meanness came from unexpected places—an ex-con who heard rumors about a wealthy farmer, a family member such as Andrews, or handsome soldiers (York and Latham) offering directions or appearing stranded by the roadside. All together these crimes implied that anyone could suffer a similar fate.

Seeking Safety: Small-Town America and Suburbia in *In Cold Blood*

Although aspects of the heartland seemed strange to Capote, he was actually quite familiar with communities like Holcomb. Capote spent his most significant childhood years in a rural Alabama town, and as a teenager he lived in a Greenwich, Connecticut, suburb. This community, like so many suburbs, had elements inspired by a nostalgia for rural, small-town life: "A private policeman patrolled its pretty, winding streets, and its ninety or so houses were, like the Capotes', all built in traditional Tudor styles. To give it a rural appearance, the people who laid it out in the twenties had left reminders of the country: hills, trees, streams, and two large lakes. . . . Small as it was, the community had its own country club, to which only residents could belong" (Clarke 50–51). The streams, trees, and lakes of this upper-middle-class suburb provided "reminders of the country" in an attempt to mimic the landscape one might find there. The country club and other resortlike amenities, however, reassured prospective buyers that the rural atmosphere was not accompanied by any of the real hardships associated with living off the land. Furthermore the community's private security promised safety, and the sameness of the homes, though a practical aspect of construction, offered a comforting image of conformity and belonging. Ultimately Capote's experiences in the rural South and suburbia helped him understand their shared values and fears, and he would make these elements central to the terrors evoked by *In Cold Blood*. Just as small towns were supposedly free of the dangers of city life such as poverty, delinquency, and ethnic diversity, suburbanites sought the same protections. Capote's message is clear, however: neither space provided safety from the threat of invasion and annihilation. *In Cold Blood* even suggests that the suburban ideal, which became an integral part of the American Dream in the 1950s, contributed to the disillusionment fueling violent crime.

Suburbia, which expanded tremendously during the 1950s, became one of the defining features of that decade. Government policies spurred its unprecedented growth after World War II: "In 1945, 98 percent of American cities reported shortages of houses, and more than 90 percent reported shortages of apartments. By 1947, 6 million families were doubling up with relatives or friends" (May 160). An estimated 5 million residences were needed to fill the initial postwar demand, and the federal government responded with a law providing federally backed mortgage insurance for white veterans. Specifically, the Servicemen's Readjustment Act of 1944 established the Veterans Administration mortgage program, and "this law gave official endorsement and support to the view that the 16 million GIs of World War II should return to civilian life with a home of their own" (Jackson 233). In addition to job training, education, and unemployment compensation, over 1 million veterans received low-interest loans for houses, farms, and small businesses. With the government insuring these home loans, providing new tax benefits for home owners, and subsidizing massive suburban developments such as those of William Levitt, private citizens eagerly entered the housing market. All of these incentives actually made it less expensive to buy than to rent. A thirty-year mortgage in Levittown with no down payment, for example, cost fifty-six dollars per month, whereas an apartment rental in the city typically cost ninety-three dollars monthly (May 161). The construction of single-family homes, which totaled only 114,000 in 1944, jumped to 1,692,000 in 1950 (Jackson 233). In New York City alone, an estimated 1.5 million migrated to the suburbs between 1950 and 1960 (Miller and Nowak 134), and "between 1950 and 1970, the suburban population doubled, from 36 million to 74 million" (May 162).

Capote draws numerous parallels between rural towns and suburbia to suggest that similar idealizations characterized both in the 1950s. Many critics have discussed the ways in which the Clutters embodied various mythologies about America. Galloway observes of the victims that "first of all, we know the Clutter family already—immortalized as they have been in Norman

Rockwell illustrations, Coca-Cola advertisements, and as 'the folks next door' in countless Hollywood movies. Herb Clutter was the embodiment of the self-made man" (157). The Clutters, in other words, represented American life as endlessly replayed by Hollywood films, consumer advertising, and other forms of popular art. Clutter's identity as a white, Christian, family man who had achieved economic and social success through hard work and with moral integrity reflected the best aspects of the American Dream. Geography and suburbia could easily be added to Galloway's list here. In Capote's rendering, the Kansas town of Holcomb embodied all small towns: "It seems just another fair-sized town in the middle—almost the exact middle—of the continental United States" (33). The indistinguishable features of towns in middle America were reminiscent of some the uniform features characterizing many suburban communities at the time. Planned communities became so similar after Levittown that "by the 1960s the casual suburban visitor would have a difficult time deciphering whether she was in the environs of Boston or Dallas" (Jackson 240).

To give the Clutter murders a broader national significance, Capote wanted to evoke suburbia in his depiction of Holcomb, and he highlights aspects of the town that many suburbanites would recognize. For instance, Holcomb, which has only two "apartment houses" for low-income workers such as the local teachers, is composed primarily of single-family detached houses "with front porches" (4). A certain sameness characterizes most Holcomb residences as well—even the more affluent ones such as the Clutters'. They share a similar taste in furniture: "As for the interior [of the Clutter house], there were spongy displays of liver-colored carpet intermittently abolishing the glare of varnished, resounding floors; an immense modernistic living-room couch covered in nubby fabric interwoven with glittery strands of silver metal; a breakfast alcove featuring a banquette upholstered in blue-and-white plastic. This sort of furnishing was what Mr. and Mrs. Clutter liked, as did the majority of their acquaintances, whose homes, by and large, were similarly furnished" (9). This uniformity of taste, a defining feature of suburbia, included personal preferences as well, for the residents of the town felt "quite content to exist inside an ordinary life—to work, to hunt, to watch television, to attend school socials, choir practice" (5). These characteristics present small-town America and the suburbs as sharing a common vocabulary. They held many identical values and desires, and both spaces were commonly associated with achieving some version of the American Dream—including success, security, and stability. The connection between Holcomb and suburbia suggests that the Clutters represented the suburban ideal.

Yet the Clutter murders exposed the fragility of this dream, highlighting its inherent artificiality and dangerous politics of exclusion—particularly in regard to class and race. The characters who longed to be part of suburbia found it both entrapping and dispiriting. Dick first married at the age of nineteen and bought into the American suburban ideal as much as he possibly could. In 1949 his job as a mechanic and painter enabled him and his wife to rent a "good-size house," but they spent too much money on consumer goods such as a "fancy car." As Dick's father observed, "They was in debt all the time" (166). His son, like millions of other working-class families, invested in suburbia and other consumer goods as an opportunity to feel as if they were part of a higher social class. As Rosalyn Baxandall and Elizabeth Ewen have argued, places such as Levittown transformed its residents into the middle class: "Whether a household's breadwinner was a mechanic, factory worker, low-level engineer, white-collar employee, salesman, or small businessman scarcely mattered. . . . What mattered was that his home bore the trappings of middle-class life—a new house, new car, new television. It was what one consumed—not what one produced—that was important" (147). The Cold War certainly provided a broader political rational for mass consumption. Purchasing things, as the historian Tom McCarthy notes, became "proof not just of the productive superiority of the American economy but evidence of a growing economic egalitarianism that would make the United States a 'classless society' where people enjoyed a material standard of living far above that of the Soviet Union" (106). This failed to be true for working-class men such as Dick and countless poor people in the United States, however. Dick's expenses eventually became so overwhelming that he turned to crime, and yet his arrest did not dull his appetite for the suburban dream. After getting parole, he moved back with his parents, stayed home at nights, and took a job in "the suburban village of Olathe" (167). His renewed attempt to achieve a middle-class suburban life did not last long. Within a matter of months, he was forging checks again and planning the Clutter robbery. Suburbia did not guarantee happiness and security. Instead it was something people struggled to achieve (if they could get access at all) and to maintain.

For Capote, the homogeneity of small-town America and suburbia served as a troubling reminder for the contemporary realities of racial segregation. Racism certainly shaped the development of suburbia throughout the twentieth century. The post–World War I boom stemmed in part from a reaction among whites against the growing ethnic diversity of the city as a result of the war and the massive migration of African Americans in search of work. Soon suburban developments established restrictive covenants, legal restrictions against "undesirable activities" (such as construction that might damage the aesthetics of a planned community) and "undesirable residents" (namely racial minorities and poor people), to appeal to white home owners.[6] Even though the Supreme Court determined racial covenants to be illegal in 1948 (Shelley v. Kraemer), other types of covenants (such as prohibiting multiple-family occupancy, forbidding the subdivision of homes into apartments, and making it impossible to take on boarders) continued into the 1950s. These policies insured that less well-to-do African Americans could not afford to buy homes. Furthermore banks as well as the Federal Housing Authority typically rejected loan applications from African Americans.[7] In the late 1950s, 55 percent of whites outside of the South claimed that they would leave a neighborhood if a significant population of African Americans moved in.[8] A similar attitude about racial segregation shaped Levittown as well, which refused to sell to African Americans. Even in 1960 "not a single one of the Long Island Levittown's 82,000 residents was black" (Jackson 241). Such practices forced most African Americans to remain in dilapidated, inner-city dwellings, and as the historian Thomas J. Sugrue has persuasively argued, deindustrialization in the 1950s, white flight, and ghettoization trapped most blacks in poverty. Furthermore "increasing joblessness, and the decaying infrastructure of inner-city neighborhoods, reinforced white stereotypes of black people, families, and communities" (Sugrue 8).

Throughout *In Cold Blood,* Capote captures the impact of such stereotypes through Perry's self-loathing and his violent response to being denied a white, middle-class suburban life. Perry's ethnic identity as half Cherokee troubled him throughout his life. Most people viewed Perry as an ethnic other, "a foreigner, a Mexican maybe" (167), and from an early age he was persecuted for his ethnicity. One nurse at the Salvation Army called him "a 'nigger' and say [sic] there wasn't any difference between niggers and Indians" (132). Perry found this association infuriating. While discussing his father, for instance, he flew into a rage: "I was his nigger. . . . That's all. Somebody he could work their guts out and never have to pay them one hot dime" (185). Like Dick, Perry viewed himself as economically disenfranchised, but he also considered his abuse from various people in racial terms. Capote makes compelling use of the association between Native Americans and African Americans here—groups that have shared a long history of marginalization and victimization as a result of U.S. imperialism and broken legal promises. By the end of the text, Perry realized that his ethnicity would continue to define and limit him in white America. He would never be able to achieve wealth or a place of his own, and this realization eventually seeped into his dream fantasies about being a music singer: "The dream's geographical center was a Las Vegas night club where, wearing a white top hat and a white tuxedo, he strutted about a spotlighted stage playing in turn a harmonica, a guitar, a banjo, drums"; after the performance, he looked out at the silent audience filled with thousands of people, mostly African American men: "Staring at them, the perspiring entertainer at last understood their silence, for suddenly he knew that these were phantoms, the ghosts of the legally annihilated, the hanged, the gassed, the electrocuted—and in the same instant he realized that he was there to join them" (319).

Capote juxtaposes Perry's whiteness in this dream, as emphasized by his clothing and the spotlights onstage, with the blackness of the audience. Perry's fantasies about musical stardom were inextricably linked with his desire for whiteness, but at this moment he recognized an important connection between himself and African Americans: both become the "legally annihilated" in white America. The role of ethnicity here provides another way to understand his decision to kill the Clutters: "Maybe it's just that the Clutters were the ones who had to pay for it" (290). In the context of Perry's ethnic identity and the prejudice he experienced, Capote implies that part of this "payment" came from the legacy of racism in America. Perry gained access to the Clutter home, which embodied the white, suburban middle-class ideal and which most nonwhites did not get to see because of segregation, and for the first time he realized the full extent of his marginalization.

"You Can't Catch Me": The Car Culture of *In Cold Blood*

The exodus to suburbia in the 1950s would not have been possible without the automobile industry.[9] Most people needed cars to live in the suburbs, and automobile production along with highway construction expanded the reach of suburban development. Yet car culture at the time, which represented prosperity and freedom for millions of Americans, also enabled the dangers that rolled into Holcolm, Kansas, on the night of November 15, 1959. Americans purchased approximately 7 million cars annually throughout the 1950s, and a record 7.9 million were sold in 1955.[10] As Miller and Nowak explain, "By 1958 over 76.4 million cars and trucks were in use, more than one for every household. (Nearly 12 million families, mostly in the suburbia, had two or more cars.)" (139). Between 1945 and 1960 the annual miles driven in passenger cars jumped an astonishing 194 percent from "200 billion to 587 billion" (Tom McCarthy 152).

The government facilitated this growth in part through the passage of the National Defense Highway Act in 1956, which authorized the construction of 41,000 miles of high-speed roads as part of a cross-country highway system.[11] Congress justified the $25 billion public works project (which amounted to 90 percent of the cost) in the name of national security, arguing that the armed forces would need to move supplies, equipment, and troops quickly from one place to another during a national emergency. As President Eisenhower remarked, "In case of atomic attack on our key cities, the road net must permit quick evacuation of target areas" (quoted in Jackson 249).[12] The automobile lobby—along with the steel, rubber, petroleum, and construction industries—put tremendous pressure on Congress to pass the law. These industries were a crucial part of the U.S. economy at the time. In 1958, "85,000 automobile dealers employed over 700,000 persons; 206,755 service stations gave 465,500 persons jobs and did $14 billion worth of business; highway construction and maintenance costs that year alone came to $5.5 billion" (Miller and Nowak 139). Perhaps it was not surprising that Charles E. Wilson, President Eisenhower's secretary of defense and a strong proponent of the National Defense Highway Act, said, "What was good for our country was good for General Motors, and vice versa" (quoted in Lubin 150). The automobile industry in America benefited indeed. General Motors, Ford, and Chrysler controlled 95 percent of the market in the 1950s (Tom McCarthy 100).

Buying shiny, hulking, overpriced American cars that could hardly fit in typical garages seemed to be a national craze in the first half of the decade.[13] Elvis Presley owned three Cadillacs by 1956 (in canary yellow, pink and black, and white respectively), and advertising for the automobile industry, the biggest television sponsor of the decade, sent a clear message that nothing communicated social status and economic success like owning an American car. As the *Chicago Tribune*'s director of motivational research explained at the time, "The automobile tells us who we are and what we think we want to be. It is a portable symbol of our personality and our position, the clearest way we have of telling people of our exact position" (quoted in Marling 136). The most effective and wide-reaching medium for this message was television. Not only did many of America's favorite television characters, for example Ward Cleaver, drive American cars on family shows, such as *Leave It to Beaver,* but also a great deal of advertising was integrated explicitly into television programming. As Karal Ann Marling explains in *As Seen on TV: The Visual Culture of Everyday Life in the 1950s,* variety shows such as Ed Sullivan's often featured small-scale Motoramas—automobiles displayed on rotating pedestals.

Sales for behemoth cars did dwindle toward the end of the decade, and a significant drop in sales caused a national recession in 1957–58 (Tom McCarthy 131). A desire for smaller cars emerged as a reaction against the excesses and garishness of the large automobiles with tailfins and other ornaments. The "Big Three" responded to the growing popularity of smaller cars—particularly foreign imports—by introducing the "compact" in 1960. At the same time companies such as Ford were particularly successful at convincing American families that they each needed a second car. Advertisements featuring suburban housewives as stranded while their husbands went to work sparked sales of the station wagon, which came to symbolize the baby-boom generation of the suburbs. Tom McCarthy notes that "sales soared from 100,000 to 890,000 or 15 percent of the passenger car market, between 1949 and 1957. Between a third and half of station wagon sales were to families as a second car. By 1959, 15 percent of American families had a second car, a number that grew to 31 percent over the next decade" (150). American life was being defined and shaped by the automobile.

As with the depiction of suburbia, Capote presents American car culture throughout *In Cold Blood* not merely as a reflection of contemporary life but also as another source of danger. Capote owned cars and enjoyed driving. In fact he bought a new Jaguar, which he referred to as a "Fabergé on wheels" (quoted in Clarke 340), for his trip to Kansas in 1963 with Harper Lee. Given that Dick Hickock and Perry Smith drove approximately ten thousand miles in the six-week period between the crime and their arrest, it is not surprising that Capote highlights the various ways automobiles defined American life. He notes, for instance, that Kansas boys such as Kenyon Clutter learned to drive at a young age (38), that some teachers earned extra money by driving school buses (61), and that service stations remained open late into the night (53). Capote also points out that Dick spent many years trying to make a living as a mechanic. He even worked at a car repair shop after his parole (167) and looked for similar employment in Mexico. Small details such as these saturate the text, demonstrating how car culture was a ubiquitous part of the social and professional lives of most Americans. Yet in the world of *In Cold Blood*, automobiles—particularly as images for movement and speed—function as metaphors for personal discontent and social instability. Automobile manufacturers glamorized the notion of speed, associating it with the benefits of modern life. As Marling explains, "Auto bodies styled by Raymond Lowey, Buckminster Fuller, and other well-known streamliners of the period . . . intimated that the American automobile was a machine for zooming along toward a crisp, efficient, and thoroughly modern tomorrow" (138). Yet Capote tends to highlight the negative impact of this modern technology and lifestyle. Whether in his pickup truck or an airplane, Herb Clutter was viewed as always "rushing" from one thing to another (68–69) without appreciating the people around him. Similarly, despite the happiness that his neighbors Mrs. Ashida and her children felt in Holcomb,

Mr. Hideo Ashida moved the family to Nebraska with the belief that he could "do better somewhere else" (116).

Capote links Herb's desire for movement with his wife's depression and Hideo's with a desire for greater economic opportunities. Likewise Perry and Dick used cars as a salve for their dissatisfying lives. They yearned for financial security and social stability, and they hoped at some level to find these things on the road. Their speedy cross-country drive failed to achieve either, however. Perry's aimlessness—joining the military, resorting to crime, and trying a series of low-paying jobs—revealed his desperate quest to find a place of his own. As a young man, he was "somewhat reckless and speed crazy with motorcycles and light cars" (128). Dick drove fast for similar reasons and noted on a number of occasions how quickly the two men were driving. On their way to the Clutters', he observed that the Chevrolet "hurried on across the countryside. . . . The car was going very fast" (53). Both men hoped that driving would get them to a meaningful destination—one characterized by wealth (such as the money in the Clutters' safe or the sunken treasure in Mexico). In a sense, their passion for speed reflected a longing for stasis, for belonging in a society that continually reminded them of their marginal status. Despite the celebration of freedom/movement that the automobile embodied, cars were also about going to work from the suburbs and back, about being parked in the driveway unless you were taking a Sunday drive with the family. Such things were denied to Perry and Dick, and the automobile as an image for social mobility and success only deepened their frustration.

Capote also highlights the dangers of car culture through violent accidents, and these moments capture some of the ramifications of modern, consumer culture as embodied by the automobile. Cars provided many Americans with visible means to communicate a middle-class social status; yet the real dangers of automobile culture received little media attention in the 1950s. The automobile industry spent millions developing bigger cars in the 1950s but spent almost nothing on safety. Seat belts, not required by law, were sold only as "extras" at the time. As Halberstam notes, "Highway deaths mounted—over 40,000 a year by the late fifties. Millions more were injured, some maimed for life" (141). Dick and Perry were among the millions injured, and both men found their bodies irrevocably changed as a result. Perry had been maimed in a 1952 motorcycle wreck that left him hospitalized for six months and disabled for another six: "his chunky, dwarfish legs, broken in five places and pitifully scarred, still pained him" (31). Dick's crash, which hospitalized him and left him unable to work for months (278), reshaped his face. It subsequently appeared "as though his head had been halved like an apple, then put together a fraction off center" (31). Capote notes that the 1950 car collision "left his long-jawed and narrow face tilted, the left side rather lower than the right, with the results that the lips were slightly aslant, the nose askew, and his eyes not only situated at uneven levels but of uneven size, the left eye being truly serpentine, with a venomous, sickly-blue squint that although it was involuntarily acquired, seemed nevertheless to warn of bitter sediment at the bottom of his nature" (31). Capote suggests that the physical damage caused by this accident deformed Dick in a way that revealed his sinister nature. Dick took on the characteristics of Satan, the serpent who tempted another (in this case Perry) into an evil act. Dick's father explicitly blamed the accident for his son's criminality: "I still think the reason he started doing stunts such as that was connected with the smash-up. Concussed his head in a car smash-up. After that, he wasn't the same boy. Gambling, writing bad checks. I never knew him to do them things before" (166). Dick himself described the accident as leaving him with a "sickness. . . . Spells of passing out, and sometimes I would hemhorrage [*sic*] at the nose and left ear" (279). His smashup made him reckless with himself (turning him into a thief and criminal) and with the lives of others. His influence over Perry in effect led to four callous murders, and Dick's fixation on the Clutters smashed up their lives as well. Automobile accidents in the text not only represent the dangerous forces outside of one's control, but, as Capote suggests, they also serve as metaphors for the collisions among people.

Beat Culture and *In Cold Blood*

With the publication of Allen Ginsberg's *Howl* in 1956 and Jack Kerouac's *On the Road* the following year, the Beat writers became prominent public figures and part of the ongoing debate over delinquency, violence, and disillusionment in American culture. Capote had mixed feelings about the artistic merit of the Beats' work. He famously quipped that Kerouac's "spontaneous prose" was "not writing, but typing," and in a 1964 interview, he stated that "none of the 'beat' writing interests me at all. I think it's fraudulent. I think it's all evasive. Where there is no discipline there is nothing. I don't even find that the beat writing has a surface liveliness—but that's neither here nor there because I'm sure that eventually something good will come out of it. Some extraordinary person will be encouraged by it who could never have accepted the rigid disciplines of what I consider good writing" (Inge 44). While Capote dismisses the work of Beat writers such as Kerouac and Ginsberg here, he does recognize the importance of artistic freedom and experimentation. The "extraordinary person" qualification also suggests that the Beat philosophy tended to foster poor art. Through Perry, Capote had seen how a Beat life (one driven by instinct, spontaneity, movement, and a desire to create art) could have destructive consequences. Perry shared many of the struggles of a typical Beat figure, though without the requisite genius to transcend his circumstances. He was pulled into a wild cross-country journey (which included Mexico) by a charismatic man who had abandoned his familial responsibilities to be on the road. Perry and Dick, in other words, embodied the worst possible outcome of Beat life. They never transcended the rootlessness, poverty, and artistic struggles that the Beats tended to glamorize; instead they remained in a state of never-ending transience and criminality, which ultimately left them with feelings of resentment and rage.

For many people, the unconventional lifestyles, nonconformist ethos, and criminality of the Beats seemed to be another symptom of the deepening problem with delinquency in America. As the scholar Stephen Schryer notes, readers and reviewers of Kerouac's work repeatedly made connections between his hipster figures and the growing number of disaffected teenagers in the 1950s (123–24). The writer, philosopher, and sociologist (though he disliked the latter term) Paul Goodman published a 1960 study that examined the similarities and differences among the delinquent, hipster, and Beat figures. In *Growing Up Absurd: Problems of Youth in the Organized System,* he noted the shared elements of criminality, drug use, apparent rejection of middle-class values, and danger among these groups, but he argued that the Beats' quest for spiritual transcendence distinguished them: "The risks of delinquency, criminality, and injury rouse in [the Beats] a normal apprehension, and they express a human amazement at the brutality and cruelty of some with whom they keep company" (180). Goodman quickly admitted, however, that this apprehension did not prevent the Beats from keeping such company and experimenting with self-destructive behavior.

The critic Norman Podhoretz offered a less compassionate interpretation. His scathing essay "The Know-Nothing Bohemians," which first appeared in the 1958 issue of the *Paris Review,* accused Beat philosophy—with its emphasis on instinct, primitivism, mysticism, spontaneity, and hip-hop lingo—as being fundamentally hostile to civilization. "At the one end of the spectrum," he argued, "this ethos shades off into violence and criminality, main-line drug addiction and madness" (484). He concluded by explicitly linking the Beat generation with violent delinquency: "the spirit of hipsterism and the Beat Generation strikes me as the same spirit which animates the young savages in leather jackets who have been running amuck in the last few years with their switch-blades and zip guns. . . . Even the relatively mild ethos of Kerouac's books can spill over easily into brutality, for there is a suppressed cry in those books. Kill the intellectuals who can talk coherently, kill the people who can sit still for five minutes at a time, kill those incomprehensible characters who are capable of getting seriously involved with a woman, a job, a cause" (492–93). Although Podhoretz directed his anger primarily at the group's antiintellectualism, he considered the rootlessness of Beat life, with its blatant rejection of social stability through marriage, work, and serious thought, to be another source of danger. In Capote's hands, Perry and Dick possessed the same spirit of hipsterism, and the brutality they inflicted on the Clutters would have come as no surprise to Podhoretz. They were merely succumbing to the "suppressed cry" to "kill" found in books such as *On the Road*. In this way Capote's *In Cold Blood*—when read alongside *On the Road*—can be understood as an indictment of Beat philosophy for contributing to real social dangers.

The origins of this artistic movement can help explain why Capote evoked the Beats in *In Cold Blood*. On the most basic level, the term "Beat" refers to both a status outside of normal society and a feeling of exhaustion, isolation, and despair—qualities that Perry and Dick shared. The term first gained currency after Jack Kerouac's remark "So I guess you might say we're a *beat* generation" appeared in an article for the *New York Times* magazine (quoted in Watson 3). Kerouac first heard the term from Herbert Huncke, a Times Square hustler, drug dealer, and writer, who "picked up the phrase from carnies, small-time crooks, and jazz musicians in Chicago, who used it to describe the 'beaten' condition of worn-out travelers for whom home was the road." As Brenda Knight goes on to explain, "Huncke used it to explain his 'exalted exhaustion' of life lived beyond the edge" (2). All of the writers associated with this movement—most notably Allen Ginsberg, Jack Kerouac, William S. Burroughs, Gary Snyder, Lawrence Ferlinghetti, Diane di Prima, Janine Pommy Vega, Joyce Johnson, LeRoi Jones/Amiri Baraka, and Bob Kaufman—responded to the condition of being "Beat" through a spontaneous engagement with the world.[14] Only an authentic life of immediacy could provide the foundation for artistic expression. As for the origins of the movement itself, most scholars consider the 1955 poetry reading at Six Gallery in San Francisco to be the start of the Beat cultural revolution. The event, which was covered by the *New York Times,* featured writers from both the East and West Coasts. Six poets (Philip Lamantia, Michael McClure, Philip Whalen, Allen Ginsberg, and Gary Snyder) read that night while the audience passed around wine, got drunk, and occasionally joined Jack Kerouac as he uttered "yeses" and "wows" from the back row. It was here that Allen Ginsberg first read part 1 of *Howl* (the only complete section at the time).[15] Of course the relationships among many of the Beat writers began over a decade earlier, and their experiences in the 1940s significantly shaped their art as well as the public perception of their work.

Ginsberg and Kerouac first met at Columbia University. The artistic community that built up around them actively rejected cultural norms in part by embracing aspects of criminal culture—theft, drug use, homosexuality (which was criminalized at the time), and even murder. Trouble first began in the summer of 1944 when one of their friends, Lucien Carr, murdered David Kammerer, a St. Louis schoolteacher who had come to New York in his obsessive pursuit to be Carr's lover. Carr eventually felt smothered by the demands of both his girlfriend and Kammerer, so he decided to join Kerouac aboard a ship setting sail to France. The two men were hired as part of the crew, but long before the ship left its Brooklyn dock, they were fired for unruly behavior (Campbell 29). Undaunted, the men decided to try again. When Kammerer heard about these plans, however, he began to panic. He could not imagine losing Carr and vowed to follow him wherever he went.

On the night of August 13, 1945, Kerouac and Ginsberg were drinking at the West End bar when Carr arrived. Kerouac left around midnight, and while walking across the Columbia campus to his girlfriend's apartment, he came across Kammerer and mentioned that Carr and Ginsberg were at the West End. Kammerer hurried to the bar and began pleading with Carr. After last call, "Kammerer and Carr staggered out and headed west toward Riverside Park. The volatile combination of whiskey, the days' unhinging events, and Kammerer's desperate fear of separation proved fatal" (Watson 45). The two men began arguing alongside the Hudson River. A few moments later Carr viciously stabbed Kammerer. According to the *New York Times,* "Carr, a slight youth, 5 feet 9 inches tall and weighing 140 pounds[,] was no match for the burly former physical education instructor, who was 6 feet tall and weighed 185 pounds. . . . Carr pulled out of his pocket his boy scout knife, a relic of his boyhood, and plunged the blade twice in rapid succession into Kammerer's chest" (quoted in Campbell 29–30). Carr then tried to dispose of the body by weighing it down with rocks and dumping it in the river. Kammerer's corpse would not sink, however. It floated downstream in the darkness. With blood still on his clothes, Carr hailed a cab to the Greenwich Village apartment of William Burroughs, who advised him to get a good lawyer and to argue self-defense. Carr felt too agitated to go home, so he took a taxi uptown to see Kerouac. Carr still had Kammerer's glasses and the knife with him, so Kerouac encouraged him to dispose of the evidence. Together they walked to Morningside Park, where Carr buried the glasses and dropped the knife in a subway grate. Two days later Carr turned himself in to the police. He was not charged with second-degree manslaughter until the body was found later that afternoon. The police then arrested Burroughs and Kerouac for being material witnesses to the crime. Carr pleaded guilty before a judge and was released from prison in 1946.[16]

The publicity surrounding this incident along with other acts of criminality and rebellion would fuel the association between Beat culture and criminality. As Watson observes, "Although the circle of friends disbanded in the wake of David Kammerer's death, the horrific event irrevocably branded them as members of the same unsavory tribe" (49). Not long after the murder, for example, Columbia University expelled Ginsberg for drawing obscene pictures and writing "Fuck the Jews" and "Butler has no balls" (Butler being the president of Columbia University at the time) in the dirt on his dorm windows. In 1949 Ginsberg found himself in trouble again—sitting with two friends in a car filled with stolen goods and trying to outrun the police. The car crashed, and Ginsberg fled the scene. He was later apprehended and pleaded "psychological disability," for which the court required him to receive psychotherapy at Columbia Presbyterian Psychiatric Institute (Watson 112).

Even the central muse for Ginsberg's and Kerouac's early work—Neal Cassady—was a con man and criminal. Literally born in the backseat of a car in 1926, Cassady remained obsessed with automobiles and women throughout his life. He had stolen approximately five hundred cars by the age of twenty-one, been arrested ten times, and spent several months in various reform schools: "In short, Cassady was a perfect natural sociopath, unrestrained by guilt and fueled by hedonism" (Watson 81). In the first part of *Howl,* Ginsberg famously described some of his experiences with Cassady, "who went out whoring through Colorado in myriad stolen nightcars, N.C., / secret hero of these poems, cocksman and Adonis of Denver—joy to / the memory of his innumerable lays of girls in empty lots." Unlike the suave and sophisticated playboy of Hugh Hefner's imagination, Cassady-Adonis drives stolen cars, frequents whorehouses, and engages in "empty" sexual experiences behind diners, on the rickety seats in movie houses, at gas stations, and in alleyways. Likewise the Cassady of *On the Road,* whom Kerouac named Dean Moriarty in the first published version of the book, steals cars, takes drugs, flees from his wives and children, and abandons his friends.

In another example of Beat culture and criminality, William S. Burroughs, who already had a long history of narcotic and alcohol abuse, killed his wife, Joan Vollmer, on September 6, 1951, while trying to shoot a glass of water balanced on top of her head. He spent only thirteen days in a Mexican prison for the crime. Incidents such as these became part of Beat lore. As a result, it is not surprising that many people would link Beat culture with delinquency and violence. Of course Kerouac railed against this association. "Those who think that the Beat Generation means crime, delinquency, immorality, amorality," Kerouac wrote in 1959, "don't understand history and the yearning of human souls . . . woe unto those who don't realize that America must, will, is changing now, for the better I say" (quoted in Vlagopoulos 57–58). Close examination of *On the Road* supports Kerouac's contention, but the text could not offset the group's provocative image in popular culture. Capote's *In Cold Blood* responds to this mainstream image, suggesting that some of the changes inspired by Beat culture (such as its apparent glamorization of poverty and rootlessness) could have devastating consequences.

On the Road with Dick and Perry

Despite Capote's impression that Beat writing lacked discipline, Kerouac labored intensively over the manuscript of *On the Road*. The story about his feverishly written draft still tends to overshadow the amount of planning and revision he put into it. Starting on April 2, 1951, Kerouac began a three-week marathon of continuous writing. His plan, as he explained, was to "just write it down as fast as I can, exactly like it happened, all in a rush, the hell with these phony architectures" (quoted in Watson 136). Despite pausing for the occasional Benzedrine inhaler, he did not want anything to slow him down. He did not delineate paragraphs or place periods at the ends of sentences. He even taped sheets of paper together to form a continuous roll so that he would not be hampered by inserting new pages into the typewriter. The narrative grew to 186,000 words as it spilled onto a 120-foot scroll of paper. In a May 22, 1951, letter to Neal Cassady, Kerouac described the manuscript as looking "like a road" when rolled out on the floor (quoted in Cunnell 1). Prior to this draft, however, Kerouac began working on the book in November 1948—three and a half years earlier—and he based much of it on his subsequent cross-country trip with Cassady from New York to San Francisco in 1949. After producing the 120-foot scroll, he spent several months revising it. He ultimately crafted several different versions before its publication in 1957.[17] This approach to writing, to capturing the events just like they happened, reveals Kerouac's struggle to find an artistic expression fitting for the Beat generation's lifestyle and experiences.

But what about the Beats, such as Dean Moriarty, who seemed doomed to remain on the road forever? Dean is a shell of his former self by the end of the novel—worn, ragged, nonsensical—and the protagonist, Sal Paradise, achieves a greater sense of self only by rejecting the road, falling in love, and planning to settle down. For most readers and critics, however, the celebration of Beat life in the novel tends to overshadow this rather conventional ending. As Erik Mortenson explains, "The novel introduced a new cultural movement as well, alerting society to an undercurrent of dissent and dissatisfaction with conformity of postwar life that would eventually erupt into full-scale social revolution in the sixties" (27). Capote witnessed the start of this revolution while writing *In Cold Blood*, and he used aspects of his nonfiction novel to examine it. In addition to casting Perry as a Beat figure, Capote established Perry Smith and Dick Hickock as dark alternatives to Sal Paradise and Dean Moriarty. As Kerouac did with *On the Road*, Capote made artistry, movement (as it relates to finding an authentic community, rejecting social norms, and to exploring homosexual desire), and theft central themes to his text, and these thematic elements reveal the darker, more dangerous consequences of Beat life.

While Perry's artistry aligned him with the types of figures celebrated in Beat writing, Capote presents his inability to see art as something more than a vehicle for achieving financial success as trapping him in an oppressive consumer culture and isolating him from others. Perry certainly possessed the kind of instinctual talent that the Beats, at some level, admired. As he explained, "I could play harmonica first time I picked one up. Guitar, too. I had this great natural musical ability. . . . Make up songs. I could draw. But I never got any encouragement—from [Dad] or anybody else" (133). His lack of formal training could have fostered innovation, but instead he preferred ballads in the style of Gene Autry[18] over the jazz of George Shearing. This musical preference reflected Perry's fantasies about the American West as a place for striking it rich. Even though he sang as a way to express feelings of loneliness and longing for some greater spiritual connection (including the hymn "I Came to the Garden Alone," which has the refrain "And He walks with me, and He talks with me, / And He tells me I am His own" [48]), Perry had neither the ability nor the training to create an art that would resonate with others. (Dick, for example, cannot stand listening to Perry sing.)

Music for Perry merely fueled his fantasies about gaining fame and wealth as a headliner in Las Vegas. It played into the mythology about American prosperity. Without an audience, Perry remained isolated, which, Capote suggests, contributed to his limited artistic abilities. Perry did not belong to a social or familial community that nurtured his talent. He did not have a Carlo Marx (Allan Ginsberg) with whom to exchange intellectual ideas. This isolation left him on the road without guidance or support. Capote presents this condition as something that eventually encouraged his exchanging one type of instrument for another: "Another sort of instrument lay beside it—a twelve-gauge pump-action shotgun. . . . A flashlight, a fishing knife, a pair of leather gloves, and a hunting vest fully packed with shells contributed further atmosphere to this curious still life" (22). Through this connection, Capote reveals how quickly Perry's version of the Beat life—on the road in a desperate search for belonging—could devolve into a journey of violent criminality. Without the artistic genius and a community of fellow artists to ground him in a more realistic view of society, Perry ultimately expressed himself with the only instruments/tools he had left: a gun and a knife.

Kerouac's *On the Road* presents art that builds community (spiritual and social) as both a central goal for Beat writers and a critical tool for creativity. Jazz, in its celebration of spontaneity (through improvisation) and its roots in the suffering of African Americans, offers an important example of this. It provides an avenue for achieving what Dean describes as "IT," a moment during a musical performance or at hypnotically high speeds on the highway that is "soul exploratory" (207); it enables one to transcend time and mortality. At the outset of *Howl,* for instance, Ginsberg's angel-headed hipsters seek some "heavenly connection" by "smoking in the supernatural darkness . . . [and] contemplating jazz." True to form, Kerouac has Dean seek out jazz clubs throughout the United States for a taste of that heavenly connection. Unlike Perry's solitary guitar strumming and singing, jazz in the world of *On the Road* builds social community. According to Jason Haslam, "'IT' is a moment of bridge-building and community-formation that arises from the artistic creation of one individual but is ultimately expressed as a communal feeling of transcendence: 'it's not the tune that counts but IT'" (453). The shared experience between performer and audience gives this music its power. This communal aspect helps explain why Sal's outcome is different from Perry's. Sal too lives in a naive, dream world, fantasizing about the fortunes that await him and describing the world as "the pearl [that] would be handed to me" (8) and an "oyster" waiting to be opened (138). These idealizations break down most directly in Los Angeles when Sal's illusions about having a "Hollywood career" get reduced to making cheap sandwiches in a parking lot and "spreading mustard on [his] lap in the back of a parking-lot john" (102). However, as a writer Sal has a powerful artistic outlet that connects him with a broader community. Not only is he writing the story of his experiences with Dean, but he has also recently published a book (187). Kerouac uses these details to highlight the importance of artistic expression as a tool for connecting the artist/writer with others—a connection perpetually denied to Perry.

Capote also introduces movement as an important theme in the text, and even though it has the potential to help one find a community, motion ultimately becomes emblematic of Perry's and Dick's perpetual uncertainty, instability, and frustration. Maps comprised some of Perry's most valued belongings (objects he kept in boxes for safe keeping) because they gave him hope of arriving at some meaningful destination. He even tried to convince Dick that they could locate buried treasure in Mexico with a map: "This is authentic. I've got a map" (100). For both of these men, however, maps led nowhere. Although they spent time in dozens of cities throughout the United States and visited several places in Mexico, the killers ended up in the same place—Kansas. Within six weeks Dick estimated that the two had traveled "approximately 10,000 miles" (222), a meandering journey that typified the aimless circularity of their lives. They were never able to accomplish or achieve anything lasting. While the car provided an intimate space for them, the exchanges between Perry and Dick remained stilted—a far cry from Sal's and Dean's animated conversations that rock the car and dent the dashboard. Every time Perry wanted to talk about the implications of their crime and the idea of "just one hundred percent [getting] away with it," Dick told him to "shut up!" (110). As their bond continued to deteriorate, Perry began seeking a broader social world, and he encouraged Dick to pick up hitch-hikers. At first they targeted wealthy drivers "to rob, strangle, discard in the desert" (154), but eventually Perry "was always pestering Dick to pick up the damnedest, sorriest-looking people" (207). Capote includes these details to underscore Perry's desperate desire for companionship and to depict the road as a place that fails to provide lasting human connection. It seems to perpetuate myths about the American Dream as a destination that can be found if one just keeps going.

Kerouac too presents the map as a problematic image, but unlike the experiences of Dick and Perry, movement in *On the Road* offers both community and personal growth for those who know when to stop. *On the Road* is structured around four transcontinental journeys that parallel the different stages of Sal's growth and self-understanding. Sal explains at the outset that he had "been poring over maps of the United States in Patterson for months," and this activity inspires him "to follow one great red line across America instead of trying various roads and routes" (10, 11). While relying on a map and trying to follow one single road across the country, Sal gets no farther than forty miles in the wrong direction on his first day. This failure highlights one of the central lessons he will need to learn. As Tim Hunt explains, "The reality of the road is not governed by the aesthetics of maps, and America will not turn out to be a single reality but a series of conflicting realities" (12). Some of these conflicting realities include desires for individuality and community, for movement and stasis, for condemning social norms and participating in consumer culture.

In addition to Sal's hope for spiritual transcendence and a greater under-standing of IT, his journey seems to be a quest for companionship among fellow hipsters. Sal gets excited about news that Dean is coming to Colorado and views him as a "long-lost brother" (7). He also sees the potential for deep intimacy with Dean. Sal has already witnessed the intense intellectual exchanges between Dean and Carlo Marx, for instance: "We're trying to communicate with absolute honesty and absolute completeness everything on our minds" (41). Unlike Perry and Dick, Sal hopes—and achieves—a power-ful intimacy with Dean. Sal also seeks out old friends and family throughout the country—including Old Bull Lee and Remi Boncoeur, whose window he climbs through in San Francisco. Additionally the community of transients provides another important community and an alternative to conventional social norms. One of his early experiences as a hitchhiker involved getting a lift from two Minnesota farm boys who picked up "every single soul they found on the road: farmer boys in red baseball caps, city boys, high-school football players "chewing gum, winking, and singing in the breeze" (23), and hobos. This truck, which Sal must run after to catch a ride, establishes a mo-bile community with no class or social hierarchies. As Halsam observes, "The truck . . . and the road, in general, allow Sal to break through socio-historical conditions of class and communicate with a variety of people" (448).

Apart from Dean, most of the hipster figures in the novel end up in a static place. Carlo realizes that everyone needs a "stone" (130), a solid foun-dation to come back to, and Sal falls in love. Kerouac—like Capote—views the road as a temporary space and decides that those who occupy it for too long risk ongoing marginalization and becoming dangerous. Old Bull Lee, for example, recognizes the potential violence in Dean: "He seems to me to be headed for his ideal fate, which is compulsive psychosis dashed with a jigger of irresponsibility and violence. . . . If you go to California with this madman you'll never make it" (147). Dean has a history of beating Marylou (who appears "black and blue from a fight" with him early in the text), and eventually he breaks his thumb while hitting her. Kerouac uses this injury, which gets progressively worse, to represent Dean's self-destructiveness as well as the danger he poses to others. He may never substitute his hand for a gun (as Perry exchanged his guitar for a rifle), but Dean's failure to get off the road makes him a destructive force in other people's lives. In this way *On the Road* and *In Cold Blood* offer similar warnings about the importance of viewing the road as a journey, not as a lifestyle in itself.

Capote also relates movement to sexual freedom in his presentation of on-the-road culture as tolerant of homosexuality. Like Sal Paradise in *On the Road,* Perry was drawn to the road by a charismatic man. He received a letter from Dick that began the road trip of *In Cold Blood.* After his parole, Perry had been wandering aimlessly from place to place: "months of rattling around in a fifth-hand, hundred-dollar Ford, rolling from Reno to Las Vegas, from Bellingham, Washington, to Buhl, Idaho" (44). Dick's letter made Perry feel that he mattered to someone and that he could embark on a journey for companionship and financial stability. In addition to his own desire to connect with someone, Perry admired Dick's charisma and manliness. Perry frequently noted Dick's effortless ability to charm people (especially when conning them with a bad check), and his toughness, pragmatism, and decisiveness gave him a "totally masculine" quality (124). Perry wanted to possess this type of manhood himself but could not express it through sex. In many ways Perry's sexual abuse as a child and at the hands of military men (133–34) probably prevented him from engaging in much heterosexual sex or acting on his desires for Dick.

Considering the oppressive Cold War culture of the 1950s, it is not surprising that homosexual intimacy would be muted in the text. Nevertheless Capote presents numerous details to suggest a homoerotic bond between the men. Perry's attraction to Dick's masculinity appeared to be sexually charged. In addition to keeping a scrapbook filled with magazine photographs featuring "sweaty studies of weight-lifting weight-lifters" (178), Perry treasured several nude sketches of Dick (119), and prior to his execution, he still considered Dick his most intimate companion. What he most desired after his arrest was to communicate with Dick—"to talk to Dick, be with him again. . . . Of everyone in all the world, this was the person to whom he was closest at the moment" (259–60). Likewise Dick repeatedly referred to Perry as "honey," "sugar," and "baby." He labeled Perry an "ordinary punk" (a term among prisoners that refers to "a man who serves as the passive sexual partner of a stronger male prisoner" [Voss 107]), and at one point he even compared him to a burdensome spouse: "Dick was sick of him—his harmonica, his aches and ills, his superstitions, the weepy, womanly eyes, the nagging, whispering voice. Suspicious, self-righteous, spiteful, he was like a wife that must be got rid of" (214–15). Dick's allusion to marriage suggested the extent of their closeness, while feminizing the "nagging" Perry with "womanly eyes" hinted at his homosexuality.

The critic Ralph Voss interprets the Clutter murders as motivated by Perry's closeted sexual attraction for Dick. When "Dick decided to use his shotgun-and-alcohol-fueled power over the Clutters to rape Nancy, an act that implicitly rejected Perry not only as a sexual partner but also as an ideal and loyal companion . . . [it] relegated Perry to second-rate intimacy and even, in some odd way, insulted and disgusted him. For Perry, this was the last straw" (Voss 117). Whether or not suppressed homosexuality factored into the crime, Perry's possible homosexuality certainly played into Cold War fears that ordinary people could be hiding dangerous secrets. As Capote remarks when Perry and Dick arrived at the Garden City courthouse, the crowd was "amazed to find them humanly shaped" (148). Even though road culture offered a sexual freedom for men such as Perry (a freedom that threatened the heterosexual imperatives embodied by the nuclear family), this opportunity did not bring happiness for many people. Perry's quest for belonging (for stasis) required a rejection of his latent homosexuality, and not even his high-speed travels on the road could help him escape that.

Kerouac depicts movement as integral to Sal's quest for community and self-definition, which also occurs in the context of a male relationship with homoerotic overtones. *On the Road* begins by mentioning Sal's recent divorce. In his quest to feel connected with someone, he gravitates toward Dean's frenetic energy and masculine appeal. Sal admits that he had a history of following such men: "I shambled after as I've been doing all my life after people who interest me, because the only people are the mad ones, the ones who are mad to live, mad to talk, mad to be saved, desirous of everything at the same time" (5). His journey is motivated by a desire to share Dean's energetic, mad enthusiasm for experiencing life. He notes that "every muscle [of Dean's] twitched to live and go" and that "he had become absolutely mad in his movements; he seemed to be doing everything at the same time" (113, 114). When questioned about the point of these cross-country journeys, Dean and Sal have no answer. "The only thing to do was go" (120). In a Beat framework, movement gets equated with vitality and freedom (social, intellectual, and sexual), while stillness means stagnation, conformity, and death. "True freedom," as Mortenson argues, "was not to be found in a democratic America or in consumer choice but in giving oneself over, fully and completely, to the immediacy of the present moment" (33).

Dean lives life by this code, and he expresses some of this through his sexual appetite. In addition to cars, Dean has an insatiable desire for women. He often has sex several times a day with more than one woman, which is another manifestation of his movement. His obsession with time, which is always "running, running" (43), reflects his attempts to squeeze as much experience into every moment as possible. He laments at one point that he simply has not "had the time to work in weeks" (44). Sal, on the other hand, struggles to seduce women: "I tried everything in the books to make a girl ... without success" (73). Early in the text, Sal envies Dean's sexual prowess, yet Sal's sexual relationships on the road remain unsatisfying. He is either too "impatient" to please a woman (57) or too quickly dissatisfied because of his need to be "on the road again" (101). As illustrated by Dean's and Sal's adventures, movement in *On the Road* is the freedom to pursue different sexual partners and to reject cultural norms regarding marriage. Dean—like Dick—abandons his wives and children to hit the road, and he enjoys sex with prostitutes in Mexico. Kerouac, however, decided to leave Dean's (Neal Cassady's) bisexuality out of the novel.[19] He did not mention, for instance, the sexual relationship between Carlo Marx (Ginsberg) and Dean, which had sadomasochistic elements.[20] Kerouac may have had similar reasons as Capote for such a choice—a response to the cultural climate surrounding homosexuality and a desire to produce marketable fiction. Given Kerouac's aspirations to be a widely read author, it seems likely that he did not want to court the same kind of controversy that Ginsberg did with his explicit descriptions of homosexual sex in *Howl*.[21] Despite Sal's progressive enlightenment at the end of each journey, he retreats into conventional, heterosexual environments—such as the family kitchen at his aunt's home in New York and the plan to move in with his girlfriend at the end of the novel. Kerouac thus implies that the sexual and social freedoms of their journeys do not exist off the road.

Theft emerges as another central motif throughout Beat literature, and Capote uses it to expose the limitations of this practice for rejecting conventional attitudes regarding ownership and work; instead theft reveals the inability of Perry, Dick, and arguably all people on the road to escape consumer culture. Capote regularly reminds readers of the ubiquitous nature of American crime. He quotes a newspaper editorial lamenting the ways people forget about acts of serious violence, which is "a sad commentary on the state of crime in our nation" (271). Masked bandits robbed the Garden City post office almost a year after the Clutter murders (87–88), and the text recounts the details of Dick and Perry's crime spree. The killers committed some of the same petty thefts (for food, consumer goods, and cars) that enabled Sal and Dean to continue their road trip, and yet Capote draws a chilling analogy between theft and murder in *In Cold Blood*. Perry ascribed to the philosophy that "all crimes were only 'varieties of theft.' Murder included. When you kill a man, you steal his life" (291). While Perry's acts of violence were to some extent a reflection of the violence done to him (one psychiatrist, for example, argued that Perry viewed Clutter as a representation of various figures who had hurt him, such as his father, the orphanage nuns, and his army sergeant), his various forms of thievery clearly functioned to reject the conventions of a society that repeatedly marginalized him. Perry simply could not envision a future for himself in mainstream society. One of his inmate friends, Willie-Jay, described him as "a deeply frustrated man striving to project his individuality against a backdrop of rigid conformity" (43) and "an unconventional person" (143). Perry's sister wrote him a letter criticizing his nonconformity: "all of us are responsible to the community we live in & its laws. . . . For surely you can realize what a mess the world would be if everyone in it said 'I want to be an individual, without responsibilities, & be able to speak my mind freely & do as *I* alone will'" (142).

Not surprisingly, the movement, nonconformity, and free expression prized by the Beats were condemned by the suburban housewife here. Perry's choices ultimately proved her right, however. His brand of nonconformist individuality led to nonstop motion and violence. It ended up inspiring him to reject community and law completely. Capote depicts the consumer drives of Dick and Perry as undermining the freedoms that they hoped to achieve through theft. When Dick and Perry picked up the boy hitchhiker who collects Coca-Cola bottles on the side of the road, the killers enjoyed both the "treasure-hunt excitement" (208) of it as well as the $12.30 they earned in refund money. In many respects the collection of Coke bottles paralleled their use of consumer goods throughout *In Cold Blood*. Dick wrote bad checks to purchase television sets, cameras, cuff links, and other items not for his personal use but rather to buy other consumer goods—namely prostitutes and alcohol. These details revealed how a consumerist ethos contributed to their inability to reject conventionality. Furthermore Dick subsequently abandoned the boy and the grandfather because they had no money. His need to pursue pleasure through "goods" such as "vodka and women" (119), which provided him with only temporary pleasure, prevented his being part of a broader community. Like Dick's consulting a map while abandoning the hitchhikers, Dick's and Perry's endless search for money through stealing and selling consumer goods kept them perpetually on the road.

Theft functions as an integral part of Beat existence in *On the Road,* and while Kerouac uses thievery as an image for rejecting social norms, he also depicts its dangers and limitations. Early in the novel Sal admits that his friends are comprised of either intellectuals or thieves, implying a connection between the two. Both reject conventional notions of law and order. Intellectuals did so through art/words that critiqued American culture at a time when it was dangerous to do so, and they presented unconventional practices that the law considered obscene (as it did with the publication of *Howl*). Thieves, on the other hand, literally take the property of others throughout the novel. Dean steals cars—sometimes for the need to keep moving, sometimes for the mere thrill of it. Sal initially celebrates Dean's actions— "his 'criminality' was not something that sulked and sneered; it was a wild

yes-saying outburst of American joy" (7). Its roots in exuberance and the
desire to live life fully negate its "criminality," as the quotes suggest, and it
also introduces Sal to the theft all around him.

He observes that Remi Boncoeur compulsively stole things as a form of
payment for the losses of life: "He was out to get back everything he'd lost;
there was no end to his loss; this thing would drag on forever" (70). As Sal
spends more time on the road, he comes to the conclusion that "everybody in
America is a natural-born thief" (72), an attitude which helps him justify his
own criminality. Part of this participation makes sense given Sal's awareness
of the pressures to conform. He notes that police are suspicious of juvenile
delinquents ("gangs of youngsters . . . without a cent in their pockets" [165])
and try to punish any example of unconventionality: "The American police
are involved in psychological warfare against those Americans who don't
frighten them with imposing papers and threats. It's a Victorian police force;
it peers out of musty windows and wants to inquire about everything, and
can make crimes if the crimes don't exist to its satisfaction" (137). Unconventionality of any kind—even if it is not technically criminal, such as driving
across the country for no apparent reason—is considered dangerous behavior in America. As Kerouac suggests, nonconformist behavior among adoles-
cents in particular has inspired a psychological battle between young and old,
repression and freedom, individual autonomy and social norms. Nevertheless
Kerouac questions theft as an effective mode for unconventionality. The narrator notes that Remi's life of stealing would "drag on forever," and Dean's
deterioration (which includes dangerous speeding and car crashes) suggests
the flaw with this belief system. Stealing makes up an essential component of
life on the road, but without an end point, Kerouac presents it as something
corrosive. It perpetuates resentment (feeling that a person can never regain
one's losses) and continual dissatisfaction. It fosters distrust. (Sal initially
worries that Terry might be "a common hustler who worked the buses for
a guy's bucks" [83], and Terry even wonders if Sal might be a pimp.) And it
ultimately harms others.

Furthermore the attempt to reject the norms of consumer culture through
theft fails to help Sal escape his part in the American economic system. Unlike Perry, Sal has money—an aunt who never fails to mail him cash when
he needs it—and he frequently consumes pie and ice cream. He even buys his
aunt a refrigerator—"the first one in the family" (107)—and this appliance,
which stores Sal's favorite foods, clearly serves as a marker of social status.
Dean, on the other hand, seems more aware of the dangers of consumerism. He argues that poorly made consumer goods serve a broader economic
agenda: "They prefer making cheap goods so's everybody'll have to go on

working and punching timeclocks and organizing themselves in sullen unions and floundering around" (149). Constant movement and trying to get the most out of each moment become Dean's primary tools for rejecting American capitalism. He possesses, as Mortenson argues, "an economy of ecstasy, not of oppression" (31). Yet Kerouac notes that this life comes at a personal cost for Dean, who appears decimated at the end of the novel. He has also caused considerable pain for the wives and children he repeatedly abandons for these trips. Sal appreciates such insights about consumerism, but he eventually recognizes that Dean is a problematic model. Sal grows tired of the "nightmare road" (254) and wants an end point defined by family, ice cream, pie, and love. Unlike Perry and Dick, who were forced into stasis as prisoners, Sal chooses to settle down. The lessons of his journey show a need to balance some form of community (through romantic love and friendship) as well as movement. *On the Road* concludes with Sal and his girlfriend planning to move to San Francisco and settle down.

Conclusion: What Is So Dangerous about *In Cold Blood*?

During the 2010–11 school year, a teacher at Glendale High School in California submitted a request to teach *In Cold Blood* the following year as part of her eleventh grade AP literature class. She believed that the book would offer a provocative way to debate the death penalty, the American judicial system, and other contemporary topics. Almost immediately, however, the request met with resistance. While the English Curriculum Study Committee for the district approved the choice, many members of the Secondary Education Council balked at the idea. The latter group, comprised of high school principals, believed the content to be too violent. According to a spokesperson for the Glendale Unified School District, "The thought amongst the reluctant members of the board was that it's a grim story, a somewhat graphically told story, by 1960s standards, that they felt they did not want to subject students to, while recognizing the discussion value the teacher intended to address" (Shaw). The Parent Teacher Association wholeheartedly agreed, and the organization recommended against teaching the text.

On September 13, 2011, the school board convened to vote on the matter, and after much debate, the group remained evenly divided over the issue. One of the dissenting voices felt that students were "subjected to enough violent images in other arenas of their life" and that "the school curriculum didn't necessarily have to be one of those places" (Shaw). When describing the book and her concerns about it, this board member also stated that "'chilling' is far too benign a word to use" (Kellog). The split decision forced Vice President Christine Walters to cast the deciding vote, but she declined to do so because she had not read the book. Instead she rescheduled the meeting to give herself time to peruse *In Cold Blood*. This delay prolonged the controversy, which had been going on for months among faculty, school officials, parents, students, and the news media. On October 11 the board reconvened and decided to approve its use in the class (with one member abstaining from the final vote).

Certainly Capote's poetic rendering of the Clutter killings is horrific and tragic. Yet most would agree that the violence of *In Cold Blood* is far less graphic than the average episode of *Law and Order*, which for years advertised its content as "ripped from the headlines." Even *Law and Order* is tame compared to most video games. So why did so many parents and members of the board view the book as being too violent for teenagers? Perhaps the district's initial reaction can best be understood as a response to the way Capote crafts these killings as a metaphor for a broader assault on American culture. Many of the fears in the text still resonate with Americans. Cold War concerns about annihilation and invasion share many parallels with the anxieties that have shaped American life since 9/11. Poverty, which has certainly worsened since the 2008 economic collapse, continues to raise troubling questions about economic inequality in the United States. The housing crisis at the heart of this collapse has profoundly shaken the cultural investment and idealization of home ownership, and it has exposed ongoing lending practices by banks that have hurt the poorest Americans—most notably African Americans. Adolescent disaffectedness, delinquency, and dissatisfaction never cease to puzzle and concern parents. Like the characters in the film *Rebel without a Cause*, teenagers still occupy a subculture (whether virtual or actual) that mystifies adults. The prospect of "good" kids going bad unsettles American society just as much today as it did in the 1950s. And violent crime continues to be fueled by economic deprivation and disillusionment that have terrifying implications for a country increasingly divided in terms of class. When considering all of these things, I would agree with the comment by one of the board members who disapproved of bringing *In Cold Blood* into the classroom: "'Chilling' is far too benign a word [for this book]." Indeed.

CHAPTER 8

Three Stories, *Answered Prayers*, and Capote in the Twenty-First Century

Throughout *Understanding Truman Capote,* my approach has been to situate Capote as a writer shaped by and deeply engaged with the social, cultural, and political climate of the 1940s and 1950s. When placed in this context, his work—with its depictions of nostalgia, racism, sexuality, the Cold War, poverty, juvenile delinquency, and violence—takes on a new significance. It condemns the practices that limited social equality and stifled individual expression. It criticizes the social and political disengagement of those who clung to isolation and nostalgia. And it shares great affinities with the works of contemporary writers such as Flannery O'Connor and Carson McCullers, writers whom scholars have typically seen as far more politically engaged. This approach for understanding Capote also challenges some of the ways that literary criticism has inadvertently contributed to his marginalization in the canon. Analyses anchored in New Criticism have positioned Capote as a stylist, not a cultural critic. As a result his work continues to be omitted from anthologies and is increasingly left off course syllabi.

My chapter on *Breakfast at Tiffany's and Three Stories* does not include an analysis of the three short stories published with the novella in 1958, and I would briefly like to address that decision—as well as these stories—here. Their omission from chapter six was based on two issues. The first involved the 1961 film. This adaptation continues to have an important place in the American cultural imagination, and any discussion of the book needs to account for the differences between the two versions. With this focus for the chapter, any discussion of the stories would have felt extraneous. Second, unlike *A Tree of Night and Other Stories,* the short fiction included with *Breakfast at Tiffany's* was not conceived as a whole. Capote's tendency to write novellas posed a challenge for publishers, and Random House felt the need to publish *Breakfast at Tiffany's* with some additional material. Certainly, the stories share elements found throughout Capote's oeuvre, but I believe they can be more fully appreciated in the context of their original publication dates.

Given that Capote published "House of Flowers" and "A Diamond Guitar" in 1950, it is not entirely surprising that they reflect many of the social concerns explored in both *A Tree of Night and Other Stories* (1949) and *The Grass Harp* (1951). "House of Flowers" was inspired by the author's trip to Haiti in 1948, and he based the story on an anecdote that he included in a travel sketch for *Local Color.*[1] Like Holly Golightly, Ottilie is an orphaned girl from the rural country who gets seduced by city nightlife (in this case Port-au-Prince) and remakes herself largely through her sexuality. She starts working as a prostitute at the Champs Elysèes brothel and quickly becomes a favorite among patrons, who shower her with gifts including alcohol, silk dresses, green satin shoes, good teeth, and jewelry. Despite the appeal of this tawdry world, she is not happy. The source of her dissatisfaction does not become clear until she falls in love with Royal Bonaparte. She immediately recognizes the appeal of their shared rural roots ("she could see that he was from the mountains" [120]) and admits that "nostalgia touched her with its far-reaching wand" (121). The couple soon gets married and moves to Royal's hillside abode, which is enveloped by wisteria lilacs. This fairy-tale "house of flowers" even comes with its own witch. Royal's grandmother, Old Bonaparte, lives with the newlyweds, and she torments Ottilie in a variety of ways, including casting spells to make her ill. The young bride circumvents this voodoo magic by secretly cooking the animals used for the spells (for example, lizards, snakes, spiders, the head of a cat) and feeding them to the old woman. After learning of Ottilie's treachery, Old Bonaparte dies instantly. Her presence lingers, however, and Ottilie is convinced that the grandmother is haunting the house. As a solution, her husband suggests that she be tied to a tree for one day to appease (and hopefully cast out) the ghost.

Capote ultimately portrays marriage in "House of Flowers" as limiting the social and sexual freedom of women, which aligns it with some of the issues raised in *Breakfast at Tiffany's* (see chapter six) and *A Tree of Night and Other Stories* (see chapter two). Ottilie never expresses moral reservations about her decision to work at the Champs Elysèes, in part because she is not ashamed of her sexuality. Much like Holly, she enjoys the company of men. She relishes gifts, enjoys alcohol, and takes pleasure in gossiping with the other prostitutes. Ottilie and Holly also share a willingness to give up the trappings of city life and social independence for the idea of love. Ottilie's friends at the brothel find such a choice inconceivable: "to think of it, a gorgeous piece like you suffering far away from those who love you" (133). These women define love through female community, not marriage, and despite Capote's comical portrait of the other prostitutes, he endorses this message through his critical portrait of married life. Ottilie embraces domesticity despite the fact that it curtails her freedom. Her daily schedule of cooking, cleaning, caring for farm animals, and carrying water to Royal in the cane fields keeps her "too busy to be lonesome" (125). Capote also contrasts her restrictive routine with Royal's social freedom. After five months of marriage, he begins staying out late with his male companions and spending Sundays at cockfights. He even ties her to a tree by force at the end of the story. All of these details present marriage as a problematic institution that reinforces patriarchal power.

Like Capote's portrait of same-sex desire in *The Grass Harp,* his muted treatment of homosexuality in "A Diamond Guitar" can best be understood in the context of homosexual persecution during the Lavender Scare (see chapter four). Set in a remote southern jail, the story focuses on Mr. Schaeffer, who is serving a life sentence for killing a man. Despite being surrounded by over two hundred prisoners, Schaeffer has withdrawn from the world: "he seems to have no friends beyond the prison, and actually he has none there" (140). The arrival of a new inmate, however, transforms the emotionally numb, solitary lives of Schaeffer and the other prisoners. Tico Feo, a Cuban teenager with golden hair, sky-blue eyes, an infectious smile, and a voice "soft and sweet as a banana" (142), brings an unexpected brightness to the prison. These characteristics also remind the men of their lives before incarceration. In addition to his personality, Tico owns a guitar adorned with glass diamonds. His nightly performances in the jailhouse enchant the men, inspiring them to dance and laugh. Although most of the inmates feel affection for Tico, Schaeffer falls in love with him, and the narrator explicitly describes the pair as lovers—despite the fact that they do not become physically intimate. This love blinds Schaeffer to Tico's selfishness and manipulation. The young convict uses him to get more food, cigarettes, and a better bed near the furnace. He also needs Schaeffer's help with his escape. Tico knows that the older man will not be able to keep up with him during a prison break, and when Schaeffer gets injured during the attempt, Tico abandons him as planned. Like Randolph in *Other Voices, Other Rooms,* Schaeffer is haunted by memories of lost love that leave him shattered, lonely, and isolated.

As with some of the stories in *A Tree of Night and Other Stories* (see chapter two), *The Grass Harp* (see chapter four), and *The Muses Are Heard* (see chapter five), Capote presents gossip in "A Diamond Guitar" as a tool for perpetuating Cold War prejudices and fears. The prisoners use this tool against Tico: "Because [the men] were jealous, or for more subtle reasons, some of them told ugly stories. Tico Feo seemed unaware of this" (145–46). The narrator does not specify the rationale for these rumors, nor does he reveal any details, but two possibilities seem likely given the social climate of the period: sexuality and race. Although his relationship with Schaeffer does not involve sex, homosexuality is part of prison life: "Except that they did not combine their bodies or think to do so, though such things were not unknown at the farm, they were lovers" (146). Capote's narrative later undercuts the idea that the men did not "think to do so." Schaeffer notes the "tender pressure" of Tico's hand on his, and in the closing moments of the story, he strums the guitar as if to caress Tico. Regardless, homophobic gossip would certainly make sense during the Lavender Scare and with the stigma associated with homosexuality in the South at the time. Thus Tico's lack of awareness about these rumors parallels Schaeffer's inability and/or unwillingness to hear them. They remain disconnected from the realities of homophobia outside of the prison even though Schaeffer has access to this information: "[The Captain and Schaeffer] would talk together about things they had read in the newspaper" (141–42). The same can be said about Schaeffer's attitude toward race. He does not address or question the racial hierarchies shaping prison life—hierarchies that mirror contemporary racist practices in the South. The narrator notes, for example, that whites sleep in separate buildings from nonwhites, which include African Americans and a Chinese man. Tico's sleeping arrangement with the other white men should raise questions about his ethnicity, and most likely this is the second source of gossip. Schaeffer, however, refuses to acknowledge it. Like the depiction of race in *Other Voices, Other Rooms* (see chapter three) and *The Muses Are Heard*, Capote includes these details to underscore the way social prejudices prevent community. Segregation certainly contributes to the aloofness of these men and the fractured community of the prison. While Tico breaks down these barriers for a short time, the rigid hierarchies return in his absence.

Like *The Grass Harp*, "A Christmas Memory" draws on Capote's experiences with the Faulk family to portray one boy's holiday ritual in the 1930s. First published in *Mademoiselle* in 1956, the story appeared amid intense anxieties about the Cold War, and this nostalgic tale certainly played into American idealizations about rural life in a time before World War II.

Specifically the story recalls the relationship between a seven-year-old boy named Buddy and his elderly cousin. A recluse in her sixties, this woman lives in a world completely removed from mainstream society and adult responsibilities: "In addition to her never having seen a movie, she has never: eaten in a restaurant, traveled more than five miles from home, received or sent a telegram, read anything except funny papers and the Bible, worn cosmetics, cursed, wished someone harm, told a lie on purpose" (163). She is completely uncorrupted by the outside world and has remained, in a sense, frozen in time—which was certainly the underlying fantasy of isolationism. She has not been altered by financial responsibilities, social prejudices, or the local/national/global dangers that rob adults of this innocence. The tale begins in the late fall when Buddy and his cousin begin gathering the ingredients for making fruitcakes. This annual ritual is something they prepare for every year, saving money for their "Fruitcake Fund" through a variety of enterprises such as killing flies for neighbors and operating Buddy's backyard "Fun and Freak Museum." The two cousins collect the ingredients, which include buying whiskey from a bootlegger named Mr. Haha Jones,[2] make thirty-one cakes, and send them to people they hardly know, including President Roosevelt and his wife. This ritual is followed by an account of the annual preparations for Christmas. Buddy recalls their adventures finding a tree, making decorations, and preparing gifts. When the holiday arrives, they exchange beautiful paper kites—the same gifts they give each other every year. As this "memory" comes to an end, Capote reminds the reader that this moment has passed, that the events occurred twenty years ago when his cousin and his dog were still alive. Like Capote's other nostalgic fiction, this beautiful tale about childhood captures the sense of loss that many Americans felt as a result of social and political changes after World War II. The narrator's reminiscences reflect a longing for comforting rituals and safety, for a time without the specter of war. Yet he recognizes that time has changed the world irrevocably. The fragile paper kites, images for childhood and innocence more broadly, have long since drifted into the sky, leaving only memories.

Capote in the Twenty-First Century

It appears that Capote's uncanny knack for publicity has continued well into the twenty-first century. After setting aside his first attempt at a novel, *Summer Crossing,* he returned to this early manuscript in 1949 and worked steadily on it for several months. He made significant progress, but in several letters to his editor, he expressed serious reservations: "[The book] has turned into quite a different, infinitely more complex novel than I originally proposed, and to pull it into shape will be a monumental effort" (quoted in Long 34). His frustrations with *Summer Crossing* caused him to turn his attentions elsewhere once again. In 1950 he began writing *The Grass Harp,* and that shift seemed to be the end of *Summer Crossing*—the story of a New York debutante who rebels against the affluent world of her parents, in large part by falling in love with a Jewish parking-lot attendant. By 1953 Capote even claimed to have torn up the manuscript. However, it appeared—along with several photographs and other personal belongings—for auction at Sotheby's in 2004.

The story of the manuscript's discovery is compelling in its own right. Capote's lengthy travels often required him to hire a house sitter for his residence in Brooklyn Heights. When he decided to give up this apartment for a place at the ritzy United Nations Plaza, he asked his former superintendant to dispose of any possessions left behind. Unbeknownst to Capote, the house sitter did not feel comfortable destroying manuscripts and other memorabilia. He simply could not bring himself to toss them out with the rest of the garbage, so he kept them. His nephew inherited the papers decades later and sold them at the 2004 auction.

This was not the only time someone rescued Capote memorabilia from the garbage. In 2003 Ron Nye noticed several file boxes next to the trash bins at his mother's house. His father, Harold Nye, had been one of the lead investigators for the Clutter murders in 1959, and he kept extensive notes from the case. Among other things, the boxes contained a signed copy of *In Cold Blood,* Nye's personal notebooks at the time, and the original Kansas Bureau of Investigation file, which included crime-scene photographs, the confessions of the killers, and other information pertaining to the case. The Nye family's decision to put the papers up for auction in July 2012 started a fierce legal battle. Members of the Clutter family threatened to file a lawsuit, claiming that the release of these materials would be painful for them, and after the Kansas attorney general argued in court that the file belonged to the state, a judge temporarily blocked the auction in October 2012.

Two months later the December 2012 issue of *Vanity Fair* published a recently discovered vignette from Truman Capote's unfinished novel *Answered Prayers.* "Yachts and Things" was the title for one of the seven chapters intended to comprise the book. Until now scholars assumed that Capote never wrote a word of that chapter. As his biographer Gerald Clarke remarked about this discovery, "I don't know why this one was not published. My guess is that he thought it fell short in some way" (quoted in Kashner 208). Like the other parts of *Answered Prayers,* the setting and characters in "Yachts and Things" offer a snapshot of life among exorbitantly wealthy

Americans. The vignette recounts the experiences of the narrator and Mrs. Williams while they were taking a three-week Mediterranean cruise on a friend's chartered yacht. Capote aligns the yacht—with its attentive staff, plentiful supply of delicious food and drink, and a captain who wears a "crisply tailored white uniform"—with an idyllic description of the Greek islands, which the narrator likens to "a Rousseau forest" (208). This luxurious lifestyle, in other words, seems to fit naturally with the sumptuous landscape. When the narrator and Mrs. Williams notice a celebration taking place on a beach not far from their anchored yacht, they decide to row ashore to investigate. Dozens of Turks greet them, offering tea and hashish, and they invite them to join their "very special family celebration" (209). After a time, the patriarch of the family (none of whom speak English) communicates his desire to come aboard the yacht, and soon the entire family wants to go. Once onboard everyone gets high and dances to American music. The playful cultural exchange is only temporary, however. The Turks have left by the time the narrator wakes up the next morning. Like the Turkish porpoise that will not follow the ship into Aegean waters, the Turks have returned to their community. Capote juxtaposes this clan with the absence of family for the two Americans on the yacht. The narrator and Mrs. Williams never reference kin and merely cling to their newfound friendship during the trip. The man who has chartered the boat has experienced a family death that prevents him from participating in the cruise, and another guest, the politician and ambassador to the United Nations Adlai Stevenson, died just before the trip. As with the rest of *Answered Prayers,* Capote portrays elite, society life as isolated and alone in many respects. These wealthy individuals continually seek a community that falls short of what this Turkish family inherently possesses.

Some hints of Capote's narcissistic P. B. Jones, the narrator from *Answered Prayers,* can be seen in "Yachts and Things." The narrator expresses utter indifference to the idea of sightseeing and history: "one old rock is just another old rock" (209). He later mocks Mrs. Williams for exploring the Turkish interior: "It's lots better than stamping around in the heat sweating your nuts off looking at a lot of old rocks. . . . Of course, we must always be improving our minds"; and she responds, "You're such a hedonist. It's intolerable" (209). Although the narrator expresses "sorrow" over the death of Stevenson, his heart "sinks" only with the thought that the cruise might be cancelled (208). Nevertheless this version of the narrator comes across as far less calculating and conniving than the one depicted throughout the rest of the book.

The Jones of *Answered Prayers* is a hustler and a bisexual prostitute who tries to achieve fame as a writer by cultivating influential people to promote his career. By and large Jones's scathing portrait of the ultrawealthy reveals them to be miserable, unfaithful, and dishonest. They gossip ruthlessly and care little about the feelings of others. Capote intended *Answered Prayers* to be a Proustian portrait of elite American society in the 1960s, and he was particularly well suited to write it. Capote spent most of his adult life as the darling of café society, and he had been a confidant to some of the most prominent women in America. Recounting the stories he had learned in confidence as well as the pretensions of this social circle was one thing, but making it clear who he was writing about was another. When three chapters appeared in *Esquire* between 1975 and 1976, they caused a firestorm of controversy. Capote, for instance, brought renewed attention to the shooting death of William Woodward by his wife Ann (named Ann Hopkins in the novel). She claimed to police that she thought her husband was an intruder on the night she killed him with a rifle. Although she was subsequently acquitted of murder, Capote's chapter "La Côte Basque, 1965" essentially convicts her of the crime. It dredged up the case in gossip circles, and just days before its publication, Ann Woodward killed herself. As her mother-in-law later remarked, "Well, that's that. She shot my son, and Truman murdered her. So now I suppose we don't have to worry about that anymore" (quoted in Kashner 211).

The most shocking anecdote from *Answered Prayers* refers to William and Babe Paley, who were close friends with Capote. The narrator describes one of William's affairs with the heavy-set wife of New York's governor (most likely Nelson Rockefeller's second wife). After trying to have sex in the dark, he discovers that her menstrual blood has left a stain "the size of Brazil" on his sheets. Fearing that his wife would return within a matter of hours, he must clean the sheets, soaking them in hot bath water and scrubbing the stain with soap. Most of his wealthy friends, including Babe, ostracized Capote after that—a reaction that shocked and devastated him.

The emotional pain of these severed relationships exacerbated Capote's troubles with writing the manuscript. In addition to suffering from writer's block, he had been abusing alcohol and cocaine for years. He was increasingly unable to focus on his writing. In 1979 he did get enough control over his drinking to complete *Music for Chameleons*—a collection of short fiction, profiles of people such as Marilyn Monroe, personal reminiscences, and the novella "Handcarved Coffins." Capote declined steadily after that, however. On August 25, 1984, one month before his sixtieth birthday, he died of an overdose of painkillers.

NOTES

Chapter 1—Understanding Truman Capote

1. Her divorce from Arch became official on November 9, 1931, and on February 14, 1935, Lillie Mae's legal petition for complete custody was granted. "Joe [Capote] became a father, and at the age of ten Truman Streckfus Persons was renamed Truman Garcia Capote" (Clarke 38).

2. This was not Capote's first experience with sexual abuse. At Trinity School for boys, for example, one of the teachers would walk Truman home and stop at a movie theater. "They would sit in the privacy of the back row, and while the teacher fondled him, Truman would masturbate the teacher" (Clarke 44).

3. Clarke 63.

4. Clarke 158.

5. Reumann 21.

6. Reumann 97.

7. Clarke 363.

8. See "'Some Unheard-of Thing': Freaks, Families, and Coming of Age in Carson McCullers and Truman Capote."

9. See Hassan, "The Daydream and Nightmare of Narcissus."

10. See Garson's *Truman Capote: A Study of the Short Fiction.*

11. In the most basic sense, I am using the word "canon" to refer to literary works being actively taught in a university setting today.

12. Capote made these comments in reference to his 1958 plans to return to Moscow. He decided not to finish this second journalistic project because of fears that the people he profiled with pro-Western views might be punished.

Chapter 2—A Tree of Night and Other Stories

1. Clarke 74–77.

2. Capote described writing short fiction this way to Andrew Lyndon in a letter on May 15, 1950: "I'm so happy to be writing stories again—they are my great love" (Truman Capote Papers, New York Public Library, Box 23A, Folder 2, Letters to Andrew Lyndon, 1947–1952).

3. Kennedy 427.

4. It should be noted that inflation and stagnant wages made it difficult for many Americans to participate in this culture of spending. Massive strikes over working conditions, pay, and pension plans resulted. Toward the end of November 1945, for example, "225,000 auto workers at General Motors went on strike. Two months

later they were joined by 174,000 electrical workers, and then 800,000 steel workers. Within a year of V-J Day more than 5 million men and women walked off the job" (Chafe 93–94). The subsequent settlements between corporations and unions such as the United Auto Workers helped move the United States more fully into a consumer-based economy.

5. According to Richard Rhodes, "the most recent estimates place the number of deaths [at Hiroshima] up to the end of 1945 at 140,000. The dying continued; five-year deaths related to the bombing reached 200,000" (734). In Nagasaki 70,000 died by the end of 1945, "and 140,000 altogether across the next five years" (741–42).

6. Kennedy 779.

Chapter 3 — *Other Voices, Other Rooms*

1. The photograph was taken by Harold Halma. Even though Capote's editor, Robert Linscott, ultimately chose the photo, he did so with Capote's strong recommendation. Both men wanted to generate publicity for the book.

2. For additional analyses on these statistics, see Reumann 165–67.

3. Although human curiosities had been common attractions in taverns and public squares since the 1700s, these itinerant performers began appearing in dime museums in the nineteenth century. Here audiences could gaze at freaks alongside dioramas, menageries, stuffed animals, jugglers, historical wax tableaux, cabinets filled with curious objects, and other oddities. Live performers soon became central to the dime museum's appeal, and this form of entertainment reached its apex with P. T. Barnum's American Museum in 1841. Located in the heart of New York City near the Astor Hotel and Delmonico's Restaurant, Barnum's dazzling establishment became a fashionable public attraction. Due to the prominence he gave freak performers and the unprecedented scope of his promotional efforts, he helped make the freak show a national pastime.

4. Tom Thumb, born Charles Sherwood Stratton in 1838, was one of Barnum's most famous and financially successful exhibits. Barnum initially offered the impoverished Stratton family three dollars a week to display Charles at the American Museum. Soon afterward they toured throughout the United States and Europe. (In 1844, for example, Queen Victoria invited him to the palace twice.) Barnum advertised Tom Thumb as a twelve-year-old dwarf; though he exaggerated his age, Thumb was apparently twenty-five inches and fifteen pounds when Barnum first met him in 1842. He most likely had ateliotic dwarfism—"his diminutiveness resulted from a deficiency of the growth hormone that is normally produced by the pituitary gland" (Saxon 124).

5. Born in 1811 in Siam, Chang and Eng Bunker were joined together at birth "at the xiphoid [the lowest portion of the sternum] by a band of tissue just a few inches long" (Alexander 66). As Robert Bogdan explains, "Chang and Eng were the vanguard of joined twins. They were the first put on display in this country, and it is to them we can attribute the term *Siamese Twins*" (201). In fact Barnum first gave Chang and Eng the label "Siamese Twins," and this term has been synonymous with conjoined twins ever since. One night, at the age of sixty, Chang died in bed, and his brother, legend has it, died several hours later of "fright." In an article for the *North Carolina Medical Journal*, Dr. Eben Alexander Jr. argues that Chang and Eng actually died of exsanguination: "The vascular connection between the two may not have been

very large, but we know that Eng's heart was still beating after Chang's had stopped, and the connection was sufficient to let Eng's blood drain away over the two to four hours it took him to die. It seems clear: Eng died of blood loss" (67).

6. For more on the history of freak shows in American culture, see Robert Bogdan, *Freak Show: Presenting Human Oddities for Amusement and Profit*; Rosemarie Garland Thomson, *Extraordinary Bodies: Figuring Physical Disability in American Culture and Literature* and the essay collection *Freakery: Cultural Spectacles of the Extraordinary Body*; Rachel Adams, *Sideshow U.S.A.: Freaks and the American Cultural Imagination*; Leslie Fiedler, *Freaks: Myths and Images of the Secret Self*; Daniel Mannix, *Freaks: We Who Are Not As Others*; and Frederick Drimmer, *Very Special People: The Struggles, Loves and Triumphs of Human Oddities*.

7. Bogdan 224–29.

8. Bogdan explains in *Freak Show* that African Americans with this condition were often "cast as 'missing links' or as atavistic specimens of an extinct race" (112). Also see his section on William Henry Johnson (134–42).

9. Throughout his career Barnum also had to shift his "stories" about Joice Heth in response to shifting anxieties about race (see Benjamin Reiss, "P. T. Barnum, Joice Heth, and Antebellum Spectacles of Race"). To offer one early example, Bluford Adams's *E Pluribus Barnum: The Great Showman and the Making of U.S. Popular Culture* discusses the ways Barnum juxtaposed his racial freak exhibits with some of the more controversial dramas appearing in his Lecture Room. The display of "What Is It?" between acts of Boucicault's *The Octoroon* essentially made this play "safe for even the most anti-abolitionist of patrons" (Bluford Adams 163).

10. For more on the decline of the freak show, see Bogdan; Rosemarie Garland Thomson, "Introduction" to *Freakery*; and Thomas Fahy, *Freak Shows and the Modern American Imagination*.

11. Thomson, *Extraordinary Bodies*, 77–78.

12. For more on Capote's return to Monroeville, see Clarke 78–81.

13. The details of this rape—including Wilson's statement—are detailed in the first chapter of McGuire, *At the Dark End of the Street*.

14. The same was true in the aftermath of World War II, when the United States wanted to expand its sphere of influence during the Cold War. As Mary L. Dudziak argues in *Cold War Civil Rights: Race and the Image of American Democracy*, "In the years following World War II, racial discrimination in the United States received increasing attention from other countries. Newspapers throughout the world carried stories about discrimination against nonwhite visiting foreign dignitaries, as well as against American blacks. At a time when the United States hoped to reshape the postwar world in its own image, the international attention given to racial segregation was troublesome and embarrassing. The focus of American foreign policy was to promote democracy and to 'contain' communism, but the international focus on U.S. racial problems meant that the image of American democracy was tarnished" (12).

15. The large migration of African Americans from rural to urban spaces in the South made it much easier for the African American community to get news about issues and to rally around them. According to Stephan Thernstrom and Abigail Thernstrom in *America in Black and White: One Nation, Indivisible*, "the farm population of the South plunged 20 percent between 1940 and 1945, while the number of southern city-dwellers grew by almost 30 percent, a rate of urban growth unparalleled

elsewhere in the country in those years. . . . The tremendous growth of the black population in southern cities laid the foundation for the emergence of an aggressive civil
rights movement with an urban base in the postwar years" (77). Franklin Roosevelt's
1941 Executive Order to end discrimination in federal defense plants had a similar
rallying effect for African Americans. This order and the Fair Employment Practices
Committee it created resulted from pressure by A. Philip Randolph, president of
the Brotherhood of Sleep Car Porters. He scheduled a march on Washington, and
"the prospect of one hundred thousand Negroes in the streets of the capital rattled
Franklin Roosevelt" (Kennedy 767). Employment of blacks increased dramatically
as a result of Roosevelt's order: "The number of black workers in shipyards leaped
from 6,000 to 14,000, in aircraft from 0 to 5,000, in government service from 60,000
to 200,000. Overall, the number of Negroes employed in manufacturing grew from
500,000 to 1.2 million" (Chafe 18). It was difficult to enforce this Executive Order,
however, and racial tensions skyrocketed, leading to riots across the country. As the
historian William Chafe argues, "To many, the Detroit riots symbolized not only the
rawness of race relations in America, but also a new spirit of militancy and assertive-
ness among American blacks. War had provided a forge within which anger and
outrage, long suppressed, were seeking new expression. The searing contradiction
between the rhetoric of fighting for democracy and the reality of racism at home
galvanized black anger" (21). Last, the impressive record of African Americans in
military service inspired President Truman to desegregate the armed forces in 1948. As
Jacqueline Foertsch notes, "it was primarily the lobbying efforts and forthright reporting of NAACP executive secretary, Walter White, that inspired Truman to desegregate
United States armed forces. White's detailed and persuasive *A Rising Wind* (1945)
documented the frustrations of willing, well-trained black soldiers sent to Europe and
North Africa on combat missions, only to find themselves demoted to the status of
port battalions and quartermasters" (13).

    16. For more on the Great Migration of African Americans during the twentieth
century, see James Gregory, *The Southern Diaspora: How the Great Migrations
of Black and White Southerners Transformed America;* and Isabel Wilkerson, *The
Warmth of Other Suns: The Epic Story of America's Great Migration.*

Chapter 4 — *The Grass Harp*

    1. Anna Stabler possessed all of these qualities (Clarke 19).

    2. As he recalled in a 1957 interview with Pati Hill, "I have a passion for news-
papers . . . read all of the New York dailies every day, and the Sunday edition of
several foreign magazines too. The ones I don't buy I read standing at newsstands"
(26–27).

    3. When Truman arrived, his mother had remarried and changed her name to
Nina Capote (just as Lulamae would rename herself Holly Golightly in *Breakfast
at Tiffany's*). Her divorce from Arch became official on November 9, 1931, and on
February 14, 1935, Lillie Mae's legal petition for complete custody was granted. "Joe
became a father, and at the age of ten Truman Streckfus Persons was renamed Truman
Garcia Capote" (Clarke 38).

    4. Capote was working on *Summer Crossing* at the time, but he ultimately aban-
doned the text. The manuscript was discovered and published in 2004. As Robert
Emmet Long explains, "It emerged . . . with a collection of newly found Capote

material—letters, photographs, manuscripts—offered to Sotheby's for auction. With it came an account of how this trove of material became available that reads like fiction" (34).

5. Truman Capote Papers, New York Public Library, Box 23A, Folder 2, Letters to Andrew Lyndon, 1947–1952.

6. Letter dated December 15, 1950 (Truman Capote Papers, New York Public Library, Box 23A, Folder 2, Letters to Andrew Lyndon, 1947–1952).

7. Letter dated January 1951 (Truman Capote Papers, New York Public Library, Box 23A, Folder 2, Letters to Andrew Lyndon, 1947–1952).

8. For more on nuclear technology and weapons development in America and the Soviet Union at the time, see David Halberstam, *The Fifties*, 25–48.

9. McCarthy did not get married until 1953.

10. In 1947 the State Department published its security principles; this quotation comes from that document (qtd. in Johnson 21).

11. For more on this, see Johnson, *The Lavender Scare*, 20–23.

12. Terry 342–43.

13. Whittaker Chambers, a former member of the Communist Party, appeared before HUAC and testified that Alger Hiss, a former State Department official, was a Communist. The high-profile case included accusations that Hiss and Chambers shared an intimate relationship and that Chambers was acting like a jealous lover. Hiss was ultimately convicted of perjury and spent forty-four months in a federal prison. See Halberstam 11–16; and Johnson 32–33.

14. For more on this, see Johnson 79–87.

15. For a trenchant analysis of this document, see John D'Emilio, "The Homosexual Menace: The Politics of Sexuality in Cold War America."

16. In the context of the judge's playful romance with the girl, the subsequent revelations of romance by the other tree dwellers, and the fact that other labels such as "madness" would not offend him (he cheerfully refers to himself as a fool in a tree and falls in love with Dolly, whom the town considers "mad"), it seems clear that the judge overheard his sons saying that he was some kind of sexual deviant or "pervert" (to use the term typically applied to this at the time).

17. See Eve Kosofsky Sedgwick, *Between Men: English Literature and Male Homosocial Desire,* chap. 1, "Gender Asymmetry and Erotic Triangles."

18. Levitt helped transform the housing crisis of World War II into a booming industry, and nearly 1.7 million single family startups were built in 1950 alone. As Kenneth T. Jackson, *Crabgrass Frontier,* notes, "By 1950 the national suburban growth rate was ten times that of central cities, and in 1954 the editors of *Fortune* estimated that 9 million people had moved to the suburbs in the previous decade" (238).

19. Prior to these comments by Holly Golightly, she discusses her attraction to women: "And of course I am [a bit of a dyke myself]. Everyone is: a bit" (22).

20. As an effeminate gay man, Capote was acutely aware of the ways in which other people, particularly his mother, perceived him, and he could understand this desire among homosexuals and lesbians in contemporary America to pass as heterosexual.

21. Capote explicitly condemns this history disenfranchisement through white characters that reject racism, Judge Cool's criticism of antimiscegenation laws, and

Catherine's own sentiments about labor: "If you sweep a house, and tent its fires and fill its stove, and there is love in you all the years you are doing this, then you and that house are married, that house is yours" (31).

Chapter 5 — *The Muses Are Heard*

1. It appeared in the October 20 and 27 issues of the *New Yorker* in 1956, and Random House published it in book form at the end of the year.

2. The troupe subsequently performed in Moscow on January 10, 1956, which concluded their trip to the Soviet Union.

3. Interview in the *Paris Review*, http://www.theparisreview.org/interviews/4867/ the-art-of-fiction-no-17-truman-capote.

4. For more, see Clarke 292–95.

5. Capote made these comments in reference to his 1958 plans to return to Moscow. He decided not to finish this second journalistic project because of fears that the people he profiled with pro-Western views might be punished.

6. This is quoted in Salmond 434.

7. This term was used in the mid-1950s by Robert Patterson, the organizer of the first Citizens' Council. See Bacon 94.

8. Halberstam 540.

9. "Although this was a radical and unflinching challenge to the principle of white supremacy, the concrete changes the organizers of the boycott sought at the outset were remarkably modest. King spoke passionately of the need to obtain 'justice on the buses of this city,' but by 'justice' he did not mean an entirely segregated bus system. The principal demand of the boycotters at this point was only that Montgomery adopt the somewhat milder form of segregation that was used on the buses in Mobile, Alabama. In Mobile your race determined where you were allowed to sit when you first boarded, but no African American was required to move after having settled into a seat" (Thernstrom and Thernstrom 109–10).

Chapter 6 — *Breakfast at Tiffany's*

1. Even the series as a whole operates as an anti–*Breakfast at Tiffany's*. Nothing is elegant about the lives portrayed in *Seinfeld,* and lasting romantic love eludes the central characters.

2. Barthes's "The Face of Garbo" was published in his 1957 book *Mythologies.* At the end of the essay he compares Garbo's to Hepburn's: "Viewed as a transition the face of Garbo reconciles two iconographic ages, it assures the passage from awe to charm. As is well known, we are today at the other pole of this evolution: the face of Audrey Hepburn, for instance, is individualized, not only because of its peculiar thematics (woman as child, woman as kitten) but also because of her person, of an almost unique specification of the face, which has nothing of the essence left in it, but is constituted by an infinite complexity of morphological functions. As a language, Garbo's singularity was of the order of the concept, that of Audrey Hepburn is of the order of the substance. The face of Garbo is an Idea, that of Hepburn, an Event" (57) (trans. Annette Lavers [New York: Noonday Press. 1991]). Hepburn's role in *Breakfast at Tiffany's* four years after the publication of this essay radically changed her public image. She went from embodying innocence ("woman as child") to representing urbanity. The now iconic image of her staring into the window at Tiffany's

made Hepburn's face, body, and fashion an idea as well—an idea to which millions of women would aspire.

3. Altschuler 70.

4. Marilyn Monroe did not pose for the magazine per se. Hefner bought these images from a photographer named Tom Kelley, a friend of Monroe's. "In 1949 she agreed to do a nude shoot for a photographer friend named Tom Kelley. He paid only fifty dollars, but she was living hand to mouth and she owed him a favor—he had lent her five dollars on an earlier occasion for cab fare" (Halberstam 567).

5. *Stag* magazine filed an injunction against using the name *Stag Party.* "Shortly before *Stag Party* went to press, Hefner received a warning letter from the attorneys of *Stag* magazine compelling him to find another name. *Top Hat, Bachelor, Gent, Gentlemen, Satyr,* and *Pan* received brief consideration, until a friend remembered an automobile called 'Playboy,' a name Hefner found reminiscent of the 'Roaring Twenties.' In fact, it was also the name of a short-lived publication from that decade. With its F. Scott Fitzgerald connotations, Hefner decided it had the sound he wanted, and *Playboy* hit newsstands in November 1953" (Fraterrigo 20).

6. Fraterrigo 20.

7. Fraterrigo 25.

8. Halberstam 280.

9. Reumann 97.

10. Reumann 165–66.

11. Clarke 314.

12. Tison Pugh makes this argument in his notes about the novel: "Descriptions of Joe Bell's bar also subtly hint that it is a gay bar: its anonymity suggests that it is hidden from general view; the narrator remarks that it has no neon sign to attract attention to itself. Gay bars did not advertise themselves as such in the 1950s, and patrons had to learn about their locations through word of mouth. Furthermore, the narrator mentions that the windows of the bar are mirrors. Mirror windows allow patrons to see outside but do not allow passersby to look in; to this day many gay bars have such mirror windows to protect the privacy of their patrons. Though we see very few customers inside the bar besides Holly and the narrator, two men enter together when the narrator prepares to leave after conversing with Joe Bell" (53).

13. Most scholars consider Holly's name a play on the word "holiday"—which captures her carefree approach to living.

Chapter 7—*In Cold Blood*

1. For some examples of this critical debate, see Kazin; and Galloway.

2. See Nuttall.

3. See Christensen; and Hickman.

4. See Fahy "Hobbes"; and Voss.

5. See Doherty.

6. Fogelson 117–33.

7. Sugrue 46.

8. May 11.

9. This title comes from the Chuck Berry song "You Can't Catch Me" (1956).

10. Tom McCarthy 100.

11. It eventually grew to 42,500 miles of road (Jackson 249).

12. President Eisenhower also listed three other reasons for signing the act into law: "current highways were unsafe; cars too often became snarled in traffic jams; poor roads saddled business with high costs for transportation" (Jackson 249).

13. In regard to cost in the early 1950s, "many Americans rejected automobiles advertised as low-priced for fear of the public loss of face that ownership of such vehicles involved . . . After World War II consumers no longer got more for less. They got more for more" (Tom McCarthy 107).

14. As Erik Mortenson explains, "For the Beats, capturing true immediacy involves focusing attention on desire and action as they spontaneously respond to the material conditions of each passing moment. This attention allows the beats to establish an authentic connection to the world that forms the basis for a poetics of presence" (1).

15. As Jonah Raskin describes in *American Scream: Allen Ginsberg's* Howl *and the Making of the Beat Generation,* the poetry reading started at 8 P.M. with an intermission at 11 o'clock. Ginsberg read after the intermission. He "was in the bathroom, which faced the main room. Suddenly the door opened and there he was sitting nonchalantly on the toilet. After pulling up his trousers, he made his way to the stage and began to read Part I of *Howl* in a 'small and intensely lucid voice.' At that point, Part III did not exist at all, and Part II was only beginning to take shape" (Raskin 17–18).

16. Carr's lenient sentence can be understood as a reflection of homosexual persecution during the Cold War. As Raskin explains, "everyone in the know conspired to keep Carr's bisexuality a secret. He didn't discuss it with the police [and] neither did Kerouac, Burroughs, Ginsberg, or his girlfriend, Celine Young. Everyone insisted that Carr was an innocent, clean-cut kid who had been stalked by a predatory homosexual and that he had defended his own honor. The police bought the story and so did the press. . . . Ginsberg hovered in the wings, absorbed, taking notes. To his brother, Eugene, he wrote that Carr would probably serve less than two years. (In fact he was released in 1946.) Allen added emphatically that it was 'what I call getting away with murder!' To Ginsberg, the lesson seemed to be that if you concealed your homosexuality, anything was possible, even homicide" (53–54).

17. Viking actually published the fourth version of the manuscript in 1957. Kerouac's fifth (and final) version would later be published as *Visions of Cody.*

18. The clean-cut Autry, who wore cowboy garb and rode a horse named Champion, was a matinee idol of the 1930s, 1940s, and 1950s, and he was famous for crooning tunes such as "Tumbling Tumbleweed," "You Are My Sunshine," and "Back in the Saddle Again."

19. As Penny Vlagopoulos notes in "Rewriting America: Kerouac's Nation of 'Underground Monsters,'" "all blatant references to sexuality—especially homosexuality—were edited out of the 1957 edition. Sex acts are more explicit and egalitarian in the scroll" (61).

20. Raskin discusses this element of their relationship: "What Kerouac declined to describe in *On the Road*—despite his insistence on candor—was the homosexual relationship between Ginsberg and Cassady, and the sexual games they played, in which Ginsberg was the sex slave and Cassady the sex master. . . . Neal was also plain brutal. He inflicted cruel and unusual punishment—both physical and mental—on Ginsberg, though Allen was no simple victim. Servitude in bed would serve him well as a creative artist—or so he believed. Indeed, he turned the agony of their relationship into the ecstasy of art" (71–72).

21. This aspect of the poem prompted a U.S. Customs agent to seize 520 copies of the second edition of the poem on March 25, 1957, and though the San Francisco district attorney refused to prosecute Ginsberg and Ferlinghetti (who authorized its American publication through his bookstore and publishing house City Lights), the San Francisco police eventually arrested Ferlinghetti. The obscenity charges were later dismissed in the wake of a Supreme Court ruling that literature was not obscene if it held redeeming social value.

Chapter 8 — Three Stories, *Answered Prayers*, and Capote in the Twenty-First Century

1. See Clarke 260.
2. The narrator remarks that it was illegal to buy alcohol in the state at the time.

BIBLIOGRAPHY

BOOKS BY TRUMAN CAPOTE

Other Voices, Other Rooms. New York: Random House, 1948.
A Tree of Night and Other Stories. New York: Random House, 1949.
Local Color. New York: Random House, 1950.
The Grass Harp. New York: Random House, 1951.
The Muses Are Heard. New York: Random House, 1956.
Breakfast at Tiffany's and Three Stories. New York: Random House, 1958.
Observations (with Richard Avedon). New York: Simon and Schuster, 1959.
Selected Writings of Truman Capote. New York: Random House, 1963.
In Cold Blood: A True Account of a Multiple Murder and Its Consequences. New York: Random House, 1966.
A Christmas Memory. New York: Random House, 1966.
House of Flowers. New York: Random House, 1968.
A Thanksgiving Visitor. New York: Random House, 1968.
The Dogs Bark: Public People and Private Places. New York: Random House, 1973.
Music for Chameleons. New York: Random House, 1980.
One Christmas. New York: Random House, 1983.
Three by Truman Capote. New York: Random House, 1985.
Answered Prayers: The Unfinished Novel. New York: Random House, 1987.
A Capote Reader. New York: Random House, 1987.
The Complete Stories of Truman Capote. New York: Random House, 2004.
Too Brief a Treat: The Letters of Truman Capote. Ed. Gerald Clarke. New York: Random House, 2004.
Summer Crossing. New York: Random House, 2005.
Portraits and Observations: The Essays of Truman Capote. New York: Random House, 2007.
"Yachts and Things" (recently discovered excerpt from *Answered Prayers)*. *Vanity Fair* (December 2012): 208–9.

Secondary Sources

Adams, Bluford. *E Pluribus Barnum: The Great Showman and the Making of U.S. Popular Culture*. Minneapolis: University of Minnesota Press, 1997.
Adams, Rachel. *Sideshow U.S.A.: Freaks and the American Cultural Imagination*. Chicago: University of Chicago Press, 2001.
Alexander, Eben, Jr. "The Original Siamese Twins: We Know Why Chang Died, but Why Did Eng?" *North Carolina Medical Journal* 63.2 (March/April 2001): 66–68.
Allen, Brooke. "Capote Reconsidered." *New Criticism* 23.3 (2004): 10–16.

Allmendinger, Blake. "The Room Was Locked, with the Key on the Inside: Female Influence in Truman Capote's 'My Side of the Matter.'" *Studies in Short Fiction* 24.3 (1987): 275–88.

Altschuler, Glenn C. *All Shook Up: How Rock 'n' Roll Changed America*. New York: Oxford University Press, 2003.

Bacon, Jon Lance. *Flannery O'Connor and Cold War Culture*. New York: Cambridge University Press, 1993.

Barthes, Roland. *Mythologies*. 1957. Trans. Annette Lavers. New York: Noonday Press, 1991.

Baxandall, Rosalyn, and Elizabeth Ewen. *Picture Windows: How the Suburbs Happened*. New York: Basic Books, 2000.

Bibler, Michael P. "Making a Real Phony: Truman Capote's Queerly Southern Regionalism in Breakfast at Tiffany's: A Short Novel and Three Short Stories." In *Just Below South: Intercultural Performance in the Caribbean and the U.S. South*, ed. Jessica Adams, Michael P. Bibler, and Cécile Accilien, 211–38. Charlottesville: University of Virginia Press, 2007.

Bloom, Harold. "Editor's Note." In *Bloom's Modern Critical Views: Truman Capote, New Edition*, ed. Harold Bloom, vii. New York: Infobase, 2009.

———. "Introduction." In *Bloom's Modern Critical Views: Truman Capote, New Edition*, ed. Harold Bloom, 1–2. New York: Infobase, 2009.

Bogdan, Robert. *Freak Show: Presenting Human Oddities for Amusement and Profit*. Chicago: University of Chicago Press, 1988.

Breakfast at Tiffany's. Dir. Blake Edwards. Perf. Audrey Hepburn and George Peppard. Paramount Pictures, 1961.

Campbell, James. *This Is the Beat Generation: New York—San Francisco—Paris*. Berkeley: University of California Press, 1999.

Chafe, William H. *The Unfinished Journey: America since World War II*. 4th ed. New York: Oxford University Press, 1999.

Christensen, Peter G. "Capote as Gay American Author." In *The Critical Response to Truman Capote*, ed. Joseph J. Waldmeir and John C. Waldmeir, 61–67. Westport, Conn.: Greenwood, 1999.

———. "Major Works and Themes." In *The Critical Response to Truman Capote*, ed. Joseph J. Waldmeir and John C. Waldmeir, 221–29. Westport, Conn.: Greenwood, 1999.

Clarke, Gerald. *Capote: A Biography*. New York: Carroll and Graf, 1988.

Cloward, Richard, and Lloyd Ohlin. *Delinquency and Opportunity: A Theory of Delinquent Gangs*. New York: Free Press, 1960.

Cohen, Albert K. *Delinquent Boys: The Culture of the Gang*. New York: Free Press, 1955.

"The Couch." *Seinfeld*. NBC. October 27, 1994. Television.

Cunnell, Howard. "Fast This Time: Jack Kerouac and the Writing of On the Road." In *On the Road: The Original Scroll*, ed. Howard Cunnell, 1–52. New York: Penguin, 2007.

Daniel, Pete. *Lost Revolutions: The South in the 1950s*. Chapel Hill: University of North Carolina Press, 2000.

De Bellis, Jack. "Visions and Revisions: Truman Capote's In Cold Blood." *Journal of Modern Literature* 7.3 (September 1979): 519–37.

D'Emilio, John. "The Homosexual Menace: The Politics of Sexuality in Cold War America." In *Making Trouble: Essays on Gay History, Politics, and the University,* ed. John D'Emilio, 57–73. New York: Routledge, 1992.

Doherty, Thomas. *Cold War, Cool Medium: Television, McCarthyism, and American Culture.* New York: Columbia University Press, 2003.

Drimmer, Frederick. *Very Special People: The Struggles, Loves and Triumphs of Human Oddities.* New York: Bantam, 1973.

Dudziak, Mary L. *Cold War Civil Rights: Race and the Image of American Democracy.* Princeton, N.J.: Princeton University Press, 2000.

Eagleton, Terry. *Literary Theory: An Introduction.* 3rd ed. Minneapolis: University of Minnesota Press, 2008.

"Employment of Homosexuals and Other Sex Perverts in Government" (1950). Repr. in *We Are Everywhere: A Historical Sourcebook of Gay and Lesbian Politics,* ed. Mark Blasius and Shane Phelan. 241–51. New York: Routledge, 1997.

Fahy, Thomas. *Freak Shows and the Modern American Imagination: Constructing the Damaged Body from Willa Cather to Truman Capote.* New York: Palgrave Macmillan, 2006.

———. "Hobbes, Human Nature, and the Culture of American Violence in Truman Capote's *In Cold Blood.*" In *The Philosophy of Horror,* ed. Thomas Fahy, 57–71. Lexington: University Press of Kentucky, 2010.

———. "'Some Unheard-of Thing': Freaks, Families, and Coming of Age in Carson McCullers and Truman Capote." Reprint. *Bloom's Modern Critical Views: Truman Capote, New Edition,* ed. Harold Bloom, 151–71. New York: Infobase, 2009.

Fiedler, Leslie. *Freaks: Myths and Images of the Secret Self.* New York: Simon and Schuster, 1978.

Foertsch, Jacqueline. *American Culture in the 1940s.* Edinburgh: Edinburgh University Press, 2008.

Fogelson, Robert M. *Bourgeois Nightmares: Suburbia, 1870–1930.* New Haven, Conn.: Yale University Press, 2005.

Fraterrigo, Elizabeth. *Playboy and the Making of the Good Life in Modern America.* New York: Oxford University Press, 2009.

Galloway, David. "Real Toads in Real Gardens: Reflections on the Art of Non-Fiction Fiction and the Legacy of Truman Capote." 1986. Repr. in *The Critical Response to Truman Capote,* ed. Joseph J. Waldmeir and John C. Waldmeir, 143–54. Westport, Conn.: Greenwood, 1999.

Garson, Helen S. "From Success to Failure: Capote's *The Grass Harp.*" *Southern Quarterly* 33.2–3 (1995): 35–43.

———. *Truman Capote: A Study of the Short Fiction.* New York: Twayne, 1992.

Gilbert, James. *A Cycle of Outrage: America's Reaction to the Juvenile Delinquent of the 1950s.* New York: Oxford University Press, 1986.

Ginsberg, Allen. *Howl and Other Poems.* 1956. San Francisco: City Lights, 2001.

Goddu, Teresa A. *Gothic America: Narrative, History, and Nation.* New York: Columbia University Press, 1997.

Goodman, Paul. *Growing Up Absurd: Problems of Youth in the Organized System.* New York: Random House, 1960.

Graebner, William S. *The Age of Doubt: American Thought and Culture in the 1940s.* Boston: Twayne, 1990.

Gregory, James N. *The Southern Diaspora: How the Great Migration of Black and White Southerners Transformed America.* Chapel Hill: University of North Carolina Press, 2007.

Halberstam, David. *The Fifties.* New York: Villard Books, 1993.

Harrington, Michael. *The Other America: Poverty in the United States.* 1962. Reprint. New York: Penguin, 1982.

Hartmann, Susan M. *American Women in the 1940s: The Home Front and Beyond.* Boston: Twayne, 1982.

Haslam, Jason. "'It Was My Dream That Screwed Up': The Relativity of Transcendence in *On the Road.*" *Canadian Review of American Studies* 39.4 (2009): 443–64.

Hassan, Ihab B. "The Daydream and Nightmare of Narcissus." 1960. Reprint. In *The Critical Response to Truman Capote,* ed. Joseph J. Waldmeir and John C. Waldmeir, 49–60. Westport, Conn.: Greenwood, 1999.

Hickman, Trenton. "'The Last to See Them Alive': Panopticism, the Supervisory Gaze, and Catharsis in Capote's *In Cold Blood.*" *Studies in the Novel* 37.4 (Winter 2005): 464–76.

Hill, Pati. "Truman Capote, the Art of Fiction No. 17." *Paris Review* 16 (Spring–Summer 1957). http://www.theparisreview.org/interviews/4867/the-art-of-fiction -no-17-truman-capote (15 July 2013)

Hunt, Tim. *Kerouac's Crooked Road: The Development of a Fiction.* 1981. Reprint. Carbondale: Southern Illinois University Press, 2010.

Inge, M. Thomas, ed. *Truman Capote: Conversations.* Jackson: University Press of Mississippi, 1987.

Jackson, Kenneth T. *Crabgrass Frontier: The Suburbanization of the United States.* New York: Oxford University Press, 1985.

Johnson, David K. *The Lavender Scare: The Cold War Persecution of Gays and Lesbians in the Federal Government.* Chicago: University of Chicago Press, 2004.

Jones, Landon Y. *Great Expectations: America and the Baby Boom Generation.* New York: Ballantine, 1980.

Kashner, Sam. "Capote's Swan Dive." *Vanity Fair.* Vol. 628 (December 2012): 200–214.

Kazin, Alfred. *Bright Book of Life: American Novelists and Storytellers from Hemingway to Mailer.* New York: Little, Brown, 1973.

Kellog, Carolyn. "Glendale School Board May Block 'In Cold Blood.'" *Los Angeles Times,* September 27, 2011. Web, September 3, 2012.

Kennedy, David M. *Freedom from Fear: The American People in Depression and War, 1929–1945.* New York: Oxford University Press, 1999.

Kerouac, Jack. *On the Road.* 1957. Reprint. New York: Penguin, 2003.

Knight, Brenda. *Women of the Beat Generation: The Writers, Artists, and Muses at the Heart of a Revolution.* Berkeley, Calif.: Conari, 1996.

Krämer, Peter. "The Many Faces of Holly Golightly: Truman Capote, *Breakfast at Tiffany's,* and Hollywood." *Film Studies: An International Review* 5 (Winter 2004): 58–65.

Levine, Paul. "Truman Capote: The Revelation of the Broken Image." 1958. Reprint. In *The Critical Response to Truman Capote,* ed. Joseph J. Waldmeir and John C. Waldmeir, 81–97. Westport, Conn.: Greenwood, 1990.

Long, Robert Emmet. *Truman Capote—Enfant Terrible*. New York: Continuum, 2008.

Lubin, David. *Shooting Kennedy: JFK and the Culture of Images*. Berkeley: University of California Press, 2003.

Malin, Irving. "From Gothic to Camp." 1964. Reprint. In *The Critical Response to Truman Capote*, ed. Joseph J. Waldmeir and John C. Waldmeir, 95–97. Westport, Conn.: Greenwood, 1999.

Mannix, Daniel P. *Freaks: We Who Are Not As Others*. 1976. Reprint. New York: Juno Books, 1999.

Marling, Karal Ann. *As Seen on TV: The Visual Culture of Everyday Life in the 1950s*. Cambridge, Mass.: Harvard University Press, 1994.

May, Elaine Tyler. *Homeward Bound: American Families in the Cold War Era*. 1988. Reprint. New York: Basic Books, 2008.

McAleer, John J. "*An American Tragedy* and *In Cold Blood:* Turning Case History into Art." 1972. Reprint. *The Critical Response to Truman Capote*, ed. Joseph J. Waldmeir and John C. Waldmeir, 205–19. Westport, Conn.: Greenwood, 1999.

McCarthy, Joseph. *McCarthyism: The Fight for America*. New York: Devin-Adair, 1952.

McCarthy, Tom. *Auto Mania: Cars, Consumers, and the Environment*. New Haven, Conn.: Yale University Press, 2007.

McGuire, Danielle L. *At the Dark End of the Street: Black Women, Rape, and Resistance—A New History of the Civil Rights Movement from Rosa Parks to the Rise of Black Power*. New York: Knopf, 2011.

Miller, Douglas T., and Marion Nowak. *The Fifties: The Way We Really Were*. New York: Doubleday, 1977.

Mitchell-Peters, Brian. "Camping the Gothic: Que(e)ring Sexuality in Truman Capote's *Other Voices, Other Rooms*." *Journal of Homosexuality* 39:1 (2000): 107–38.

Mortenson, Erik. *Capturing the Beat Moment: Cultural Politics and the Poetics of Presence*. Carbondale: Southern Illinois University Press, 2011.

Norden, Eric. "*Playboy* Interview: Truman Capote." 1968. Repr. in *Truman Capote: Conversations*, ed. M. Thomas Inge, 110–63. Jackson: University Press of Mississippi, 1987.

Nuttall, Nick. "Cold-Blooded Journalism: Truman Capote and the Non-Fiction Novel." In *The Journalistic Imagination: Literary Journalists from Defoe to Capote and Carter*, ed. Richard Keeble and Sharon Wheeler, 130–44. New York: Routledge, 2007.

O'Connor, Alice. *Poverty Knowledge: Social Science, Social Policy, and the Poor in Twentieth-Century U.S. History*. Princeton, N.J.: Princeton University Press, 2001.

Parsons, Talcott. "Psychoanalysis and the Social Structure." In *Essays in Sociological Theory*, rev. ed., 336–47. Glencoe, Ill.: Free Press, 1954.

Perry, J. Douglas, Jr. "Gothic as Vortex: The Form of Horror in Capote, Faulkner, and Styron." 1973. Repr. in *Bloom's Modern Critical Views: Truman Capote, New Edition*, ed. Harold Bloom, 43–56. New York: Infobase, 2009.

Plimpton, George. "The Story Behind a Nonfiction Novel." 1966. Repr. in *Truman Capote: Conversations*, ed. M. Thomas Inge, 47–68. Jackson: University Press of Mississippi, 1987.

Podhoretz, Norman. "The Know-Nothing Bohemians." 1958. Repr. in *Beat Down to Your Soul: What Was the Beat Generation?*, ed. Ann Charters, 479–93. New York: Penguin, 2001.

Pugh, Tison. "Capote's *Breakfast at Tiffany's*." *Explicator* 6.1 (Fall 2002): 51–53.

Raskin, Jonah. *American Scream: Allen Ginsberg's* Howl *and the Making of the Beat Generation*. Berkeley: University of California Press, 2006.

Reiss, Benjamin. "P. T. Barnum, Joice Heth, and Antebellum Spectacles of Race." *American Quarterly* 51.1 (March 1999): 78–107.

———. *The Showman and the Slave: Race, Death, and Memory in Barnum's America*. Cambridge, Mass.: Harvard University Press, 2001.

Reumann, Miriam G. *American Sexual Character: Sex, Gender, and National Identity in the Kinsey Reports*. Berkeley: University of California Press, 2005.

Reynolds, David S. *John Brown, Abolitionist: The Man Who Killed Slavery, Sparked the Civil War, and Seeded Civil Rights*. New York: Knopf, 2005.

Rhodes, Richard. *The Making of the Atomic Bomb*. New York: Simon and Schuster, 1986.

Richards, Gary. *Lovers and Beloveds: Sexual Otherness in Southern Fiction, 1936–1961*. Baton Rouge: Louisiana State University Press, 2005.

Salisbury, Harrison E. *The Shook-Up Generation*. New York: Harper and Row, 1958.

Salmond, John. A. "The Great Southern Commie Hunt: Aubrey Williams, the Southern Conference Educational Fund, and the Internal Security Subcommittee." *Southern Atlantic Quarterly* 77.4 (Autumn 1978): 433–52.

Saxon, A. H. *P. T. Barnum: The Legend and the Man*. New York: Columbia University Press, 1989.

Schryer, Stephen. *Fantasies of the New Class: Ideologies of Professionalism in Post–World War II American Fiction*. New York: Columbia University Press, 2011.

Schrynemakers, Ilse. "Truman Capote's *In Cold Blood* in the Atomic Age." In *Reading America: New Perspectives on the American Novel*, ed. Elizabeth Boyle and Anne-Marie Evans, 48–62. Cambridge: Cambridge Scholars, 2008.

Schultz, William Todd. *Tiny Terror: Why Truman Capote (Almost) Wrote* Answered Prayers. New York: Oxford University Press, 2011.

Sedgwick, Eve Kosofsky. *Between Men: English Literature and Male Homosocial Desire*. New York: Columbia University Press, 1985.

Shaw, Alexis. "*In Cold Blood* Approved by Glendale School Board." NBC, October 13, 2011. www.nbclosangeles.com, September 3, 2012.

Steinem, Gloria. "'Go Right Ahead and Ask Me Anything.' (And So She Did)." 1967. Repr. in *Truman Capote: Conversations*, 3 ed. M. Thomas Inge, 86–104. Jackson: University Press of Mississippi, 1987.

Sugrue, Thomas J. *The Origins of the Urban Crisis: Race and Inequality in Postwar Detroit*. Rev. ed. Princeton, N.J.: Princeton University Press, 2005.

Terry, Jennifer. *An American Obsession: Science, Medicine, and Homosexuality in Modern Society*. Chicago: University of Chicago Press, 1999.

Thernstrom, Stephan, and Abigail Thernstrom. *America in Black and White: One Nation, Indivisible*. New York: Simon and Schuster, 1997.

Thomson, Rosemarie Garland. *Extraordinary Bodies: Figuring Physical Disability in American Culture and Literature*. New York: Columbia University Press, 1997.

————. "Introduction: From Wonder to Error¾A Genealogy of Freak Discourse in Modernity." In *Freakery: Cultural Spectacles of the Extraordinary Body*, ed. Rosemarie Garland Thomson, 1–19. New York: New York University Press, 1996.

————, ed. *Freakery: Cultural Spectacles of the Extraordinary Body*. New York: New York University Press, 1996.

Tompkins, Phillip K. "In Cold Fact." 1966. Repr. in *Truman Capote's* In Cold Blood: *A Critical Handbook,* ed. Irving Malin, 44–58. Belmont, Calif.: Wadsworth, 1968.

Vlagopoulos, Penny. "Rewriting America: Kerouac's Nation of 'Underground Monsters.'" In *On the Road: The Original Scroll,* ed. Howard Cunnell, 53–68. New York: Penguin, 2007.

Voss, Ralph F. *Truman Capote and the Legacy of* In Cold Blood. Tuscaloosa: University of Alabama Press, 2011.

Wagner-Martin, Linda. *The Mid-Century American Novel 1935–1965: A Critical History.* New York: Twayne, 1997.

Wasson, Sam. *Fifth Avenue, 5 A.M.: Audrey Hepburn,* Breakfast at Tiffany's, *and the Dawn of the Modern Woman.* New York: Harper, 2010.

Watson, Steve. *The Birth of the Beat Generation: Visionaries, Rebels, and Hipsters, 1944–1960.* New York: Pantheon Books, 1995.

Wilkerson, Isabel. *The Warmth of Other Suns: The Epic Story of America's Great Migration.* New York: Random House, 2010.

Zacharias, Lee. "Living the American Dream: 'Children on Their Birthdays.'" *Studies in Short Fiction* 12 (1975): 343–50.

INDEX

9/11, 148
1920s, 1, 9, 47
1930s, 2, 9, 18, 61, 152, 164n18
1940s, 5, 9, 11–13, 15, 17–18, 20–21,
    23–30, 39, 41, 44–45, 47, 54, 66,
    75, 82, 93, 96–97, 99, 102–3, 105–6,
    109, 115, 117, 121, 124, 126–28,
    135–37, 149–50, 153, 157n4, 158n5,
    159n15, 164n18; and the climate
    of uncertainty, 17–18, 42; and
    fragmented individuals, 12, 17, 41;
    and labor unrest, 26, 157n4, 158n4;
    and the literature of the anti-dream,
    11; and loss of innocence, 25, 30;
    social anxieties during, 11–12, 29–30,
    39, 41; and unemployment, 19
1950s, 5, 7, 11–15, 19–20, 25, 62–69,
    70–76, 78–84, 93, 96–103, 108,
    112–18, 120–22, 124, 127–34, 136–
    37, 142, 148–50, 152, 154, 161n18,
    162n7, 163n5, 163n12, 164n18; and
    car production, 19, 128–31, 164n13;
    and home ownership, 19, 74, 117,
    161n18; and the literature of the anti-
    dream, 11; national recession during,
    129–30; and social anxieties, 11–12,
    25, 67–69, 114, 120
1960s, 2, 6–8, 10, 63, 96–98, 101–2,
    109, 113–14, 116–18, 124–25, 127–
    28, 130, 132–33, 138, 147, 149, 156

abandonment, 2, 7, 32, 38, 59, 63, 97,
    106–7, 111, 133, 136, 144–45, 147,
    151, 160n4
"Abbeville Affair," 53–54
Abbeville, Alabama, 53

abortion, 1, 3, 7, 100
abuse, 121, 127; emotional, 63;
    physical, 2–3, 41, 50, 53, 85; racial,
    58; sexual, 3, 52, 55, 58, 60, 142,
    157n1; spousal, 44, 57; verbal, 2–3,
    41, 50, 85
addiction, 3, 6, 8, 118, 136
adultery, 2, 7, 43, 72, 100–101
advertising, 33, 52, 100, 125, 129–30,
    148, 158n4, 163n12, 164n13
African American women, 2, 4, 13,
    31, 44, 52–54, 59, 76, 84; violence
    against, 13, 44–45, 52–60, 84
African Americans, 3, 6, 13, 41, 44–47,
    51–57, 59, 61, 64, 75, 78, 81, 83–85,
    90–92, 94, 126–28, 139, 148, 152,
    159n8, 159n14, 159n15, 160n15,
    162n9; as man-animals, 47, 52; as
    freakish, 44–47, 51, 159n9; soldiers,
    54, 122, 160n15; as "undesirable
    residents," 127
Alabama, 1, 4, 6, 13, 16–17, 29, 40,
    53–54, 61, 84, 123, 162n9. See also,
    Abeville; Monroeville; Montgomery
alcohol, 17, 28, 50, 77, 80, 89, 96, 103,
    105, 134–35, 142, 145, 150, 153,
    156, 165n2
alcoholism, 3, 6, 8, 66, 118, 136, 156
Alexander, Jason, 95
alienation, 4, 8, 37, 90
Alvarez, Pepe (*Other Voices, Other
    Rooms*), 44, 50
American Dream, 51, 116–17, 119–20,
    124–26, 140
American Tragedy, An, 113
American West, 24, 71, 88, 134, 138

America: culture, 7, 11–12, 14–15,
    18–19, 21, 25, 27, 31, 35–36, 38, 42,
    44, 51, 53, 55, 58–60, 68, 74–75, 77,
    82, 88, 91, 94, 96–104, 106, 108–11,
    122–23, 132, 144–45, 148–49,
    159n6; delinquent subculture, 12,
    14, 25, 120–22; economy, 18–20,
    35–37, 53–54, 64, 85, 92, 102, 106,
    116–18, 120–21, 125–27, 129, 131,
    146–48, 157n4, 158n4; government,
    8, 19, 25, 54, 58, 65–70, 74, 76–78,
    80–87, 117, 124, 128, 140, 156, 160;
    idealization of, 12, 15, 30–31, 33, 36,
    65, 124, 148, 152; lifestyle, 5–6, 12,
    18, 21, 29, 62, 114, 125, 130, 148;
    and outward appearances, 14, 35, 98,
    106–8; and popular culture, 30–31,
    36–37, 39–40, 95, 107, 137,
    159n9
Amos 'n' Andy, 83
Andrews, Lowell Lee, 122–23
Angela Lee (*Other Voices, Other
    Rooms*), 49, 55
Answered Prayers, 8–9, 15, 154–56;
    controversy, 156; reaction from
    wealthy friends, 8, 156
Appleseed ("Jug of Silver"), 34–36
art, 3–4, 14–15, 17, 25, 31, 37–39,
    49–50, 55, 64, 79–82, 90–94, 100,
    112, 125–26, 132–35, 137–39, 142,
    145, 164n20
Ashida, Hideo (*In Cold Blood*), 131
Ashida, Mrs. (*In Cold Blood*), 130
atomic age, 12–13, 17–18, 20, 26, 31,
    38, 93, 114–16; and bomb shelters,
    115; fear during, 20, 27, 115; and
    loss of innocence, 31
Atomic Energy Commission, 115
atomic weapons, 20, 25, 27, 31, 64–65,
    82, 115–16, 120, 129
Aunt Eunice ("My Side of the Matter"),
    40–41
"Aunt" Liza, 2
Aunt Olivia-Ann ("My Side of the
    Matter"), 40–41
automobile industry, 128–31
Autry, Gene, 138, 164n18

bachelor life, 98, 100–101
Ball, Lucille, 81
Barnes, Fred (*Breakfast at Tiffany's*), 97,
    99, 107–8, 110
Barnes, Lulamae (*Breakfast at Tiffany's*).
    See Golightly, Holly
Barnum, P.T., 1, 45, 47, 52, 158n3,
    158n4, 158n5, 159n9
bars, 89, 103, 135; gay, 105, 162n12
Barthes, Roland, 96, 162n2
bearded ladies, 45–46, 49, 58
Beat culture, 14–15, 132–39, 143–47,
    164n14, 164n15; criticisms of, 132–
    33; and the glamorization of poverty,
    15, 133, 137; writers, 134–35, 139
Beat the Devil, 5–6, 109
Bell, Joe (*Breakfast at Tiffany's*), 105,
    163n12
Bikini Atoll, 93
Bill (*In Cold Blood*), 145
Billy Bob ("Children on Their
    Birthdays"), 31
bisexuality, 37, 39, 144, 155, 161n19,
    164n16. *See also* female sexuality;
    heterosexuality; homosexuals; male
    sexuality; sexuality
Black and White Ball, 8
black comedy, 9–10, 29, 42
Blick, Roy, 67–68
Bloom, Harold, 8–9
Blue Express, 79, 88, 91–92
Bluebell ("My Side of the Matter"), 41
Bobbit, Lily Jane ("Children on Their
    Birthdays"), 29–30
bodies, 23–24, 28, 44–46, 48–49,
    51–52, 55, 57, 73, 89, 99, 105, 131,
    135–36, 152, 163n2
Bogart, Humphrey, 5, 9, 109
bogeyman, 11, 27–29, 40; representing
    war, 29
Bonaparte, Old ("House of Flowers"),
    150
Bonaparte, Royal ("House of Flowers"),
    150–51
Boncoeur, Remi (*On the Road*), 141,
    146
Brando, Marlon, 6

Brazil, 97, 107, 111, 156

Bread Loaf Writers' Conference, 16

Breakfast at Tiffany's (novella), 3–4, 6, 14–15, 75, 95–111, 149–51, 160n3, 162n1, 162n2; film adaptation, 7, 95–96, 99, 109–11, 149; superficial transformations in, 102, 106–8

"Breakfast at Tiffany's" (song), 96

Breen, Mrs. ("The Muses are Heard"), 93

Brest Litovsk, 80–81, 88

Brooklyn, New York, 5, 135, 154

Browder v. Gale, 84

Brown v. Board of Education, 84–85

Brown, Helen Gurley, 98, 101

Brown, John, 56

Brown, John (*Other Voices, Other Rooms*), 56

Brown, Keg (*Other Voices, Other Rooms*), 56–57

Buddy ("A Christmas Memory"), 152–53

Burroughs, William S., 134–36, 164n16

Buster, Mrs. (*The Grass Harp*), 77

Buster, Reverend (*The Grass Harp*), 70, 76–77

C, Mr. ("Children on Their Birthdays"), 30

Candle, Sheriff Junius (*The Grass Harp*), 62, 70, 75–77

capital punishment, 7–8, 56, 81, 113–14, 128, 142, 147

capitalism, 12, 35, 117, 147. *See also* consumerism

Capote (film), 9

Capote, Joe (stepfather), 3, 157n1, 160n3

Capote, Nina (mother), 1–4, 61, 63, 102, 157n1, 160n3, 161n20; affairs, 2

Capote, Truman: addiction, 8, 156; as apolitical, 63; calling to be a writer, 3; charm of, 5; on cultural differences, 13–14, 79–80, 82, 86, 88, 92–94, 155; and "daylight stories," 9–10, 42; death of, 8, 156; as a fiction writer, 4–6, 8–12, 16–17, 36, 41–42, 54,

80–81, 89, 104, 110, 113, 144, 150, 153, 156, 157n2, 161n4; flamboyance of, 5, 16; as a journalist, 5–7, 13, 54, 80–81, 90–91, 113–14, 157n12, 160n2, 162n5; and the literary canon, 8–9, 11, 15, 149, 157n11; living overseas, 5, 62; memorabilia, 154, 161n4; mother's disapproval of, 3, 6, 63, 161n20; neglect from parents, 2–3, 61; and "nocturnal stories," 9–10, 42; as a painter, 17; and self-promotion, 112–13; sexual abuse, 3, 157n2; and sexual politics, 10, 54; as a "southern writer," 10; as a student, 4; and writing for the stage, 6

Captain, the ("A Diamond Guitar"), 152

cars, 38, 53, 72, 76, 89, 100, 123, 126, 128–32, 136, 140, 142, 144–46, 163n5, 164n12, 164n13; accidents, 131–32; culture, 128, 130–31; negative impact of, 130–32; theft, 120. *See also* automobile industry

carnivals. *See* circus; freak shows

Carr, Lucien, 135–36, 164n16

Cassady, Neal, 136–37, 144, 164n20

Chaplin, Charlie, 4

childhood, 4, 6, 16, 23–27, 29–30, 32–37, 40, 45, 61–64, 69–70, 73, 85, 88, 93, 105, 111, 119, 121–23, 130, 135–36, 142, 144, 147, 152–53, 162n2; idealizations of, 25–26, 29, 32

"Children on Their Birthdays," 29–31, 34, 37; and devil imagery, 31; and performance, 30–31

"Christmas Memory, A," 2, 152–53

circus, 13, 25, 32–33, 37, 44–45, 47–49, 55. *See also* freak shows

civil rights, 56, 59, 65, 75, 78, 82–84, 90–91, 159n14; movement, 13, 52–54, 160n15

Clare, Myrtle (*In Cold Blood*), 115

Clarke, Gerald, 10, 61, 102, 112, 154

Cleaver, June, 102

Cleaver, Ward, 129

Cloud Hotel, 51, 56

Cloward, Richard, 120

Clutter, Bonnie (*In Cold Blood*), 112,
    125, 131
Clutter, Herb (*In Cold Blood*), 112,
    114, 116, 119, 123, 125, 130–31,
    144; as the embodiment of the self-
    made man, 125
Clutter, Kenyon (*In Cold Blood*), 112,
    130
Clutter, Nancy (*In Cold Blood*), 112–
    13, 119, 142–43
Coca-Cola, 125, 145
Cold War, 6–8, 12–14, 18, 25–27, 42,
    63–65, 67, 70, 78–94, 101, 104,
    114–15, 123, 126, 142–43, 148–49,
    152, 159n14, 161n15, 164n16; and
    cultural climate, 6, 8, 25, 63, 114,
    142; and disillusionment, 13, 65; fear
    during, 7, 20, 63–64, 76, 78, 81–84,
    86–87, 90–92, 114–15, 123, 143,
    152; propaganda, 12, 79, 86–90, 93
Columbia Pictures, 7
Columbia University, 135–36
Colvin, Claudette, 84
Communism: 12–14, 17, 27, 42–43,
    63–67, 74, 81–90, 99, 101, 114, 117,
    159n14, 161n13
community, 10, 18, 20, 30, 35, 49, 54,
    59, 62, 64, 72, 74, 84–85, 92–93,
    112–13, 123, 127, 135, 138–41, 143,
    145, 147, 151–52, 155, 159n15
conformity, 6, 13, 42, 46, 61, 65–66,
    68–69, 73–77, 107, 123, 133, 138,
    143, 145–46
consumerism, 14, 19–20, 26, 28, 30,
    34–36, 40, 42, 100, 107, 116, 125,
    128–31, 138, 140, 143–48, 157n4,
    158n4, 164n13; and the anxiety of
    choice, 19–20
consumption, 7, 19, 95, 98, 101, 121,
    126
contraception, 98, 102
Cool, Judge Charlie (*The Grass Harp*),
    62, 69–70, 72, 74, 76–77, 161n16,
    161n21
Costanza, George, 95–96
County, Mrs. (*The Grass Harp*), 75–76
Creek, Catherine (*The Grass Harp*), 2,
    61–62, 75, 77, 162n21

crime, 14–15, 22–23, 25, 54, 56, 66,
    68, 70, 73, 77, 112–14, 116, 118–24,
    126, 130–33, 135–46, 148, 154,
    156
Cronkite, Walter, 115

D.J. (Headless Hawk"), 37–40; as a
    doppelganger, 39
death, 8, 10, 20, 22–25, 27–30, 40, 43,
    56, 62, 76–77, 93, 97, 108, 116, 119,
    121–22, 131, 136, 139, 143, 147,
    155–56, 158n5; fear of, 20, 22, 24,
    28. *See also* murder
Deep Blue Something, 96
Destronelli, Mr. ("Headless Hawk"),
    37, 40
Dewey, Alvin (*In Cold Blood*), 113–14,
    116
"Diamond Guitar, A" 150–52
discrimination. *See* racism
Dolores (*Other Voices, Other Rooms*),
    50
domesticity, 14, 21, 70, 97–98, 101–2,
    107, 111, 151
dreams, 1–3, 11, 13, 26–27, 31–32, 35,
    39, 45, 54, 57, 71, 73, 126–28; *See
    also* American Dream
Dreiser, Theodore, 113
dropsy cure, 2, 61–62
drug: addiction, 8, 136, 156; dealer, 97,
    134; use, 133–36, 139, 155
"Duke and His Domain, The," 6
Dunphy, Jack, 5
Durkheim, Emile, 120

East Berlin, Germany, 79, 87–88
Edwards, Blake, 110
effeminacy, 2–3, 34, 44, 49, 71, 110,
    161n20
Eisenhower, President Dwight D., 85,
    114, 129, 164n12
equality, 12, 25, 36, 45, 57, 78, 81,
    83–85, 90, 101, 118, 148–49
Esquire, 8, 100, 113, 156
Estelle ("Master Misery"), 24
Europe, 5, 19, 63, 76, 158n4, 160n15
Everyman Opera Company, 6, 13,
    79–80, 86, 89–94

Falls, Heather (*The Grass Harp*), 69
Father Knows Best, 7
fatherhood, 6–7, 30–33, 39, 41, 43–44,
    48, 51, 69, 71, 105, 118–19, 121,
    125–27, 132–33, 136, 138, 144, 154,
    157n1, 160n3. *See also* motherhood;
    parenthood
Faubus, Orval, 85
Faulk, Callie, 2, 6, 61, 152
Faulk, Jennie, 2, 6, 61, 152
Faulk, Lillie Mae. *See* Capote, Nina
    (mother)
Faulk, Sook, 2, 6, 61, 152
Faulkner, William, 11
fear, 2–3, 5, 7, 12–14, 17–24, 26–29,
    31, 33–34, 39–42, 49, 56, 61, 63–64,
    68, 71, 74, 76–78, 81–82, 86–94,
    98, 105, 114–15, 120, 122–24, 135,
    143, 148, 152, 156, 157n12, 158n5,
    162n5, 164n13
Federal Bureau of Investigation (FBI),
    68, 83, 114, 120
Federal Civil Defense Administration
    (FCDA), 115
Federal Housing Authority, 127
female autonomy, 7, 14, 24, 95–98,
    101, 103–4, 106–8, 150–51
female sexuality, 6–7, 14, 24–26,
    70, 73, 97, 98–103, 109–11,
    143–44, 150. *See also* bisexuality;
    heterosexuality; homosexuals; male
    sexuality; sexuality
Fenwick, Collin (*The Grass Harp*), 6,
    61–62, 68–76
Feo, Tico ("A Diamond Guitar"),
    151–52
Ferlinghetti, Lawrence, 134, 165n21
Fever, Jesus (*Other Voices, Other
    Rooms*), 48, 51, 54
Fever, Missouri "Zoo" (*Other Voices,
    Other Rooms*), 13, 44–45, 49, 52–60
financial: hardships, 110; independence,
    101; resources, 100; responsibility, 2,
    66, 153; security, 14, 98, 131, 142;
    success, 100, 138, 158; support, 85;
    value, 35
Fitzgerald, F. Scott, 96, 163n5
Ford, 129–30, 142

Foucault, Michel, 113
freak shows, 12–13, 32–33, 44–47, 49,
    51–52, 58–59, 158n3, 158n4, 159n6,
    159n9, 159n10
freaks, 12–13, 28–29, 32, 37, 44–49,
    51–52, 58–59, 71, 153, 157n8,
    158n3, 158n4, 158n5, 159n6, 159n8,
    159n9, 159n10; and medical science,
    32, 52
"Fred" (*Breakfast at Tiffany's*), 95–97,
    103, 105, 107–8, 163n12
Frost, Robert, 16
Fuchs, Klaus, 82

Garbo, Greta, 96, 104, 162n2
Garson, Helen S., 10–11, 23, 73
gender, 10, 12, 33, 42, 44, 46, 48–49,
    51, 58–59, 73, 77, 91, 95, 101, 111
General Motors, 26, 129, 157n4
Gershwin, George, 13, 79, 94
Gershwin, Ira, 86–88, 91–92
Gillespie, Dizzy , 93
Ginsberg, Allen, 132, 134–36, 138–39,
    144, 164n15, 164n16, 164n20,
    165n21
Golightly, Doc (*Breakfast at Tiffany's*),
    107, 111
Golightly, Holly (*Breakfast at Tiffany's*),
    3–4, 6–7, 11, 14, 75, 95–99, 102–11,
    150–51, 160n3, 161n19, 163n12,
    163n13; as the biblical Eve, 103;
    as an escort, 97, 108, 110; as a
    gold digger, 7; inspiration for, 102;
    phoniness of, 14, 98; and profanity, 7
Gordon ("Headless Hawk), 38–39
gossip, 13–14, 32–33, 40, 69–72, 75,
    82, 86–87, 123, 150–52, 156; types,
    69, 71
gothic fiction, 9, 11, 29, 113; in
    America, 11
Grass Harp, The, 2–3, 6, 11, 13, 61–78,
    104, 150–52, 154; and guns, 77–78;
    and the private world, 75, 78; and
    self-discovery, 61, 74; as a theatrical
    adaptation, 6; and the tree house, 3,
    11, 61–62, 64, 69–70, 73–78, 104,
    161n16
Great Depression, 18, 20, 26

Great Gatsby, The, 96
Great Pasha, the, 1–2
Greenwich, Connecticut, 3–4, 123

Haiti, 150
Hall, Martha Lovejoy ("Headless Hawk"), 40
Hamurabi, Mr. ("Jug of Silver"), 34–36, 75
"Handcarved Coffins," 156
Harper's Bazaar, 4, 7, 17, 37, 109
Harper's Ferry Raid, 56
Hawthorne, Nathaniel, 11
"Headless Hawk," 17, 37–39
hedonism, 100, 136, 155
Hefner, Hue, 98–102, 136, 163n4, 163n5
Helvick, James, 109
Henderson, Riley (*The Grass Harp*), 62, 69, 72–78
Hepburn, Audrey, 7, 96, 99, 109–11, 162n2, 163n2
hermaphrodites, 45–46, 58, 71
heterosexuality, 14, 46–48, 50–51, 58–60, 68, 72, 74–75, 96, 104, 109–11, 142–44, 161n20
Hickok, Dick (*In Cold Blood*), 14–15, 112, 114, 116, 118–19, 122–23, 126–27, 130–34, 137–45, 147, 154; car crash, 131–32; deformity, 132; effect of poverty on, 118, 127, 131, 133
Hickok, Walter, Sr. (*In Cold Blood*), 126, 132
hierarchy: class, 35, 51, 107, 121, 141; economic, 53, 102, 106, 116; gender, 21, 42, 111; patriarchal; 20, 41; racial, 44, 47, 55–57, 68, 126, 152; sexual, 41; social, 54–56, 77, 102, 116, 141
Hiroshima, 20, 31, 158n5
Hiss, Alger, 13, 43, 65–66, 81–82, 161n13
Hitler, Adolf, 18, 40
Hoey, Senator Clyde, 67
Holcomb, Kansas, 7, 112–13, 115–16, 119, 123, 125, 128, 130, 140
Hollywood, 5, 25, 30–31, 36, 64, 66, 82, 96, 106–7, 110, 125, 139

Holocaust, 20, 23, 25
homophobia, 3, 5–6, 12–13, 33, 44–45, 48, 50, 59–60, 65–68, 70–73, 76, 78, 104–5, 110, 144, 151–52, 164n16
homosexuality, 3, 5–6, 10, 13–14, 32–33, 43–45, 47–51, 59–60, 63–68, 70–78, 97, 99–101, 104–6, 108, 110–11, 135, 138, 141–44, 151–52, 161n13, 161n20, 163n12, 164n16, 164n19; as freakish, 44–45, 47, 49, 51, 59, 71; and orgasm, 5, 43, 67, 100; as a threat to traditional American values, 68, 143
Honey, Sister Ida (*The Grass Harp*), 70, 72–73
Hopkins, Ann (*Answered Prayers*), 156
horror, 11, 18, 22–23, 25, 28–29, 113, 124
Hotel Astoria, 80, 87, 93
"House of Flowers," 6, 150
House Un-American Activities Committee (HUAC), 43, 65–66, 81–82, 114, 161n13
Howl, 132, 134, 136, 139, 144–45, 164n15, 165n21
Huncke, Herbert, 134
Huston, John, 5, 109

identity, 6–7, 12–13, 17, 30, 36, 41, 46, 48, 50, 63, 65, 71, 73–74, 97–98, 101, 103–4, 106–8, 125, 127–28, 137, 140
In Cold Blood, 6–9, 11, 15, 80–81, 112–48, 154; controversy, 147–48; and factual accuracy, 113–14; and canonical status, 8–9; and Clutter murders, 11, 14, 112–20, 122, 124–26, 128, 131–32, 134, 142, 144, 148, 154; as a "non-fiction novel," 7, 112–13, 138
individuality, 12, 17–20, 22, 26–27, 30, 33, 38, 40, 42, 46, 55, 65, 67, 74, 82, 108, 114, 121, 139–40, 145–46, 149, 155, 162n2
Infamous, 9
Innocents, The, 6
integration, 6, 83, 85, 90–92. *See also* segregation

Iron Curtain, 80
Irving ("Shut a Final Door"), 32, 34
Irving, Washington, 11
isolationism, 2, 12, 17–19, 21–24,
	26–33, 37–41, 44, 47, 50, 55, 59, 75,
	104, 112, 117, 134, 138, 149, 151,
	153, 155

Jackson, Earl Bruce (*The Muses are
	Heard*), 92
jail, 30, 54–56, 64, 70, 76–77, 97,
	107–8, 114, 118, 121, 136, 142, 145,
	151–52, 164n16. *See also* Sing Sing
Japan, 18, 20, 31
Jazz Age, 5, 62, 100
jazz, 4–5, 17, 62, 92–93, 100, 134,
	138–39
Jesus, 31, 70, 89
Jim Crow laws, 53–54
Johnny (*In Cold Blood*), 145
Johnson, Barbara (*In Cold Blood*), 145
Jones, Mr. Haha ("A Christmas
	Memory"), 153
Jones, P.B. (*Answered Prayers*), 155–56
Journalism, 5–7, 13, 54, 67, 80–81, 87,
	91, 113–14, 157n12, 162n5
"Jug of Silver," 17, 34–37; and the
	destruction of false hope, 36; and
	snow imagery; 34
juvenile delinquency, 14, 25, 116, 120–
	24, 132–33, 135–38, 146, 148–49;
	fear of, 120; parents role in, 121;
	types of, 120–21

Kammerer, David, 135–36, 164n16
Kansas Bureau of Investigation, 113,
	154
Kay ("A Tree of Night"), 27–29
Kazin Cathedral, 89
Kefauver Committee on Juvenile
	Delinquency, 120
Kendall, Ellen (*Other Voices, Other
	Rooms*), 43, 50–51
Kennedy, Jacqueline, 8–9
Kennedy, President John F., 117
Kerouac, Jack, 15, 132–37, 139, 141,
	145–47, 164n16, 164n17, 164n19,
	164n20

King, Martin Luther, Jr., 84–85, 162n9
Kinsey, Alfred, 5, 7, 13, 43, 65, 67–68,
	98–100, 102, 104
Knox, Joel Harrison (*Other Voices,
	Other Rooms*), 5, 12–13, 43–44,
	47–52, 54–56, 58–60, 73
Korean War, 63–64, 114
Ku Klux Klan, 3, 84

"La Côte Basque, 1965," 156
Lardner, Ring, Jr., 66
Las Vegas, Nevada, 128, 138, 142
Latham, James Douglas, 122–23
Lavender Scare, 65, 67, 151–52
Law and Order, 148
Lazarus ("A Tree of Night"), 28
Leave It to Beaver, 7, 129
Lee, Nelle Harper, 2–3, 7, 61, 130
Lee, Old Bull (*On the Road*), 141
Legrand, Amos (*The Grass Harp*),
	71–72
Leningrad, 20, 79–80, 87, 89
Levitt, William J., 74, 124–27, 161n18
Levittown, New York, 74, 124–27
Lilly, Doris, 102
literary criticism: 15, 54, 149;
	biographical, 9; New Critical, 9–10,
	149
Little Rock, Arkansas, 85
Little Sunshine (*Other Voices, Other
	Rooms*), 48, 51
Local Color, 5, 150
loneliness, 4, 23, 71, 117, 138, 151
Long Island, New York, 74, 127
Long, Robert Emmet, 10, 160n4
Los Angeles, California, 106, 139, 141
Lyndon, Andrew, 63, 157n2
Lyons, Leonard (*The Muses are Heard*),
	87–88, 93

Mademoiselle, 4, 17, 152
male sexuality, 5, 13, 25, 31, 65,
	99–100, 143. *See also* bisexuality;
	female sexuality; heterosexuality;
	homosexuals; sexuality
Manzer, Clyde (*Summer Crossing*), 4,
	154
Marcus, Carol, 4, 102

Margaret ("Shut a Final Door"), 32–34

Marge ("My Side of the Story"), 40–41

marginalization, 10, 12, 20, 35–36, 45, 47, 51, 59, 70, 73, 78, 104, 121, 127–28, 131, 141, 144, 149

marriage, 1, 3, 14, 24, 40, 45, 50–51, 62, 68, 70–71, 74–76, 80, 92, 97–103, 105–8, 110–12, 126, 130, 134, 142–44, 150–51, 162n21; gay, 97, 104, 106, 108, 110

Marshall, Ed ("Jug of Silver"), 34–36

Marx, Carlo (On the Road), 138, 141, 144

Marylou (On the Road), 141

masculinity, 5, 34, 40–41, 44, 48, 53, 121, 142–43; threats to, 33–34, 40–41

"Master Misery," 24–27, 29–31

materialism, 6, 14, 61, 73–74, 98, 101, 107

McCarthy, Joseph R., 64–67, 81–82, 161n9

McCarthyism, 6, 14, 63–67, 69–70, 76, 81–88, 114–15

McCullers, Carson, 4–5, 9, 11, 42, 149, 157n8

McDonald, Susie, 84

McNeil, Grady (Summer Crossing), 4, 17, 153–54

McPherson, Rufus ("Jug of Silver"), 35

media, 4–5, 13, 21–22, 26, 35, 38–39, 53–54, 60, 62–64, 66–67, 82–83, 85, 88, 90, 97, 100, 105, 107, 114–16, 120, 131, 142, 144, 148, 152, 159n14, 159n15, 160n2, 163n5

Mexico, 119, 130–31, 133, 136, 140, 144

Middy ("Jug of Silver"), 36

Miller, H.T Mrs. ("Miriam"), 21–24, 26, 28, 32, 37, 40; appearance, 21–22; madness of, 23

"Miriam," 4, 17, 21–24, 26, 28–29, 32, 37, 40, 42; and the doorbell, 22; and snow imagery, 23–24

Miriam ("Miriam"), 22–24, 32, 40; appearance, 22; mother of, 22–23; physicality of, 24

miscarriage, 97, 102, 108, 110–11

miscegenation, 76, 83, 161n21

misogyny, 33–34, 40, 73

monogamy, 96, 109

Monroe, Marilyn, 7, 9, 98–99, 109, 111, 118, 156, 163n4

Monroeville, Alabama, 1–4, 6, 13, 16–17, 53, 123, 159n12

Montgomery, Alabama, 53–54, 84–85, 91; bus system of, 84, 162n9

morality, 18–19, 22–23, 25–26, 31, 35, 50, 52, 65–67, 74, 76–77, 96–97, 99, 101, 108–10, 125, 137, 150

Moriarty, Dean (On the Road), 136–41, 143–47

motherhood, 1–3, 6, 22–23, 27, 29, 43–44, 49, 52–53, 69–70, 75, 101–3, 107–8, 121, 154, 156, 160n3, 161n20. See also fatherhood; parenthood

movement, 3–4, 14–15, 23–24, 29, 42, 54–55, 84, 106, 108, 113, 115, 117–19, 121, 126–27, 129–31, 133–34, 137–45, 147, 150, 161n18, 162n9

murder, 7, 11, 14–15, 35, 40, 50, 112, 113–20, 122, 125–26, 132, 134–36, 139–40, 142, 144, 154, 156, 164n16

Murphy, Maudie Laura (The Grass Harp), 71

Muses Are Heard, The, 6, 11, 14, 79–94, 152; and cannons, 79, 86, 92, 94; fictionalized elements in, 81; and human nature, 81; part I of, 79, 86, 94; part II of, 80; and Ski-Glasses, 87–89

Music for Chameleons, 8, 15, 156

"My Side of the Matter," 17, 40–41

myth, 11, 14–15, 27, 29–30, 33–34, 36–37, 82, 86–87, 92; of American prosperity, 15, 36, 114, 116, 119–20, 124, 126, 138, 140

NAACP, 53–54, 84, 160n15

National Defense Highway Act, 128–29, 163n11, 164n12

National Geographic, 52

Native Americans, 127

neglect. See abandonment

New Criticism, The, 9

New Journalism, 113
Noon City, 54, 59
North, the, 34, 54–57
Nye, Harold (*In Cold Blood*), 154
Nuclear family, 51, 68, 74, 101, 104, 143
nostalgia, 6, 12–13, 18, 25–27, 29–30, 32–34, 36, 61–65, 68–69, 73, 78, 96, 123, 149–50, 152–53
New Yorker, 4, 6–7, 16, 79, 113, 162n1
New Orleans, Louisiana, 1, 5, 17, 31–32, 76
New York City, 1–5, 8, 17, 24, 32, 62–63, 94, 96–98, 102, 108–9, 124, 135, 137, 144, 154, 156, 158n3, 160n2; as a "diamond iceberg," 5; nightlife of, 4, 96, 102, 108, 135
Nagasaki, 20, 31, 158n5
New York Times, 5, 7, 22, 39, 43, 112, 134–35

Ohlin, Lloyd, 120
Olathe, Kansas, 126
O'Connor, Flannery, 9, 11, 42, 149
O. Henry Award, 17, 31
O'Neill, Eugene, 4, 102
O'Neill, Oona, 4, 102
"Operation Castle," 115
Oreilly ("Master Misery"), 26–28
Orlov, Stefan (*The Muses are Heard*), 89, 94
On the Road, 14–15, 132, 134, 136–47, 164n19, 164n20; and "IT," 139, 141; and the police, 146
Other, the, 24, 46, 82, 88, 127
Other Voices, Other Rooms, 3–6, 10–13, 17, 43–60, 73, 75, 104, 110, 151–52; critics reaction to, 5, 43; and the jacket photograph, 5, 43, 158n1; and the slave bell, 55–56; and snow imagery, 54, 57
Ottilie ("House of Flowers"), 150–51
"Our Gal Sunday," 105

Paley, Babe (*Answered Prayers*), 156
Paley, William (*Answered Prayers*), 156
panopticism, 113
Paradise, Sal (*On the Road*), 137–47; relationship with aunt, 146

Paramount Pictures, 109, 111
parenthood, 1–3, 74, 99–101, 148, 154. *See also* fatherhood; motherhood
Parker, Sarah Jessica, 96
Parks, Rosa, 53–54, 84–85, 91
Parsons, Talcott, 121
patriarchy, 20–21, 34, 41, 53, 103, 108, 151, 155
patriotism, 20, 30–31, 38, 66, 74, 90
Peacock at the Hermitage, 92–93
Pearl Harbor, 18, 23
pedophilia, 50, 69–70, 122, 161n16
Peppard, George, 95
Persons, Arch (father), 1–2, 157n1, 160n3
Peurifoy, John, 66–68
Pierce, Phoebe, 4, 102
Playboy, 7, 98–102, 136, 163n4, 163n5
Plaza Hotel, 8
Plessy, Homer, 91
Poe, Edgar Allen, 11
politics, 6, 9, 10, 11–12, 14, 18–19, 31, 38, 54, 56, 61–64, 66–67, 72, 76, 78, 81–86, 90–94, 97, 101, 117, 120, 126, 149, 153, 155; democracy, 54, 58, 78, 82, 143, 159n14, 160n15; geopolitics; 18, 33; global politics; 18; political conformity, 66; political corruption, 120; political isolationism; 18; racial politics, 81, 90–91; sexual politics, 10, 54; sociopolitical issues, 9, 12, 59, 109; southern politics, 84
popular entertainment, 39–40, 44, 47, 51, 58, 86, 95–96, 109, 128, 158n3
Porgy and Bess, 6, 13, 79–81, 90–92, 94
poverty, 7, 12, 14–15, 36, 90, 107–8, 114, 116–21, 124–27, 133, 137, 148–49
pregnancy, 1, 3, 40–41, 70, 97, 108, 110–11
premarital sex, 7, 98, 100–101
Presley, Elvis, 98, 129
propaganda, 11–12, 14, 20, 22, 79, 82, 86–90, 92, 94. *See also;* myths
prostitution, 53, 110, 118, 122, 144–45, 150–51, 155
psychiatry, 3, 37, 40, 68, 136, 144

psychology, 8, 10, 19–21, 23, 32, 39, 41, 75, 85, 89, 113, 116–17, 120–21, 136, 141, 146, 161n16

Queenie ("A Christmas Memory"), 153
queer theory, 10, 113

racism, 3–4, 6, 12–14, 21, 40–41, 44–47, 51–60, 76–79, 81–85, 88–92, 94, 104, 126–28, 149, 152–53, 159n14, 160n15, 161n21.
Randolph (*Other Voices, Other Rooms*), 5, 44, 47–51, 55, 56, 59, 73, 75, 151; and cross-dressing, 44, 49, 51; physical features of, 44
Random House, 4, 62, 150, 162n1
Ranney, Walter ("Shut a Final Door"), 31–34; relationship with father, 32–33
rape, 4, 12–13, 25, 44, 52–60, 120, 142–43, 159n13
Rebel Without a Cause, 25, 148
religion, 11, 30–31, 37, 39, 53, 70, 77, 84, 89, 120, 125, 153
Revercomb, Mr. ("Master Misery"), 26–27, 31
Riordan, Maude (*The Grass Harp*), 69, 72, 74
Ritz, Morris (*The Grass Harp*), 62, 71
Roberta, Miss (*Other Voices, Other Rooms*), 48–49
Rockefeller, Nelson, 156
Roman Holiday, 99
romance, 7, 14, 31, 38, 62, 72, 74, 96–99, 103, 107, 109–11, 147, 151, 161n16, 162n1
Roosevelt, Eleanor, 153
Roosevelt, Franklin, 18–19, 153, 160n15
Rosenberg, Ethel, 81
Rosenberg, Julius, 64, 81
Rosie the Riveter, 20–21
rural life, 13, 65, 72, 102, 123–24, 150, 152, 159n15
Russian Ministry of Culture, 79–80, 90–92
Russians, 6, 63–64, 79–94. *See also* Soviet Union

Sabrina, 99
sadomasochism, 144, 164n20
safety, 12, 17–18, 39, 65–67, 72, 74, 82, 107, 114–15, 123–26, 129, 131, 153, 161n10
San Francisco, California, 121, 134, 137, 141, 147, 165n21
Sansom, Edward R. (*Other Voices, Other Rooms*), 43–44, 48, 50–51
Saratoga, New York, 4, 32
Schaeffer, Mr. ("A Diamond Guitar"), 151–52
segregation, 45, 54–55, 59, 64, 72, 76, 81–85, 90–92, 104, 117, 120, 126–28, 152, 159n14, 160n15, 162n9. *See also* integration
Seinfeld, 95–96, 111, 162n1
Seinfeld, Jerry, 95
Senate Appropriations Committee, 66
Senate Internal Security Subcommittee, 83
Senate Permanent Subcommittee on Investigations, 65, 82
Servicemen's Readjustment Act of 1944, 124
Seven Year Itch, The, 99, 110
Sex and the City, 96
Sex and the Single Girl, 98, 101
sexism, 33–34
Sexual Behavior in the Human Female, 98, 100, 104
Sexual Behavior in the Human Male, 5, 43, 65, 67, 99
sexual freedom, 56, 96, 98, 103–4, 110, 141, 143, 150
sexual perversion, 65–70, 72, 74, 161n16
sexual repression, 14, 32, 71, 103, 105–6, 108, 111, 146
sexuality, 12–13, 28, 32, 44, 46, 48, 50–51, 58–59, 65, 68–72, 75, 77, 95–99, 102–6, 108–10, 136, 142–44, 149–52, 156, 161n16, 164n19. *See also* bisexuality; female sexuality; heterosexuality; homosexuals; male sexuality
Shearing, George, 138

Shepherd, Richard, 110
Shotgun (musician), 5
"Shut a Final Door," 31–34, 37
siamese twins, 46, 48, 158n5, 159n5
Sinatra, Frank, 8
Sing Sing, 107
singlehood, 14, 96, 98–99, 101–2, 108
Skully, Amy, 44, 47–48, 55–56, 58;
  gloved hand, 44
Skully's Landing, 43, 47, 50–52, 54–56,
  59
slavery, 11, 55–56
Smith, Mary Louise, 84
Smith, Perry (*In Cold Blood*), 14–15,
  112–14, 116, 118–23, 127–28,
  130–34, 137–47, 154; deformity, 131;
  desire for companionship, 140, 142;
  effect of poverty on, 119, 127, 131,
  133; and ethnic identity, 127–28;
  motorcycle accident, 131; and musical
  ability, 138–39; preoccupation with
  maps, 119, 139–40
Smith, Tex John (*In Cold Blood*), 119,
  138, 144
social class, 12, 26, 32, 35–36, 46,
  51, 54–55, 57, 72, 91–92, 96–97,
  99–100, 104, 106–7, 114, 116–17,
  120–21, 123, 125–29, 131, 133, 141,
  146, 148; lower class, 55, 106, 120,
  125, 127, 131; middle class, 12, 36,
  46, 51, 96, 99, 116, 121, 123, 126–
  28, 131, 133; upper class, 32, 91,
  100, 104, 107, 126; working class,
  36, 57, 117, 121, 126
social norms, 25, 47–50, 65, 75, 98,
  103–4, 108, 111, 120, 134, 138,
  140–41, 144–46
soldiers, 17, 54, 58, 80, 85, 93, 107,
  122–24, 131, 142, 144, 160n15
Sook ("A Christmas Memory"), 153
south, the, 1, 4, 10, 13, 29, 45, 53–60,
  71–72, 83–85, 90–91, 102–3, 123–24,
  127, 150–52, 159n15, 160n15
Southern Conference Education Fund
  (SCEF), 83
Southern Literary Studies, 10
Soviet Union, 6, 13, 18, 20, 64, 79–94,

115–16, 126, 157n12, 161n8, 162n2,
  162n5; and cultural differences
  with America, 79–80, 82, 86, 88;
  government, 86; socioeconomic
  hardships of, 79–80, 88; surveillance
  of Americans, 86–89
Sparks, Chauncey, 54
Stabler, Anna, 2, 61, 160n1
Stag Party, 100, 163n5
State Department, 64, 66, 68, 79,
  81–82, 161n10, 161n13
station wagon, 130
Steinem, Gloria, 45, 63
Stevenson, Adlai (*Answered Prayers*),
  155
Stowe, Harriet Beecher, 91
Strawberry Woman (*The Muses Are
  Heard*), 89
suburbia, 3, 15, 74–75, 78, 116–17,
  123–28, 130–31, 145, 161n18;
  homogeneity of, 125–26
Sullivan, Ed, 83, 129
Summer Crossing, 4–5, 16, 153–54,
  160n4
Supreme Court, 84–85, 127, 165n21
Sylvester (My Side of the Matter"),
  40–41
Sylvia ("Master Misery"), 24–28, 30,
  32; friendship with clown, 24–25

Talbo, Dolly (*The Grass Harp*), 61–62,
  70–71, 73, 75–77, 161n16
Talbo, Verena (*The Grass Harp*), 61–62,
  70–72, 75–76, 78
Taormina, Sicily, 62–63
Taylor, Recy, 13, 53–54, 60
television, 7–8, 19, 25, 64, 66, 81, 83,
  85, 96, 115–17, 120, 125–26, 129,
  145
Temple, Shirley, 66
Terry (*On the Road*), 146
theft, 15, 25, 27, 59, 77, 118, 120–22,
  126, 135, 138, 144–46
Thigpen, Miss (*The Muses are Heard*),
  91–92
Thompkins, Florabel (*Other Voices,
  Other Rooms*), 48–49

Thompkins, Idabel (*Other Voices, Other Rooms*), 3, 44, 48–51, 59; clothing of, 48–49, 51
Tiffany's, 107, 162n2
Time, 43, 63
To Kill a Mockingbird, 2
Toast of the Town, 83
tolerance, 13, 74, 83, 92
Tomato, Sally (*Breakfast at Tiffany's*), 97
Tompkins, Phillip K., 113
Trawler, Rusty (*Breakfast at Tiffany's*), 105–7
Treasure of the Sierra Madre, 119
"Tree of Night, A," 2, 4, 17, 27–29; and snow imagery, 28
Tree of Night and Other Stories, A 5, 12, 16–42, 151, 152
Trinity School, 3, 157n2
Truman Capote–Enfant Terrible, 10
Truman, President Harry S., 64, 82, 114, 160n15
Turks, 155

Underground Railroad, 56
Understanding Fiction, 9

Valhalla drugstore, 34–35
Vanderbilt, Gloria, 4, 102
Vanity Fair, 154
Varjak, Paul (*Breakfast at Tiffany's*), 110–11. *See also* "Fred"
Vidal, Gore, 11
Vietnam War, 63
violence, 7, 13–15, 23, 25, 28–29, 37–38, 40–41, 44–45, 50, 52–60, 70, 75–78, 84–85, 89, 113–24, 132–35, 137, 139–41, 144–45, 147–49; sexual, 45, 52–54, 57
V-J Day, 19, 26, 158n4
Vollmer, Joan, 136
voodoo, 150

"Walls Are Cold, The," 17
War Manpower Commission, 20
Warhol, Andy, 9
Warren, Chief Justice, 85
Washington, D.C., 54–55, 57–58, 67, 160

Waters, Vincent ("Headless Hawk"), 37–40; relationships with others; 38–39
wealth, 4, 7–8, 14, 28, 32, 36, 61, 71–72, 76, 91–92, 97–99, 102–5, 107, 110, 116–19, 123, 127, 131, 138, 140, 154–56
Wells, Floyd (*In Cold Blood*), 114, 123
Welty, Eudora, 42
Wheeling, West Virginia, 64, 66
whites, 7, 11–12, 41, 44–46, 51–61, 74–76, 83–85, 90–93, 116, 124–29, 152, 159, 161n21, 162n9
Wilder, Thornton, 8
Wildwood, Mag (*Breakfast at Tiffany's*), 103–4, 106–7
Williams, Mrs. (*Answered Prayers*), 155
Willie-Jay (*In Cold Blood*), 145
Wilson, Charles E., 129
Wilson, Hugo, 53, 159n13
Wisteria, Miss (*Other Voices, Other Rooms*), 49–50
wives, 1, 4, 21, 40–41, 46, 53, 69, 75–77, 97, 101, 107–8, 112, 123, 126, 130–31, 136, 142, 144–45, 147, 153, 156
Wolfert, Ira (*The Muses are Heard*), 88
Woman's Political Council, 84
Wood, Catherine, 4
Woodward, Ann, 156
Woodward, William, 156
World War I, 126
World War II, 7, 12–13, 16–18, 20–28, 31, 37–40, 42, 51, 58, 64, 97–99, 101–2, 104, 114, 124, 138, 152–53, 159n14, 160n15, 161n18, 164n13; and the Allies, 18–19; casualties, 20, 28, 39; and collective engagement, 19, 22, 31; fear during, 18, 21–23, 26–28, 37, 39, 42; opportunities for women, 20–21, 33–34; use of Morse code, 38

"Yachts and Things," 154–55
Yaddo, 4–5
Ybarra-Jaegar, José (*Breakfast at Tiffany's*), 97, 103–5, 108
York, George Ronald, 122–23